ELEVENTH
HOUR

Céleste perrino Walker
&
Eric Stoffle

a sycamore tree book

from

Pacific Press® Publishing Association
Nampa, Idaho
Oshawa, Ontario, Canada

Edited by Glen Robinson
Designed by Robert Mason

Copyright © 1998 by
Pacific Press® Publishing Association
Printed in the United States
All Rights Reserved

ISBN 0-8163-1649-X

98 99 00 01 02 • 5 4 3 2 1

Prologue

In the Atlantic near Nova Scotia

"Captain? You might want to take a look at this."

Wilma Blaine frowned. "What is it, Edward?" He never called
her "Captain" unless it was something serious. Wilma trusted
Edward implicitly. He had worked for her father from the time
he bought his very first boat, and now he was imparting to her
the wisdom he had accumulated through the years. After Wilma's
father had died from a heart attack twenty miles from shore on
a bleak autumn afternoon, Edward, the old fisherman, had transferred his loyalty to her. Maybe he believed he was only doing
what Simon Blaine had intended to do: teach Wilma everything
she would need to know.

But now, Edward's usually warm, carefree eyes were cool
and serious, and that caused her stomach to tighten. He pointed
to an area approximately two miles southeast of the *Bluenose
Blaine II*, Wilma's fishing trawler, and handed her a second pair

of binoculars. He raised his own binoculars to his gray eyes again.

It took almost two minutes for her to see what Edward wanted her to see. She gulped when she saw the yellow raft roll gently over a swell and disappear. It reappeared again on another swell. *It looks like the petal of a rose,* she mused for a second before ordering a course change.

"Edward? What do you think?"

"I don't see anyone in the raft, Willy."

Wilma smiled. His duty dispensed, he was his normal self again and called her by the nickname he had used since she was two years old.

Edward set his binoculars on his nose again and stared for several long minutes. "It's hard to tell. We're a fair piece away. There could be people aboard. Just too soon to tell."

Wilma Blaine agreed. They were still far away. There still could be someone alive, and they just couldn't tell from this distance. She hoped for survivors.

The sea wasn't choppy, but it was rolling and dangerous if you were trying to get close to another craft. If they did get too close to the raft, the whole operation could become perilous. Wilma went up to talk to François, a young mainlander she had hired two years ago and who was on the bridge steering the boat.

"Let's keep a safe distance, François. If there is someone alive, I don't want to accidentally kill them attempting a rescue. Let's just have a look first and then evaluate our options."

François smiled tensely. He had worked for her long enough to know that Wilma would take every precaution during a crisis. But he seemed to see through her calm exterior and realize how nervous she really was. He nodded and set a course for the life raft.

Wilma patted François on the shoulder and climbed down to the deck to find Edward. Fifteen minutes later, François had brought the *Blaine II* close enough to get a good look inside the raft. What she saw shocked her. But Wilma Blaine could not turn her back on a fellow human being.

"Prepare a rescue attempt," she shouted. Some of the crew members hung over the railing of the trawler watching as others made preparations to secure the lifeboat and rescue its occupant. Little did Wilma know that within weeks the effects of her compassion would ripple throughout the entire world.

Chapter One

Tuesday, November 9

Dani Talbot pulled the edges of her coat tighter together. A kick from inside her rounded belly signaled a protest against the increased pressure. She bit her lip nervously. *Maybe it was bad for the baby,* she thought, and she relaxed her grip just a little. She'd need a new coat soon.

No time to think about that now, she reminded herself. Her eyes flitted around the dingy bus station lobby, casually noticing the other occupants. An old woman muttered quietly to herself while she stroked her handbag as if it were a pet. Two teens, obviously high on something, were hooked into their Walkmans and lounging carelessly across nearly an entire row of seats. The sound coming from their headsets was so loud Dani could hear it clearly from where she sat.

The only other person in the room was the one Dani was most afraid of.

Mid-fifties, she guessed. A well-groomed and well-dressed executive. His left foot beat a rhythmless staccato out of sync with the harsh music the teenagers were listening to. The incessant tapping belied a nervousness that did not show on his face. The *Detroit Free Press* newspaper he held half shielded him from Dani's view. Its headlines screamed at her about a senseless act of violence committed at the Trust National Bank early enough in the day to make the afternoon paper. Dani's heart pounded faster. She turned away and tried to ignore the headlines, but they remained etched in her mind.

"BILLIONAIRE STAN SHULTZ SLAIN!" it screamed at her. Her eyes returned to the paper. In smaller letters she could just barely read, "Suspects sought in Mafia-style hit." Centered on the page above the victim and a police sketch of his suspected killer was a photograph of a man with short hair, hard eyes, and strong jaw, as well as a rough sketch of a nondescript young woman with long brown hair.

Dani's fingers unconsciously crept up to touch the ragged ends of her own short cut. Not a professional job. There hadn't been time. But she had managed enough of a change to make herself look less like the face in the newspaper. She closed her eyes. *Maybe,* her heart prayed, *maybe when I open my eyes again this will all have vanished. I'll be at home. Daddy will be reading aloud from the Bible, and Mom will be making popcorn.* In her mind she could envision the scene so clearly that she could almost smell the popcorn.

A raspy cough and the sound of metal on metal made her jump and glance around guiltily. Finally someone occupied the ticket booth. Clutching the edges of her coat around her stomach, she shuffled up to the dirty square of glass.

"Can I . . ." she began, but her voice whistled off into a frightened whisper. Digging her fingernails into the flesh of her palm, she tried again. "May I please have a ticket?"

The man's gray hair, a fuzzy halo that encircled his head, fluttered up and down as he nodded. "Yeah. Where to?" he asked, shifting the butt of a very old and soggy, but as yet unlit, cigar in his mouth.

Dani took a step back from the booth, trying to find the "Destinations" board. *Where to? Where to? Where are you running to?* She wanted to collapse against the window and sob. *Home, I want a ticket home.* Instead, she straightened and forced herself to ask where the next bus was headed.

"Well, this next bus is going to Burlington, Vermont." His smile was friendly.

Dani bit her lip. *Vermont?* That was way over on the north end of the East Coast someplace. Far away. Even farther from home. Well, that's what she wanted. Somewhere far away. "I'll . . . I'll take the ticket," she said, mustering a false firmness in her voice. She handed him the money, remembering at the last instant to clutch the bottom cuff of her coat sleeve to keep her wrist covered. Fear crept up her spine as he slowly figured the fare, counted out the bills, and pushed the ticket across the little shelf to her. *Had he noticed the tattoo?*

She swept up the money and turned quickly away. When she returned to her seat, the man with the newspaper was gone. In his place sat a young couple with a small child. The woman glanced briefly over at Dani and offered a warm, gentle smile. Pretending she didn't notice, Dani dropped her eyes and studied the floor.

Where was the newspaper? Had the man taken it with him? She didn't dare look up to see if it was beside the couple who were trying to keep their child happy and occupied until the bus arrived. As her eyes wandered over the shape of a stain on the floor, her mind replayed the scene at the bank.

"What are you afraid of?" Shon had barked, grabbing her wrist roughly. He pulled her over in the back seat of the car and kissed her hard. "You can tell our son that his daddy wasn't afraid to do what had to be done." Then he opened the door and stepped out. Dani remembered crying and feeling nauseous.

Glaring at her in the rearview mirror, Dietrich ordered her to shut up. His cruel eyes bored into her like a slice of pure evil. They haunted her. He got out of the car and accompanied Shon.

Dani turned to stare out the back window as they walked past the bank and hid behind the shrubbery beside the doors.

When Stan Shultz walked up to the bank, briefcase in hand, he paused before the door, searching his pockets for the keys to the door. Quickly Shon stepped out behind him and forced him to kneel. Dani watched in terrible fascination as Shultz pleaded for his life. Then Shon lowered his automatic pistol inches from the man's scalp and executed him.

So quickly, a man was dead. Before Shon and Dietrich began to race back to the car, Dani threw open her door and ran. The sound of Shon screaming at her still echoed in her head. But the dense morning fog shrouding the area had kept him and Dietrich from trying to find her and get away at the same time.

It's just a matter of time, she thought. *They'll find me.*

Headlights swept through the lobby as a bus pulled into position outside the station's glass doors. Airbrakes hissed as the driver opened the door and hopped out of the bus to find the restroom. Dani checked her ticket and stood up, reaching unconsciously to brush back her long hair and finding it gone. Instead, her fingers tangled on the thin, gold chain hanging from her neck. It had a tiny heart charm on it, a present from Shon the day he found out she was pregnant.

Gripping it tightly, she yanked it free and tossed it on the floor, stepping on it just to hear the metal crunch beneath her heel as she walked outside.

Dani breathed in a deep lungfull of air. It smelled heavily of diesel fumes, but at least it was cool. As she lingered, waiting for the bus to begin loading, she began watching the television mounted high in the corner of the lobby nearest the ticket booth. She hadn't noticed it earlier. Maybe the man in the ticket booth had just turned it on. But now the images attracted her. She couldn't hear the sound, but that didn't matter. In fact, the lack of sound helped her pretend that she could watch her own life from a distance and that maybe it was just a badly done movie or a nightmare; not real. For a moment she could pretend anyway.

When someone opened the door to go inside the depot, she caught a few words from the TV about an advertisement for a huge religious rally in Washington, D.C. Soon the driver returned, and Dani let go of the door and began to climb the steps into the bus.

"Where's your luggage, Miss?" the driver asked, eyes sweeping down her and then back up again, taking in her rundown appearance and the worn duffel bag she clutched. He looked behind her wondering, Dani decided, what a pregnant teenager was doing in a bus depot late at night without someone to either travel with, someone to be there to say goodbye. And without even any luggage to put on the bus.

"That man already put it in the coach," Dani lied, pointing to a man heaving baggage into the luggage compartment.

The driver seemed satisfied, and she brushed past him. The darkness inside made it hard for her to see which seats were empty. She found a seat two rows farther back and slid into the corner against the window to make herself as small as possible.

* * *

Speaker of the House Donald Thurgood from Massachusetts shuffled feebly to the lectern, and reverent silence rolled back to the farthest seats of the House chamber. As he prepared to begin, he raised his head and surveyed his colleagues. Many were his friends, and they were scattered throughout Democratic and Republican parties. Yet, he reflected, none of them had been in Congress as long as he had.

He'd always had the capacity to make friends easily. He formed alliances quickly and expected much from them. He was himself loyal to a fault, which drew firm loyalties in return. Thus the hush that fell over the House floor was out of a deep respect for a dying friend who had served his country for many years in exemplary fashion.

People liked to have their heroes, and they believed Donald

Thurgood was one. The voters had faithfully reelected him. Speaker Thurgood remained intact as the most senior representative, and there he would serve Massachusetts for life. *He could easily make that prediction now,* he thought.

The previous day, he had called a press conference to announce the findings of the oncology specialists he had visited two weeks earlier. The doctors told him he was dying of advanced lung cancer. If he had gone to the doctors sooner, he might have had a fighting chance. But there was a reason he had not gone when he first suspected it. Rather, there were a variety of reasons, all esoteric in nature but hinging largely on the fact that he was tired. Too tired to fight back and too old to deem such a struggle worthwhile. It was better to go out with dignity.

* * *

He looks terrible, Brian Willis thought as he watched the Speaker on television in the suite reserved for the United Religious Coalition in Boise, Idaho. He remembered when Gavin Larson introduced him to the Speaker of the House nearly seven years ago. Thurgood had looked like a bear, not like the shriveled skeleton seen now on C-Span. Shortly before that, Brian had been working part time at a soup kitchen in Boston.

He was barely earning enough at the kitchen to feed himself, but it was work he enjoyed. It was his youthful idealism and energy that had probably gotten him noticed by Thurgood's top aide, Gavin Larson. And there had to be some grand design too. Brian was sure that God had something to do with his meeting Gavin and eventually becoming the public relations director for the United Religious Coalition.

Unknown to Brian on that day back in 1994, Larson was visiting several Boston-area soup kitchens run by church organizations that received funds from the Federal government. Brian was in the midst of dishing out a helping of mashed potatoes to a regular along with a quick word or two about Jesus Christ, something he did frequently even though it was against the rules to proselytize in a government-funded program. And then he looked up to see Gavin Larson standing there beside the homeless woman, and he felt faint.

"Do they still get potatoes if they don't want to hear about the religion that's helping to feed them?" Larson asked.

"Well, uh, yeah. You noticed I served the mashed potatoes first," Brian replied. He recovered and stood tall. From the corner of his eye he could see a dozen dirty faces lined up watching him.

Larson's lips relaxed. The muscles in his granitelike jaw worked as if he were preparing to speak. Then he smiled. "I did notice." He pulled out a card and handed it to Brian. "Keep up the good work."

With that, Larson turned and strode from the kitchen, leaving Brian standing like a stone statue. Brian stared after him until he disappeared into a government car, and then he looked at the card. *Gavin Larson, Congressional Aide.* He carefully tucked the card in his wallet before dishing out more food. The next day, he made an appointment with Gavin's office. A week later, Gavin offered him a job on Thurgood's staff.

Brian looked up from the television screen and glanced around the posh room. He'd really caught a lucky break, hadn't he? When Gavin left Thurgood's staff to become president of the United Religious Coalition, he asked Brian to be the Coalition's public relations director. Brian was in constant contact with all the major television news magazine and talk shows to arrange schedules for Gavin. He wrote countless articles for religious papers and magazines and even had a syndicated feature in newspapers across the nation, all in an effort to promote the Coalition's dream of creating a great nation founded on solid, moral principles.

It was odd, he thought, that although he considered himself to be richly blessed, he couldn't shake a profound emptiness in the pit of his soul. It was as though every action, every thought, every word that came out of his mouth took with it some small droplet of his spirit. Maybe he was just too tired, and his exhaustion was keeping him from feeling God's presence. When was the last time he had taken a vacation? He couldn't even remember. His wife, Ann, and his children would probably be equally hard pressed to remember such an event.

He couldn't feel, but he certainly knew the truth. He could reason intellectually, even if he couldn't identify any emotions. He knew that his work in the Coalition was important, even if inside he felt he was missing something vital. It was just that right now he didn't have the energy to figure out why he felt empty. He was too tired for what might be a frightening exploration of his faith. Frankly, he was scared of what he might discover.

As Thurgood spoke, Brian went to the window and looked down on the city of Boise. The WestCoast Hotel threw its cold shadow onto The Grove, an open area of brick walkways, trees, and specialty shops. *Somebody ought to give you a medal, Speaker Thurgood,* Brian thought as he turned back to the television set. *It takes some guts to get up and do what you're doing.*

Suddenly, the door swung open and Gavin Larson entered wearing a dove gray Yves Saint Laurent suit. Brian was again struck by Gavin's natural magnetism. But even a close study of Gavin didn't really reveal the source of his appeal. He was exactly six feet tall, which beat Brian's 5'11" by a hardly noticeable margin. Yet he seemed much taller.

Gavin had a presence about him that seemed to fill a room and draw people to him. He gave the impression of quiet strength and presence. As usual, he was impeccably groomed, his elegant carriage and graceful bearing arresting.

These things, or the combination of them, Brian thought, *give him the ability to inspire people, to motivate them, and to occasionally put fear into them. Not in a way that threatens but in a way that informs them. Gavin Larson was the only one who had the experience, the ability, and ultimately, the power to lead them through difficult times. Politicians use those subtle scare tactics all the time against their opponents. Gavin is a master.*

Gavin paused in front of the television with his thumb resting under his chin in thoughtful repose. After a moment, he took a deep breath and smiled at Brian.

"I see our friend is giving a moving speech this afternoon."

"Yes. And in agony, too, it appears."

"Donald Thurgood has always been a fighter, Brian," Gavin said as he sat down. Brian studied Gavin further. He had a dark, healthy-looking complexion, a broad forehead and strong jawline. His hair had once been black as coal but with age and maturity had also come a distinguished-looking touch of gray at his temples.

Instantly restless, Gavin rose from his chair and turned to stare sullenly out at the traffic snaking along fifteen stories below. "What do you think, Brian? Doesn't it feel to you like the United States is on the verge of a revolution? Doesn't it feel like, as a nation, we're through spinning our wheels? That our time has come?"

Brian shoved his hands into the pockets of his slacks. It was funny that while Gavin seemed to be riding the tidal wave of a spiritual revolution, he was feeling more and more uneasy. Gavin had become increasingly secretive of late, like a cat with a mouthful of bird. Brian understood that he couldn't possibly know everything that went on, even though it was his job to sound reasonably well-informed.

Uneasy about the question, he avoided answering it by asking one of his own. "Are you prepared to meet with the pope?"

"Of course." Gavin shrugged, his hands wide, like *don't worry.*

Brian did worry. It was practically his job. "Dale Meltzer assures me that everything is nearly ready. And just in time." Brian shook his head, thinking about the logistical nightmare. It was almost as bad as preparing for the Olympics. Meltzer, whose job it had been for the past year to coordinate the rally in Washington, D.C., along with Gavin's smaller rallies across the nation, had also assured Brian that he was going on a month-long vacation when Gavin's campaign was finally over.

Gavin turned back to C-Span to catch the Speaker's closing remarks. It was apparent that the Speaker as well as his colleagues understood this to be his last speech, probably his last time in the nation's capital. Gavin had talked with him the day before and learned he planned to fly home to Massachusetts on Saturday.

Gavin shook his head sadly. "He's been a great asset to the Coalition, Brian," he said on his way to the wet bar where he set up two tumblers. "A drink?"

"Just water, please."

Gavin gave him a patronizing smile, leaving Brian with the distinct impression that he considered it a manly shortcoming not to want a stiff drink now and then. "The Coalition was actually Thurgood's brainchild. He is probably one of the few men who could mastermind such a movement in this country. But he spent a lot of years in a powerful position," Gavin said, raising an eyebrow as he took a sip of brandy. "And rather uncharacteristic of most leaders in America, he understood that building a strong political organization takes time and a great deal of patience."

Brian fiddled with his glass while Gavin replayed one of his beloved speeches.

"The Speaker specifically hired me to head the Coalition whenever it really got rolling. He used the time before it took off to groom me for leadership. You see, he always thought of himself more as a sage businessman than a charismatic leader." Gavin nodded toward the television screen. The whole House stood reverently while Thurgood shuffled away. "He's a passionate man who speaks from his heart, but he lacks eloquence. And he's an old man. He was too old when he started the Coalition." Gavin shrugged with a private thought. "It won't be nearly as easy without him," he said, toasting the retiring Speaker. Again Brian got the distinct feeling that Gavin wasn't telling him something.

Gavin set his cellular phone on the desk within easy grasp and eyed it as if he expected it to ring at any moment. Behind an impassive veneer, Brian watched his boss grow increasingly impatient, pacing near the phone as if attached to it by an invisible umbilical cord.

After several minutes, Brian found himself growing weary of the endless pacing. "Can I get you something, Gavin?"

Larson shook his head and checked his watch again. He returned to the window. "You might check on the preparations for the rally."

Grateful for the diversion, Brian headed out the door. Whatever Gavin was anxious about, Brian found himself increasingly grateful that he didn't know about it.

* * *

It was apparent the call had come much later than Gavin Larson had expected it to. It was equally obvious that he did not expect good news. Brian watched his boss study the dark circles under his eyes in the mirror as he listened to a voice on the other end of the connection. Gavin was mostly listening, and whatever he was listening to put tension in his face. Brian watched with a keen sense of interest.

"Keep me informed," Gavin said finally. He glanced at Brian and dialed to make a call. He did this as Brian got up and walked into the bathroom. Brian quietly closed the door. He stared at his hands. They were shaking. He leaned over the sink and almost heaved. *What are you up to, Gavin? What are you doing?*

Instinctively, he knew it was something that he really didn't want to know about. Little bits and pieces of conversations. Secret meetings. Little anomalies in Gavin's character all told Brian that the leader of the United Religious Coalition did not always play by the kind of Christian rules Brian had grown up believing in. Christians were of a strong character and led impeccably moral lives, loving just as Christ loved. It was a conviction Brian believed in with all his heart. It was why he loved the Coalition, after all.

He was stuck between the proverbial rock and the hard place. He was in a position to actually help make the world a better place. But his instincts were also telling him that Gavin was involved in things that were unethical and possibly even illegal. For one thing, if what Gavin was doing was truly good for the country, there would be no hesitation in getting Brian involved in it. After all, Brian was how America and the rest of the world learned about the good of the Coalition.

Brian's body trembled again. He felt a chill run through the middle of him. The only other time he had ever had a feeling like that was when he and some friends had sneaked into a movie theater showing *The Exorcist*. He remembered it was the first time he had been able to associate the name of Satan with a real entity. After that, the devil wasn't just the name of a bad guy to Brian. He was real.

I can't walk away. I'm doing a good work here, Brian thought. *Take a deep breath. That'll help.* He looked at himself in the mirror. There was fear there, all right. *Is that all? Fear?* He looked closer. No, it wasn't all fear. He could also see some anger. *Jesus, give me strength. You threw the money-changers out of Your temple. Help me do what I have to do now.*

Interestingly, the trembling stopped. He didn't feel quite so alone anymore. But certainly he was in a way. Gavin circumvented him while conducting a lot of his activities, and that was just fine with Brian. They were activities he wasn't sure he wanted to know about in the first place. He'd heard rumors, murmuring about extreme paramilitary types within the organization. They were things he put out of his mind, dismissed out of hand. It was one thing to suspect something but entirely another when you knew for sure, and he'd never been sure he wanted to go there.

There were times lately when he questioned why he was involved with the Coalition at all, but whenever he prayed about it, he seemed to receive reassurance that he was where he was supposed to be. Maybe God planned to use him to help keep Gavin from losing his focus. Could it be that Gavin was being tested in some way?

Brian rubbed his face. He flushed the toilet for effect and washed his hands before leaving the bathroom. Gavin was pacing anxiously again when he returned. "I'm going to be late. What took you so long?"

Brian rubbed his abdomen. "I felt queasy all of a sudden. I just thought for a while that it was going to get the better of me."

"Are you OK?" Gavin asked, then, not waiting for an answer, he said, "Good. Let's go. We've got a lot to do to get ready for the rally tomorrow."

Brian shut the door behind them. They shared an elevator with an elderly couple down to the first floor, and then they wove through the lobby. Finally, they were walking alone again.

"What was the call about?" Brian asked.

Gavin's face was impassive. "Stan Shultz is dead."

"Stan Shultz? He's donated millions to the Coalition for humanitarian programs." Shocked, Brian fought to keep moving, to keep pace with Gavin. "What was it? Heart attack? Stroke?"

Gavin didn't slow. "Murder." The matter-of-factness in his tone of voice betrayed the fact that not only did Shultz's death not surprise him but the manner of death may not entirely have been news either. Brian felt his mouth go dry. "I want you to issue press releases about Shultz's philanthropic endeavors through the Coalition," Gavin continued. "He was a generous man, and I want people to know how much he will be missed, especially among the homeless. I think those people will notice his absence the most."

"I'll do that. But why would anyone want to murder him? Do the police have any idea?"

Gavin shrugged. "I understand that one or more of the suspects is presumed to be a Remnant believer. That could explain some things, I think." He paused and turned toward Brian. "The Remnant Church is dying. What is left is a bunch of fanatics trying to convince people the world is going to end in some kind of Armageddon, and I think those people are getting desperate. They don't like the idea of unity and morality. They actually seem to welcome discord, and they preach against the Catholic Church as if it is in league with the devil. My meeting with the pope next week will go a long way toward silencing the Remnant Church. You know, Brian, that Stan Shultz was a wealthy, powerful man. But did you also know he was a Remnant Church believer before he became a member of the Coalition?"

Brian frowned, beginning to see it.

Gavin cracked a thin smile and nodded.

Still, Brian was troubled.

* * *

Randy Burton's boyish smile was contagious. Lately, however, he rarely smiled out of joy. His smiles were reserved for times when he felt ahead of the game. Lately, he hadn't felt like smiling.

The television had been on for one hundred thirty continuous hours. At the top of every hour he came into the room and watched until, at ten o'clock on the morning of November 9th, he saw what had to be the sign for him to begin his part of the plan.

Lynn Burton's red-rimmed eyes watched Randy's interest in the TV. "That what you've been waiting for?" she demanded. There was only one television in the house, and he wouldn't let her change the channel to watch daytime soaps.

Randy's head turned. He watched his sister for several long moments, wondering why he had allowed her to live with him while he had so much to stay focused on. Doped up, she was mellow and not too much trouble, but he was going to have to deal with the drug problem. He ignored her for the time being and went back to the kitchen.

The table was covered with a large laminated street map of Washington, D.C. Twenty-three routes were diagramed, each with a different-colored marker. Each color had a corresponding set of numbers. He looked back at Lynn. She slouched on the sofa, a weary expression shrouding her face. In the dim half-light of the living room, the scenes on the television reflected off her dull, glassy eyes, the eyes of someone using heroin. Randy returned to the map while a female reporter droned in the background about the dead crew of a fishing trawler found off the coast of Nova Scotia.

For the past ten days, Randy Burton had followed ten different buses on their routes dropping off children. Tomorrow he would observe his eleventh bus. The assassination of one of the world's richest philanthropists had happened within the time frame he had been told to expect such an event. But he hadn't been informed of any details that could have helped him save Stan Shultz. For several minutes he sat and stared blankly at the map. It was about all he could do, though inside he felt frustrated and filled with a kind of slow, deep anger. All he had been told was that the death of an influential person would become national news. This had fit a referenced time frame for a series of events yet to unfold.

Randy's problem was that he was being told only what he needed to know to do his part for the Freedom Society. He had an uneasy feeling that he would never be in a good position to know what the Freedom Society was up to before it happened. The Society was just too careful.

He hadn't been able to learn the identity of the target before the fact, and he felt bad for Shultz and his family. He tried not to think about it, reminding himself he probably had no more than a three-week window in which to do his job. There was more trouble coming in the future that he needed to worry about.

Lynn shuffled into the kitchen and began massaging his shoulders. "Lynn, please leave me alone right now," he said.

Lynn's fingers lingered for a few moments to make sure he was serious. When she was convinced, she let go and disappeared. Randy listened to her bare feet shuffle down the hallway to her room. She stayed there until the early afternoon; then Randy suddenly became aware of the front door opening and closing. He looked up from his work, thoughtfully weaving a marking pen in and out of his fingers.

* * *

Lynn's gaunt form slipped through Club Rio's doors, barely noticed by anyone on the inside. But outside Club Rio, Alice Nolan, an elderly woman, had been watching. She was hoping to get close enough to the effete woman to hand her one of the small Bibles she had been passing out. But a large, middle-aged man sideswiped her, accidentally sending her cache of Bibles to the ground. The man apologized profusely as he bent on one knee to help her retrieve the Bibles. When Alice looked up, the young woman had already gone inside.

She considered going inside then decided to wait until the young woman emerged. Then she would offer a Bible. She adjusted the padded strap of the bag on her shoulder.

She had turned sixty-seven years old two weeks ago. Her gray hair was curled and cut to the middle of her neck. Her face was narrow, soft, and her expression kind. She chose a tiny table just inside the small deli next to Club Rio after ordering a cheese sandwich and lemonade. Very few people frequented Club Rio, she decided after thirty minutes of watching the door, at least during the day. *Probably more at night,* she thought.

Then she had an idea. Maybe she could get someone to ask that woman to come outside for a moment. She might try it, and if it worked, she could give the young woman a Bible and go home before it got to be too late.

Alice grabbed her bag of Bibles and stationed herself on the street near the entrance to Club Rio. There were two men and a woman who walked by at different intervals who appeared to be going inside. But as she sucked in her breath, preparing to deliver her speech, they continued on down the street. She sank back and waited.

Ten minutes later, she was watching a tall, young man with straight, very short hair. His sharp eyes moved quickly as he approached from the west. He looked as handsome and self-assured as her Richard had been when he was young. This young man wouldn't go into such a place, she told herself. Yet she found herself taking a deep breath as she stepped out to greet him just in case. Suddenly, the young man turned toward the entrance to Club Rio, surprising her even though she was prepared.

"I was wondering if you could help me," Alice said quickly.

The man smiled easily, as if he had expected her to approach him. "Sure, ma'am."

Alice relaxed as she always did once the conversation was underway. "Well, I, ah, want to give one of my Bibles to a young woman who went inside there about an hour ago. But I've never been inside a bar, and I just can't imagine going into a place like that, especially at my age. If you're going inside, I'd like you to see if she would come outside."

The young man looked puzzled for a moment. But he seemed eager to help. "Do you know her name?"

"No. I've never met her. I just saw her and thought I should give her one of these." Alice carefully held up a paperback Bible like a box brimming with precious gems.

"I don't know how receptive she will be," the young man cautioned, as if to prepare her for disappointment. "But I can try. If you'll just tell me what she looks like, I'll ask her."

Alice's face brightened. "Oh, thank you. She's about my height, I suppose, maybe a little shorter. But she looks awfully frail, so that sometimes makes a body seem shorter. She's got straight blond hair down to her shoulders. It's sort of stringy. She hasn't washed it for a couple of days, probably." She smiled even more brightly. People fascinated her. She wouldn't tell the young man why it was so important to her that she give a Bible to the woman she was describing. There was just something about the effete woman that told Alice she was lost, and Alice Nolan reserved a large place in her heart for people who were lost in this world.

As she concluded her description of the woman, she sensed the young man becoming tense and irritable.

"I'll do my best, ma'am," he said almost tersely as he opened the door and went inside.

* * *

The interior of Club Rio smelled stale from years of soaking up cigarette smoke, liquor, and the sweat of human bodies. Randy stood near the door for a moment, letting his eyes adjust to the dim lighting. He discovered Lynn lost in a dark booth along the back wall of the club. Without a word, he slid into the booth.

"What are you doing here?" Lynn asked, fixing blurry eyes on him.

"Just looking after you."

"That's very funny. You told me to get lost earlier, and now you act like a concerned brother. Well, don't bother," Lynn snapped.

Randy shrugged. "You're my sister, and I *am* concerned about you."

Lynn snorted. "Sure you are."

"I didn't come here to argue," Randy said.

"What did you come for?"

"To take you home."

"Worried?"

"About what?"

The left corner of Lynn's mouth drew back in a tight, nervous smile. She stared at him pointedly.

Randy's underarms dripped with perspiration. So she thought she understood enough about what he was doing to try to black-mail him. And for what? More drugs? His conscience pricked him that he hadn't gotten help for her addiction, but it would be a major commitment of time and energy on his part. As soon as he was finished with his assignment, he could get her the help she needed but not until then.

"Come on. I'm sorry. I'll be better."

Lynn looked surprised. "Really?"

Randy nodded. "Sure," he said with a smile as he helped her out of the booth. "I shouldn't have acted that way."

Lynn cast an incredulous look at Randy, as if she couldn't believe that all she ever had to do was threaten to tattle on him. He knew she was probably hoping there were more drugs in the reconciliation.

Remembering the elderly woman who waited outside as he ushered Lynn toward the door, Randy hurriedly began fabricating an excuse for getting past her without letting her talk to Lynn. But he finally decided that to avoid suspicion, it would be better to allow the woman to give Lynn a Bible—if Lynn wanted one, that was.

Just as going into the dark interior of Club Rio had rendered him momentarily blind, the intense fall sunlight had just the opposite effect on his vision but with the same consequences. While he and Lynn adjusted to the sunlight, the elderly woman quickly approached them.

"Is this the young woman you wanted to give a Bible to?" Randy asked helpfully. The woman's wide smile was all the confirmation he needed.

"Yes, it is. Thank you." The elderly woman took a Bible out of her bag and held it out to Lynn. "I would like you to have this as a gift."

Impulsively, Lynn reached out and took the Bible, though Randy doubted that she really wanted it. Her fingers lightly traced the gold lettering on the paper faux leather cover of the Bible. "Thank you," she said, glancing up at the old woman questioningly.

Lynn swayed unsteadily, and Randy laid a firm hand on her

arm. Lynn shrugged him off and almost fell. The old woman reached for another Bible to give to Randy, but he realized what she was doing and held up his hand.

"No, thank you," he said.

"I understand." She gave Lynn a warm smile. "If you have any questions, or if you just want to talk, I left a card with my name and number on it inside your Bible."

"Thank you," Randy interrupted impatiently. He nodded curtly as he grasped Lynn's elbow and pulled her along after him.

Chapter Two

Wednesday, November 10

Jack Talbot walked quickly. It was part of his own therapy, one that was vital for his sanity. His left leg strained to keep pace with the good one. Each step burned with fire as he pushed his muscles harder. His breathing was painful now. It came in short, jagged spurts in and out of his lungs like breathfuls of broken glass.

He could just make it out ahead through the fog. Just a little farther now. An agonized sob escaped his throat as he threw himself the last few steps onto the bridge railing for support. He clung to the cold metal rail, his chest heaving. His leg was numb yet he knew it was improving.

He would never be a patrolman again, but to walk without pain, that would be something. He had two months to decide if he wanted to remain on the police force—probably at a desk job—or retire.

As he waited for his breathing to ease, he scanned the swirling water of the Boise River below him. Branches and debris passed swiftly beneath him. *Just like life,* he mused. Seemed as though life these days was as hard to contain as the muddy, rushing waters of the river.

He watched a man and woman in sweat suits jogging toward him from the university campus and turn right onto the bridge, perfectly in stride. Obviously happy. Obviously in love. Even the steam of their breath seemed to be in sync. The bridge echoed as they went by, and then there was silence again. He listened to the stillness. At this time of the year it was amazing how serene it could all be. The massive elms stood bent over the river as if this were their time of rest before the day's beginning. And Jack knew God was out there—he could feel it. So was Dani. He had to believe God was with her wherever she was.

"You promised to go with us where we go, Lord," he whispered. "Well, my little girl is walking through a valley full of shadows. Will You go with her?"

No thundering voice answered him. There was no flash of exhilaration or blanket of peace. There was just a small voice inside, reminding him of the magnitude of the love of God. It humbled him and strengthened him at the same time.

It was precisely his trying to convey this love to Dani, Jack realized now, that had driven her away. He balled his fists and pounded them on the metal railing, vaguely aware of the pain and the dull hollow ring that rolled away to be sucked up in the silence.

"I messed up!" he cried, his heart twisting until he felt it might explode. "I didn't show Dani how much You love her." His voice fell again to a hoarse whisper. "I didn't even show her how much *I* love her."

Angry, awful scenes of fighting echoed in his head. He could hear Dani's rebellious arguments as if each episode had happened only moments ago. "Where is your God, Daddy? Where did *He* go? He's a fake! If He can't keep all these maniacs from killing innocent people! Children! Babies! I don't want anything to do with Him!"

Ironically, he had often asked the same questions hundreds of times as a police officer. He had seen things, horrible things, that Dani had only heard about or had never known. It was her innocent idealism that angered him most, because *he knew!*

Oblivious to the tears streaming down Dani's face, he unleashed his own torrent of angry arguments. "Grow up, Dani! God isn't going to keep us like a bunch of knickknacks safe in some celestial kitchen hutch. This is a world full of sin. How are we going to see what the effect of sin is if God shields us from it?"

"You aren't doing what He wants, Daddy!" The words tore through him like shrapnel. "God is angry. Shon and his friends are *doing* something! They're doing something, not standing by and wringing their hands like you and your church. They can change the world, and you and *your* God can't."

His intuition fired into gear, and he heard himself ask the question with the hard edge in his voice he usually reserved for police work. "What do you mean, Dani? Tell me what you mean. Do you really know what you're talking about?"

She wouldn't meet his eyes. "I'm leaving, Daddy," she said simply. "I'm going to be with Shon." Her shoulders sagged in an almost helpless gesture. He wanted to protect her, to wrap her in his arms as if she were little and had just fallen and skinned her knee.

"Maybe I can help in some small way." She looked up and past him, her hand resting lightly on her stomach. "I'm going to have his baby, Daddy. And I'm going to stay with Shon."

Jack honestly couldn't remember the rest of the conversation, but judging from what his wife told him as she was packing to leave him the next day, he had been too hard on Dani. Much too hard. Dani had disappeared, not even taking a suitcase. That had been over three months ago.

Jack pushed away from the railing and turned toward home. His legs were stiff, and he struggled to make them work. *Going home.* Just the thought increased his loneliness. *What kind of home was it without a family?*

Dani had gone, and Marilyn had found her excuse to leave too. Unlike Dani's screaming and tears, Marilyn hadn't spoken a word beyond cryptic responses given in a deadpan voice that bore little resemblance to the one he had grown accustomed to during their twenty years of marriage. Recently, he had become suspicious she was involved in some kind of spiritualism or New Age movement, but he had not bothered to confront her about it. He had felt she was looking for an excuse to leave him, and so he avoided the issue. Consequently, the blowup with Dani turned into a good excuse for Marilyn too.

He sucked in breath after breath, trying to bury the pain he had felt when she left. True, their marriage had been shaky for quite some time. The beginning of the end came when he was baptized into the Remnant Church. She had drawn away then and slowly made it clear to him that if he wanted to live that kind of pious life, it was fine with her, but she wanted no part of it. The strain rent a gap in the fabric of their marriage that no amount of praying had mended. Still, it was hard not to feel that God had let him down. God didn't want Marilyn to leave. He knew that. But knowing something with your head and feeling it with your heart were two different matters.

Dove Creek subdivision was a maze of twists and turns. Taking it easy, he tried to concentrate on moving his leg naturally. He thought he was getting better, walking more like "normal." But the leg would never allow him back on patrol.

He limped up to the porch and bent down to retrieve the paper. With a groan, he dropped slowly to a seat on the top step and opened the newspaper across his lap. Mopping his forehead with the edge of one sleeve, he scanned the front page. He froze, and for a long moment he simply stared at a police artist's sketch. The eyes were a little different. The mouth was close. Still, there was something that reminded him of Dani. Something he couldn't quite put his finger on.

Finally, his mind began to function clearly enough to allow

him to scan the article attached to the picture. The girl—*was it Dani?*—was wanted by authorities in connection with the murder of billionaire Stan Shultz. Jack took a deep breath. His heart pounded faster.

A sixth sense he had long trusted in police work swept over him. After all this time wondering where Dani was, he knew he was looking at her. And if it was Dani for sure, then she would need help. She would need an attorney when she was found. Most of all, she would need her father's help—a father who would love and support her. Mentally, he tallied his available funds if he drained all his existing bank accounts. His eyes frantically scanned the article looking for the location of the murder.

Detroit, Michigan. Well, it was a start.

* * *

Jack Talbot's first call was to his friend, Casey, at the department asking him to run Dani's boyfriend, Shon Cole, through NCIC (National Crime Information Center). In the hours since he had placed the call, Jack wandered through the house, mentally culling his possessions for sale until he was left with just the bare necessities. He couldn't afford to be sentimental about all the antiques he and Marilyn had happily collected throughout their years together. They would be worth more to him converted into cash to locate Dani.

When the phone finally rang, Jack found he was afraid to pick it up. "Yeah?" he asked gruffly, catching it on the fourth ring.

"Jack? It's Casey. Look, I didn't find squat on that guy you're after. What's he done anyway?"

Jack swallowed hard. What had Shon done? He had ruined Jack's life and stolen his daughter. "Nothing I've been able to discover yet," Jack finally said. "I think he's got some ties with a militia or extremist group called The Society."

"You mean the Freedom Society?"

"That could be the group." Jack's mind sorted bits and pieces of things Dani might have said, but he wasn't really sure. Many of the smaller militias had disappeared after so much negative publicity stemming from events like the bombing of the Oklahoma Federal building. "Is the Freedom Society pretty big?"

"Yeah. It's probably the largest militia group, if you can call it a militia. The Freedom Society is quite well organized and has chapters in every state. It's not considered an extremist organization, however, so I doubt you're looking in the right place for this guy. I know a few people who are members, and I say they're more like the American patriots who founded this government in the first place."

"You're making the Freedom Society sound like the Boy Scouts, Casey."

"It's a clean group, Jack. Whenever something bad happens, like a cult goes off the deep end or some fanatic blows up a couple hundred people, all these groups, even the well-known ones, get checked out real good. There are no problems with the Freedom Society."

"There's a first time for everything, Casey." There was a weighty silence on the line.

"Jack, if I were you, I'd be *asking* for the Freedom Society's help finding Dani."

"Are you telling me not to bother with the Freedom Society?"

"I'm telling you you'd be wasting your time."

Jack sensed he was starting to step on some toes. "Dani's my daughter. I'll look where I need to to find her," he said.

"Jack, all I'm saying is don't burn your bridges. OK?"

"Thanks a lot for your help, Casey."

"I'm sorry, Jack," Casey said, as if sensing the conversation was destined to end on a negative note. "The world is changing. The mainstream shies away from extremists nowadays. In fact, we downright shun them altogether. And you know what? It works better than any kind of force we can use to shut them down. One after one, they disband. Really, all that's left is the

Freedom Society. And they're so mainstream now that people actually like them.

"What else can you tell me?" The Freedom Society was beginning to sound less and less like the kind of organization Jack was interested in, but he had been in police work far too long not to know he should check everything out. And so far, this was all he had.

"Let me see," Casey mumbled. "Oh, here it is. Have you read the paper?"

"Yeah, Casey, I did."

"Then you noticed the ad promoting a rally for the United Religious Coalition at The Grove this afternoon at four o'clock?"

"So I didn't read everything."

Casey laughed. "I know the Freedom Society is sponsoring the rally and providing some of the security, so why don't you go check it out?"

"Thanks again." Jack hung up the phone. *Could the Freedom Society be the group Dani was a part of?* He wasn't so sure now that he knew it was affiliated with the United Religious Coalition. He wished he had paid more attention to Dani when she raved about Shon and his friends.

Jack hastily checked his watch. It was only four-thirty. He had time. He grabbed his coat and headed for the door. The pain in his bad leg made him wince. Too much exercise in one day. He'd pay for it tomorrow.

His car, a 1984 Ford Tempo, nearly croaked for good before it finally turned over. When the engine caught, it idled rough. He would be lucky if his car made it downtown, much less to Michigan. He toyed with the idea of trading it in on something more reliable. It certainly wouldn't do Dani any good for him to get stranded somewhere along the road.

Time was everything in disappearance cases. If you didn't find someone in the first couple of days, odds were you didn't find them. He had to chase the leads while they were hot and not leave it to someone else to find Dani. Even if he sold everything he had, there would barely be enough money if the search proved to be very long or difficult. And that wasn't ready money. Somehow he had to get some cash and get it fast.

Possibilities raced through his mind as he coaxed the Tempo toward downtown Boise. Inexplicably, his pastor's name kept running through his mind. Dan Reiss had been his pastor since he had joined the Remnant Church. But Jack knew perfectly well that Pastor Reiss didn't have any money either.

Maybe he doesn't have any money, a still, small voice seemed to say, *but he has a car that will easily make a trip to Michigan or anywhere else you might need to go. Confide in him. You could trade vehicles with him for a while. Go and ask.*

"Lord," breathed Jack. "Could it really be that simple? You lead, Lord; I'll follow."

When he reached The Grove, he was surprised to see not only the parking lots and garages completely full but cars parked, some illegally, up and down both sides of the streets. He made several passes, looking for a spot. When none opened up, he parked much farther out than he had hoped.

Jack wasn't sure what he expected to find when he got to the rally, but with every step, he found his interest peaking. The crowd of people was enormous. To get inside, he saw he would have to pay an admission fee. He headed toward the gate on his right where a lean man with a severe military haircut stood.

"How much to get in?"

"Anything you want." Surprisingly, the attendant was civil, almost pleasant. "We encourage giving a minimum of twenty. Most people give more."

Jack nearly toppled over. "What? Twenty bucks? You're kidding!" With dismay, Jack saw immediately that he had managed to knock the attendant from civility to contempt in one fell swoop.

"Listen, if you are not serious about getting your country straightened out, don't bother going in," the attendant growled.

Jack pushed a wadded five-dollar bill, all he had, into the

man's palm and started through.

"Where do you think you're going?"

"I'd like to hear the rally," Jack said.

"Not without paying twenty bucks. Or if you had one of these, you could get in free of charge." the attendant replied. He pointed to his wrist, just above the palm of his hand where Jack saw a broken strand of wire, symbolizing, Jack supposed, freedom from some kind of oppression. Dani had one exactly like it. She'd gotten it a few months before she'd left.

"I don't have that much money on me," Jack argued, then swallowed a good dose of alarm at the man's hard look.

"Sorry, mister. Gavin Larson can't do these rallies for free. It takes a lot of money to bring about the kinds of changes it'll take to make America great like it should be. That's what we're all working and praying for. Next Friday, the biggest rally ever to hit Washington, D.C., is going to happen. Takes a lot of money to pull off something as huge as what that's going to be like. But I'll tell you," he said, toying with Jack, "if you had a tattoo that proved you were a member of the Freedom Society, I'd let you in without the money." He grinned. "Understand? You might want to think about that. A lot of people are joining the Freedom Society."

Jack nodded, backing up a few steps and fighting to control his anger. He felt a tightening in the pit of his stomach, like cold hands packing a snowball. He wandered around aimlessly in the lobby, stopped in the bathroom, and splashed water over his face. While drying off, he decided to try another gate, but the only one that remained open was the one with the man he'd already had trouble with.

After watching a few stragglers pass through with no trouble, he turned to leave. Somehow he managed to make a wrong move, and his leg nearly doubled up underneath him. As he limped back to his car, he made a decision to stop by Dan Reiss's house. Although he was disappointed, he realized that he had not made a wasted trip. He did see a tattoo that proved to him Dani had

had some association with the Freedom Society.

* * *

Dan Reiss leaned heavily on the rake he'd been using all afternoon. The sun was about to crash into the horizon in a flaming ball of orange, and he watched in reverent appreciation as spectacular colors washed the horizon. It was as if the world were giving birth to hundreds of rainbows. Absently, he wiped his brow with the back of his sleeve. His salt-and-pepper curls lay plastered to his forehead, and his damp shirt stuck to his skin under his jacket.

He surveyed his lawn in the dying light. At least he was nearly finished. Another afternoon and he'd have all the leaves and debris raked up. He would have been finished by now if he hadn't received a call from a concerned church member about the recent exodus of church members from his church.

It was hard on Dan to watch the people he loved leaving the church he loved. What could he tell the remaining members? They wanted to know what was going on. They questioned their church doctrines that set them apart from the churches that were uniting with the United Religious Coalition. They questioned God's Word when their Christian friends showed them interpretations of the Scriptures that were nothing more than compromises and taught nothing of the true character of God. It had finally come to the point where the few stalwarts who remained had begun to question his leadership. They wanted to know what he was doing about the situation.

Dan squeezed his eyes shut. *Doing?* He'd been praying practically without ceasing since the first few members left for other churches. What else could he do? He couldn't track them down and force them to attend the Remnant Church. In the beginning, of course, he had visited the families who had left and spoken to them about their decisions.

It hadn't done any good. They had all kinds of reasons and

excuses for joining the Coalition of churches, and he would not argue with them. He continued to visit them throughout the following months, but he was growing both mentally and physically tired of being ignored. Any hope he had that his members might change their minds was barely a flicker in his breast.

Dan sighed and opened his eyes, surprised to see twin points of light heading slowly down his street. The street was a dead end, and his house was the last on the road. Whoever was driving the car was either terribly lost or looking for him. He leaned his rake against the side of his house and walked slowly toward his driveway. The last thing he wanted right now was a repeat of this afternoon's conversation. He prayed that whoever wanted him didn't have this subject in mind.

He didn't recognize the car at first in the light, but when Jack Talbot stepped out he smiled and waved. "Jack! What brings you so late? There's no trouble, is there?"

"I'm sorry to disappoint you, Pastor Reiss, but I'm afraid I am in trouble. Well, not me actually. My daughter. . . ."

"Dani?" Dan interrupted with concern, a frown on his face. "She's in trouble? You've found her?" Jack shifted his weight from foot to foot. Dan noticed his restlessness and quickly took him by the arm. "Come inside where it's warm, and we'll talk."

The furniture had a worn look, and the decor was devoid of any obvious feminine touch, betraying the fact Dan Reiss had never married. Dan moved a stack of religious magazines off the couch to make room for Jack. Taking the chair opposite the couch, he leaned forward, regarding Jack soberly.

Jack ran a hand through his short brown hair. "Pastor, I think Dani's in deep trouble. I mean, *deep* trouble. She's been very involved with a young man named Shon Cole. He's her boyfriend, and he's into some militia group. I—I'm not positive which one, but I think it might be the Freedom Society. Some of its members were at a religious rally put on by the United Religious Coalition in Boise today."

Dan sucked in his breath, not so much at hearing about the

Freedom Society but at once again being made aware of the United Religious Coalition. He'd been following Gavin Larson's rise to popularity with avid interest. Looking as he was toward end-time events, Dan believed he saw a lot of potential in the smooth-talking leader as a catalyst toward the closing of earth's history. In fact, the more he saw of him, the more convinced he became that Gavin Larson would play a big role in the last days.

Jack seemed to notice the stunned expression on his pastor's face, and he became even more gloomy and desperate.

"Just how involved do you think Dani has become?" Dan asked.

Jack shrugged and wrung his hands together. "I don't know. At first I thought she was just testing me with her new friends. You know, adolescent rebellion, thinking she found some better way of life than her father knew. But then, in today's paper there was a picture of this girl. I—I think it was Dani. Authorities are looking for her in connection with a murder." Jack's head dropped, and his hands covered his face. The anguish in his voice tore at Dan's heart. "Murder," he groaned. "My little girl is wanted for murder."

Dan reached out a hand and laid it sympathetically on Jack's shoulder. "Jack, listen to me. The girl wasn't positively identified, was she? Maybe there's been some mistake. Maybe it's not even Dani. Until you know for sure, there is no sense getting all worked up about it."

Jack lifted his face, his eyes tormented. "Judging from the description in the paper and the picture of the girl, I'm sure two of the three are Dani and her boyfriend, Shon Cole."

"Have you spoken with the authorities?"

Jack shook his head. "No." He sighed. "I think I'm afraid they might confirm my suspicions. I guess I know in my heart it's Dani they're after."

"Still, don't you think it would be better to let the police find her?"

"Pastor Reiss, I know you're trying to help, but I've got to find her first. I've *got* to protect her."

Dan put a hand on Jack's shoulder.

"She'll need someone she can trust. I'm sure Dani didn't murder anyone. She's probably scared to death. She's pregnant, for crying out loud. I just can't figure out how to get out to Detroit to start looking for her."

"You don't think she'll try to come back home?" Dan asked hopefully.

"No. No way. The last time I saw her, we had a big fight. As far as she's concerned, I hate her. I'm sure she hates me."

"Then she may not trust you when you do find her."

"Just my being there will be a big step toward a reconciliation, don't you think?"

Dan smiled. "Sounds prodigal."

Jack chuckled. "Except backward. Must be a 90s thing."

Jack looked into Dan's eyes, seemed about to say something further, then glanced away as if he were embarrassed. Finally he cleared his throat. "I've been so confused by all this. And I haven't been able to figure out how I'm going to get out to Detroit to look for Dani. My car would certainly never make it. Then, it was as if God was telling me to come see you."

Dan's face reflected his bewilderment. "Me? But I don't know how to fix cars." He chuckled. "I'm afraid I'm lucky when I find the gas tank, and that's usually by accident."

"Actually, the impression I got was . . . well, do you think it would be possible for us to trade cars? Just for a little while."

"You want to take my car?"

"Yeah, I guess that's what I'm asking," Jack said quietly.

"I think that's a brilliant idea. I only wish I had some money to offer you as well." He jumped up and went to the vase on the top of the piano that took up one wall of the small living room. Reaching in, he drew out a wad of bills. "Here. This is my emergency money. I don't trust the banks too much. It's not much, but it should help for a while."

Reluctantly, Jack took the money. "Are you sure you can part with this? I'll pay you back. In fact, I was wondering if you would manage the selling of a bunch of my estate while I'm gone. Just take the money from that to repay yourself, and I'll get in touch with you to wire me the rest if I need it. About the only thing I'm hoping to keep is the house, though the only reason is so that I'll have someplace to bring Dani home to if I find her."

"*When* you find her," Dan corrected him. "Please, Jack, if I can do anything else to help, you'll let me know, won't you?"

Jack nodded, his eyes brimming with tears. "Yes, I will. Although I'll never be able to repay you for all you've done so far."

Dan waved him off. "It's the least I can do."

As he pressed the keys into Jack's hands, Dan smiled and put his hand on Jack's shoulder. "Jack, I'm glad you thought of coming to me. I really needed to know that I'm doing something worthwhile." He paused thoughtfully. "I always believed the coming of the end would be so obvious that people could not miss it. I'm beginning to change my mind. I feel that right now we are living in the very last days. But most of my congregation seems totally unaware. In fact, the whole world seems oblivious to the events that are happening."

Chapter Three

Thursday, November 11

Brian Willis paused for a considerable amount of time on the front porch of his house before opening the door. His children had stopped watching for him long ago and had grown accustomed to his long absences. During the short amounts of time he could be with them, they seemed to spend it getting reacquainted instead of enjoying being a family. And the tension building between his wife and him was not pretty.

He endured the long, accusing stares while the kids were up, only to be broadsided by harsh tongue-lashings after they went to bed. Why Ann waited until bedtime to unload was beyond him, but it made for some long, sleepless nights. And it certainly didn't spare the children. The arguments were always loud. No one slept.

Ann was absolutely going to flip out when he told her that Gavin wanted him in Washington, D.C., two days sooner than originally scheduled. Gavin's itinerary had not been set, either, which meant that Brian didn't know how long Gavin planned to remain in D.C. after the rally. Probably a couple of weeks at the most. Hopefully without Brian.

He opened the door and stepped inside quickly, closing it as silently as possible. Ann was not in the living room, probably in the kitchen or in a bedroom, he decided. Matt was playing G.I. Joes, and Hannah apparently was trying to enlist her Barbies. Matt wasn't buying it, and Hannah was clearly frustrated. Brian smiled and made a mental note to look for a female G.I. Joe because he'd heard G.I. Joe had gone equal opportunity. When they saw him, they came running over, and he kissed them. After a couple of long hugs, Brian found Ann in the bedroom folding a pile of clothes stacked on the bed.

"Hi, sweetheart," he said tentatively.

Ann smiled. "Hi. How was your trip?"

Brian sat on the edge of the bed and rubbed his face. "It was fine. These rallies are getting old, you know."

Ann latched onto that disclosure right away, but she seemed to know to tread lighter than usual. "They're getting old for the kids and me too, Hon," she said as she sat down and put her arm around him. "You spend so much time with Gavin you might as well have married him instead of me."

Ann stared at him.

Brian tried to keep a straight face then choked with laughter. He gave her a warm smile and a kiss. "I'm sorry. I know you want to talk about this. I promise, we'll talk."

"Brian. . . ." Ann sighed and reached for a pair of jeans. "All right. You're tired. Go take a shower, and I'll clear off the bed."

"Thanks, sweetheart."

Ann wanted to say something else, he could tell, but she didn't. He hurried back to the front porch, grabbed his suitcases, and carried them back to the bedroom where he unloaded his toiletries and carried them into the bathroom. He stayed in the shower for nearly half an hour, after realizing how truly tired he was and how good the hot water felt. It was good to be home.

The bedroom was dark when he came out. Ann was gone, but

he could faintly smell her and painfully realized just how much he had missed her. In the silent darkness of his own bedroom, he also felt the particular presence of God, and he knelt down beside the bed to pray for a moment before going out to find his family.

Hannah and Matthew were waiting for him. Apparently Hannah had gone to some lengths to make sure he sat down and read her a story. Her favorite, **Stories Jesus Told**, lay on the couch. Brian sat down, and Hannah hopped up beside him and snuggled underneath his left arm. Matthew climbed in close, too, but at six years old was trying to balance affection with independence. Hannah flipped through the pages until she found the story she wanted to hear. Before Brian began, he glanced up and caught sight of Ann peeking in on them. She smiled, but she looked far from content.

Later, when the dishes were washing in the dishwasher and Hannah and Matthew were in bed, Brian and Ann had the evening to themselves. They chose to spend it curled up in front of the fireplace.

Ann had been watching him all evening. "You seem upset about something, Brian."

Brian hesitated to say anything, but after a few long moments he began. "Something happened in Boise. Something I can't explain." He shrugged with a heavy sigh. "I don't even know how to put it into words."

"Didn't the rally go OK?"

"It went fine. What bothered me then, and what has been troubling me ever since, is more of a feeling . . . like God is trying to speak to me."

"God *is* speaking to you, Brian. You may not be giving speeches like Gavin or have the power that he does, but you are a leader in the Christian community. People listen to you."

"I've thought of that. Actually, I've struggled with that. I haven't felt God impress me so vividly for years though. And if God hasn't been guiding until now, who have I been following? Gavin?"

Ann burrowed closer into his chest. "I think God has always been leading you, Brian. Sometimes He just chooses not to be so visible, that's all."

"And sometimes we don't listen too well either. That's what I'm thinking."

"That's true. But you've always wanted to have God in your life. Everyone gets sidetracked. Everyone forgets. God understands."

"I guess I realized this last weekend just how far I'd gotten off the track," Brian admitted. "I haven't been following God's will so much as Gavin's."

Ann gave a comforting squeeze. "What are you going to do now? You want to do more for God than anyone I know. But if Gavin has his own agenda, what can you do about it?"

"I was thinking about that while I was in the shower."

Ann looked squarely at him. "Quit."

"Quit?"

"That's what I said. Quit. You can get a job anywhere. You could come home every evening and be with your family." She paused. She'd been thinking about this for a long time, and it wasn't the first time the conversation had come up. "Even if you didn't get a job here in Chicago, we could move someplace."

"Ann!" But before he could mount an argument, she jumped up and went to the kitchen where she began unloading the dishwasher. He rose and followed her in. "Ann."

"Ann what? Isn't it time I had a say in this?"

"You don't understand." The pause that followed was like the eye of a hurricane. And then the backside of the storm hit. Dishes crashed on the counter.

"I don't understand? Brian, I understand perfectly well! You spend practically every weekend of the year away from your family, and then half the time it's like you only drop in because a connecting flight happens to come through Chicago. I'm getting tired of taking you to the airport. I've been to O'Hare so often I could walk through it blindfolded."

Brian tried to interrupt, but Ann shot him a warning glare, which in the heat of the moment he might have disregarded had he not noticed the tears in her eyes. He swallowed hard.

Ann's voice softened. "What I don't understand anymore is you, Brian!"

The last words died slowly, but when they were gone, the house was as silent as a tomb. Speaking again for either one of them suddenly became as difficult as breaking through a concrete wall with their fingers. Brian didn't know what to do. Clearly, Ann didn't know either. She carefully stepped around the broken slivers of Corel dishware scattered on the floor and sank down at the kitchen table.

Brian came over and knelt down. He wrapped an arm around her shoulders and hugged her to him. "I'm sorry," he apologized, wrestling with a quiver in his voice, feeling both horrible for hurting her and an intense, shooting pain in his knee. "You know something? I really have been thinking seriously these past few days of quitting." He heard Ann's breathing catch.

"You have?" she asked, putting her hand on his arm and squeezing.

Brian shrugged and nodded. "Yes. Gavin isn't the same person I knew when I went to work for him in the beginning. I'm not sure what it is, exactly. I've been trying to make sense out of it, but . . . it hasn't come yet. I feel like an outsider." He paused, grimacing.

"Are you in pain?" Ann asked, suddenly curious about her husband's expression.

Brian nodded with a wry, painful smile. "I think I knelt on a shard of Corel."

"What? Stand up and let me take a look."

Brian stood and leaned against the counter while Ann bent down to have a look. "You've got blood all over the knee of your sweats."

"Then I was right." Brian grimaced again.

As Ann did minor surgery to extract the Corel shard, Brian

told her about Stan Shultz and about Gavin's suggestion that the Remnant Church may have been responsible. "Shultz donated millions of dollars to charity. He was very generous to the Coalition. The leadership of the Remnant Church could have been angry about him joining the United Religious Coalition."

"Really, Brian, you're letting your imagination get the better of you, I think. Revenge? Anger? We know people in the Remnant Church. They're some of the most Christlike people I know."

Brian shrugged. "Maybe you're right." He paused while Ann applied a Band-Aid. Then he said it. "Ann. I'll tell Gavin I'm leaving the Coalition."

Ann looked up at him as if she couldn't believe what she was hearing. He nodded to reassure her. "Oh, Brian, I'm so grateful." She practically jumped into his arms.

Now came the part he dreaded telling her. "I . . . well . . . I've got to be gone for a couple of weeks."

"You mean, for the rally in Washington, D.C?"

Brian nodded. "You know how huge this thing is. Advertisements are running all over the country—TV, newspaper, magazines. We've sunk millions of dollars into this final rally, and I really ought to stay through to the end."

"Why do *you* have to do it? You're not the only person capable of public relations in the Coalition." Ann knew this was a lost argument.

"Gavin wants to meet with some important people in D.C. He wants me there. I'll talk to him when I get there and sort of feel things out. After the rally, I'm coming home for good. I just don't know when for sure."

"I can live with that," Ann replied after a few seconds of thoughtful silence. "I won't even keep trying to negotiate. It's more than I hoped for."

Chapter Four

Friday, November 12

Jack Talbot was discovering that the best way to keep from dozing while driving was to have a bum leg stuffed underneath the dash of a Toyota Corolla. The continual low-level throbbing was enough to keep him awake, and every five or ten minutes he also experienced the incredible sensation of having a cramp shoot from his left buttock to his knee. Each time it happened, he let out a gasp and pushed his foot against the floorboard.

It was three in morning on the outskirts of Des Moines, Iowa. He turned the radio on and scanned through station after station just to be doing something that would kill some time. He liked talk radio, and if he was searching for anything, it was a broadcast where people were on the air talking about their problems. The funny thing was that he could think of a million suggestions to help other people, but at the same time he had no idea what to do about his own. He located a talk show out of New York on the topic of religion. Fingers pausing an inch from the "scan" button, he changed his mind and sat back just in time to endure another spike of pain from the first cramp of the day.

"Hello, this is Ralph Dixon, and you're listening to Christian Talk. Let's go to San Diego, California, where Liz Hoagland has been patiently waiting. Hello. Liz?"

"Hi. Mr. Dixon?"

"Yes, you're on the air, Liz."

"Thank you for taking my call. I was wondering if you think all religions can get along. I know I get along just fine with my Religious Coalition friends no matter what church we go to. Should a few doctrinal differences really be something to get all worried about? I'm talking mainly about the way the Remnant Church believes."

"*Hmmm*. I think what you are wondering is not an uncommon question. But you have to remember that the United Religious Coalition encourages unity. This is the reason it has struggled to narrow the doctrinal gap between Protestant denominations and is working so hard to unite with the Catholic Church. You're reaping the results of a strong commitment from Gavin Larson and the United Religious Coalition to bring all Christians together under one banner. It strengthens us individually, economically, and especially morally."

"I think so too," Liz agreed.

Yeah, because of simple peer pressure, Jack thought. *Don't have to do your own thinking.*

"Have you heard Gavin Larson speak about the power of America? He observes the same kind of community spirit nationally that you have noticed right in your own neck of the woods. It is this spirit of unity that Mr. Larson claims will strengthen America. Remnant believers may sincerely believe in their interpretation of the Bible, but they are not doing themselves or you and me any good by separating themselves from the Coalition. In fact, it weakens us all."

For a moment, Liz was lost to static. Then her voice returned crystal clear. "I think you're right, Mr. Dixon. I had never thought about it on such a big scale before."

Jack rubbed his leg. He thought about Dan Reiss's fears that the last days were coming. Liz's voice brought him back to the radio as the conversation moved in a more personal attack.

"Ralph, what do you think about the Remnant Church? I've met a few Remnant believers, and they give me the creeps. I'm a good person. I'm a Christian, for heaven's sake, but the Remnant Church says that you and I do not understand God's character."

There was a long moment of silence. Jack thought he'd lost the frequency again. Then Ralph's voice cut through the night. "Do you feel harassed by Remnant Church believers, Liz?"

"Uh, not harassed, exactly. Just made to feel uncomfortable. There wouldn't be so many Christians joining the United Religious Coalition if God did not approve of it. Isn't that right? So what makes the Remnant Church call the United Religious Coalition the false prophet that will rise up in the last days to turn people against Christ?"

"I agree with you, Liz. And I don't have an answer. As far as I'm concerned, the Remnant believers are a bunch of fanatics. In a way, that makes them a detriment to our society. It is a matter of record that Stan Shultz, one of the most respected financial geniuses in this century, was once a Remnant Church believer. . . ." There was a moment when the airwaves were filled with silence, a moment skillfully inserted by Ralph Dixon as he led listeners down the path of "righteous" insinuation. "Is there anything else you would like to talk about?"

"Yes. I—I just can't believe what's happened to Donald Thurgood," she said almost reverently. "I saw him on the news yesterday. My prayer group has met twice since then to pray for him."

"Good. I'm glad to hear that. I know a lot of people are praying for God to lay His healing hand on the Speaker. This country certainly needs his leadership," Ralph added.

"And pray for Dani too," Jack said aloud. "Pray that I'll find her." But Religion Talk broke away to a commercial, and Liz was gone for good.

It was near noon when Jack felt the claustrophobic pressure of thousands of automobiles jockeying for position, entering the freeway and exiting, all seeming to have been preprogrammed as they swept him along. His leg was tight and killing him, and he was afraid it might go to sleep. Edging to the outside lane, he exited at the first fairly uncomplicated exit he could find and pulled into a Wendy's parking lot.

Jack parked, grabbed the map, and headed inside. He was fortunate the young man behind the register allowed him to use the restaurant's phonebook since the one in the phone booth outside was minus the city government section. He ordered salad and took it to a section that felt like an atrium. Before eating, he located the Detective Bureau on his map.

He noticed the traffic hadn't let up much as he gauged his speed and merged back onto Detroit's freeway grid. He was not a seasoned traveler, so to him, strange cities were just that—strange. They were different, and they were unfamiliar. How, he wondered, had his daughter felt in this strange, big city alone? At least at one point she must have become alone and scared all in the same instant. It gave him a sick feeling to imagine what Dani must be feeling.

Had she thought of him? He felt sure that she must have, and he had not been there for her when she needed him.

Jack almost missed the exit that would put him on the John C. Lodge Freeway. In a moment of desperation, he shot a quick look over his shoulder and squeezed through two lanes of heavy traffic to make the junction. Thirty minutes later, he was sitting in the Detective Bureau slowly losing his patience as he waited for a Detective Coleman. Finally, he tossed away his empty can of 7UP and approached the front desk. Deputy Shaw, a black woman in her forties who had assisted him when he first came in, met him at the counter.

"Yes, Mr. Talbot?"

"I've been waiting some time to speak to Detective Coleman.

Is there any way at all you can track him down?"

Shaw frowned sympathetically. "I'm really very sorry it is taking so long." She didn't say that the Bureau was overworked, but she didn't have to. Her expression only asked that he understand. Then, with some relief, her eyes lighted up. "I think you're in luck, Mr. Talbot. Hold on." She raised her hand and waved, and Jack turned around. "Detective Coleman. Will you come over here for a moment?"

Coleman. Detective Denny Coleman, changed course and walked over, maybe a little perturbed at being interrupted but hiding it well. He was a medium-built African-American, probably in his fifties, with stern features, a well-manicured mustache, and a hairline that had long since retreated to a position on the same level with his eyes.

"Thank you," Jack said quietly to the deputy. And then he introduced himself, shaking hands with the detective. "Detective, my name is Jack Talbot. I'm a police officer from Boise, Idaho. I'd like to discuss a case you're working on."

The detective lifted an eyebrow then motioned him to follow. "What case is that?"

"The murder of the banker a few days ago. Stan Shultz. He owned Trust National Bank Corporation."

Jack was shown a chair in front of a remarkably neat desk. "What is it you want to know?"

Jack leaned forward in the chair. "I'm not here officially. I'm on medical leave."

"The limp."

Nodding, Jack rubbed the leg. "I pulled a van with stolen tags over one night and got caught in a shootout."

"I wouldn't be in a uniform again," Coleman said simply.

Jack nodded again as he glanced at a photograph sitting on the desk, a picture of the detective's wife and two grown daughters. One of the young women wore a cap and gown. Physically, she had the eyes of her father, but where hers were full of wonder and idealism, her father's eyes knew better. She was extremely beautiful. "I'm here for personal reasons, Detective. I hope you can help."

For the next quarter of an hour, Jack outlined the events surrounding the disappearance of his daughter, his description of Shon and his affiliation with the Freedom Society, and his belief that Dani might be the female suspect. As he talked, Coleman produced a file and laid it on his desk. On a legal pad, he took notes. He wore an unemotional façade that Jack knew was a defense mechanism to keep from becoming too involved with the victims whose lives he was trying to sort out.

When Jack was finished, Coleman regarded him with sad eyes. "There were three suspects involved in the shooting. We were not able to apprehend any of them, but we may know where one is. The other two were a male and a female.

"When the shooting happened there was some dense fog, so there were not many witnesses, and none of them got a clear look at any of the suspects. But we do have witnesses who say the female fled the scene on foot, leaving the two men. She may have been trying to escape. But like I said, there was fog. It's hard to say for sure exactly what happened."

"Have you been looking for the girl?"

Coleman studied the top of his desk for several moments before carefully framing his answer. "Mr. Talbot, I don't know what I want to say to that. As a law enforcement officer, it is my duty to arrest the second man and the girl. I believe the man was an accomplice. The girl is a suspect too, but she could have been a victim herself. At any rate, at the moment I am not pursuing the girl. Only the second man."

Jack had been keeping his emotions in a holding pattern ever since entering the Detective Bureau. He had not allowed himself the luxury to hope or the ability to lose hope. Now, suddenly, he felt let down. "I don't understand. That *girl* is very likely my daughter, and she's running frightened and scared. You'd be doing her *and* me a favor by finding her."

"I understand your frustration, Mr. Talbot, but think carefully about this."

Jack probed a different angle. "You said you thought you knew where one of the suspects is. Where is he, and why haven't you arrested him yet?"

"We pulled him out of a canal yesterday afternoon," Coleman replied. "He's waiting in the morgue for an autopsy."

"And you're sure he was one of the two men with my daughter?"

The detective nodded. "I'm convinced of it now. There was no identification on the body. But your description of your daughter's boyfriend fits."

Jack sucked in a deep breath, the news shocking his system. "What happened?"

Coleman shrugged. "Who knows? But it was clear his death was a homicide."

"Do you think the second man killed Shon?" Jack said.

Coleman nodded, looking grim. "That would be my guess. I assume you know your daughter is pregnant."

"Yes."

"I don't relish the idea of putting a young pregnant woman in jail when I don't believe she was a willing participant in a crime, and I certainly don't believe she's dangerous. The man who disappeared when your daughter did *is* a very dangerous man, however. I want you to understand that very clearly." Coleman looked at Jack.

"Is there a good possibility you'll catch him?"

"Yes. Most definitely. But we also have a very large worry. We think he's after the girl."

Jack stiffened. "What? Why does he want her?"

"Why? I don't know for sure, and I wish I did. But he killed his partner. I think he will do the same to the girl if he finds her."

Subconsciously, Jack had begun to rub his leg. It was something he'd started doing to ease the pain during his rehabilitation that later turned into a comfort mechanism. "Who is he?"

Jack asked.

"All I can tell you is what I suspect from the evidence I've collected so far. I believe this second man to be a felon on the FBI's most-wanted list. His name is Gunnar Dietrich. We only have a hazy description of him from witnesses in front of the bank, but it matches up pretty well with what the FBI has."

"Dani would still be safer with the authorities than on her own," Jack said.

"Maybe, but we'd have to find her first, and right now I just don't have the manpower to attempt something like that. In any case, we believe she has left the state," Coleman replied quickly. He pulled a sheet of paper out of a notebook and passed it over the desktop to Jack. It was an FBI Most-Wanted poster. "Here's what Dietrich looks like."

Jack took the paper. "You told me this man Dietrich is probably after my daughter and that *if* he found her, he probably would kill her too. You know where she went, don't you?"

"I don't know what you are talking about." The detective broke eye contact.

"I want to know the parts you left out. All I want to do is find Dani—ahead of this other guy. You told me earlier there was too much fog for anyone to get a good description of the suspects, but the sketch of Dani in the papers was accurate enough for me to recognize her. That means you talked to someone afterward who could describe her."

"Mr. Talbot—."

"I want the truth, Detective. Grant me that much, at least. I think you can imagine how you will feel should things not work out as you hope."

Coleman looked away for a moment. His hand came up, and he rubbed the bridge of his nose with his thumb and index finger. "OK. We know Dani left town on a Greyhound bound for Burlington, Vermont. It took some legwork, but we were quick to get on it, so we knew within two hours after she left. That was Tuesday evening."

"And Dietrich?"

"We talked the man at the ticket booth into telling whoever asked that the girl had gone to Albany, New York. We planned to arrest Dietrich in a controlled takedown."

Jack braced himself, feeling instantly lightheaded, knowing what was coming.

"Unfortunately." Coleman sighed heavily. "He never asked. But this guy is a professional. Believe me, by now he knows where she is."

* * *

Mara Benneton hung up her white lab coat, slipped into a long gray overcoat, and headed for the door. She swept loose strands of red hair behind her ear. It never seemed to stay up in a French braid for very long. Before she could make it out the clinic door, a voice pursued her.

"Dr. Benneton! Dr. Benneton! We just admitted another one. Do you want to do the exam yourself?"

Mara didn't even pause as she threw up her hands and called over her shoulder, "Not now, Lisa, I'm going out for some air, and a little lunch wouldn't kill me. Find Dr. Ellis. He offered to cover for me." Slamming her hands against the door, she pushed it open with such force that it rocketed against the doorjamb and coming back nearly hit her. She dodged it and stepped out onto the street.

Taking a deep breath, she closed her eyes and savored the pungent odor of fall. The tangy smell of dying leaves mixed with a cold, stiff breeze from Lake Champlain. It was invigorating. Aromatherapy, she mused as she quickened her steps and headed for Church Street.

As she turned left at the First Unitarian Universalist Society Church onto Church Street, she was again struck by how much it had changed in the last few years. Scrawled graffiti marked gang territory, and litter blew with abandon down the brick-lined street. Pedestrians no longer strolled leisurely while shopping and listening to street musicians. Instead, they scurried, wrapped up in themselves, avoiding eye contact or any gesture that might be mistaken as threatening.

Mara kept her own eyes pasted to the ground in front of her. There was no sense in provoking the gangs that patrolled these streets. Out of the corner of her eye, she saw a large group, talking and laughing in tones that carried at least half a block. *It's like they owned the world,* Mara thought. *But what they really own is misery, violence, fear, and worst of all, hopelessness.*

Dressed in cutoff army fatigues, their heads were shaved and tattoos laced their arms, heads, and faces. The girls aped the men, who swaggered and cursed. It was hard to tell them apart. Mara shuddered and lengthened her stride. Just ahead was O. Henry's, where she planned to eat lunch.

Once a very nice, upscale restaurant, the place now had an almost furtive air. The metal bars surrounding the restaurant didn't help. Garbage blowing around the streets caught in the bars, further deteriorating its appearance. A restless waiter seated her and took her order, all without ever actually looking at her.

Mara was dismayed to see that he, too, had oozing scabs on his face and hands. Some had broken open and were bleeding despite obvious attempts to conceal them. A few times he covered his mouth as his body was racked with a hacking cough. Her stomach turned. Not because she was squeamish. She had been treating people with the same symptoms for the last two weeks. Still, she couldn't help but wonder if the person about to cook her food was in the same condition.

What is the CDC doing, anyway? She suddenly realized that the only reason this man was still working was because the government was trying its best to downplay the disease, whatever it was. And to do that, they couldn't very well order businesses to send their workers home, because that *would* generate hysteria.

Mara had a clear view of the street, and depressing as it was, she stared at it. The state of deterioration defied the imagination. Mara remembered days when she spent lunch hours sitting on one of the benches lining the street, watching street musicians and feeding the pigeons. The place had been rich with culture; it had celebrated ethnicity. Now all it celebrated was destruction.

A police officer on a mountain bike pedaled past the window. The gang absorbed his attention, but Mara knew he wouldn't stop unless they were about to commit murder. Even then, the police were slow to act. Some people claimed that the police were scared of the gangs and couldn't be counted on for protection.

Mara drummed her fingers on the table impatiently. Just before she worked up enough nerve to ask when her lunch would be ready, her attention was caught by a lone figure walking quickly up the street. It was a young pregnant girl whose knuckles were stone white as she gripped the edges of an old coat that was much too small to reach around her belly. She struggled to keep the coat closed against a stiff breeze that also blew her short, ragged brown hair around her face, obscuring it from view.

As she made her way past the gang, one of the men lunged out for her arm. He made a comment that caused hoots and laughter among his comrades. The girl jerked away, stumbled, then ran blindly past them. The one who had grabbed for her looked as though he might consider chasing her down, but a possessive arm around his waist from one of the girls in the group changed his mind. The two began to make out shamelessly, and the frightened pregnant girl was forgotten.

But, Mara continued to wonder about her.

She jumped as the waiter cleared his throat to get her attention. "I'm sorry, but your order will be a little longer," he apologized.

Mara tried to hide her irritation. She felt guilty enough taking time off for lunch when they were swamped at the welfare clinic. "What's the problem?"

The waiter scuffed his feet and avoided her gaze. "Well, the cook has been sick, and the boss sent him to the emergency room. The dishwasher took over, but she's new, and she doesn't exactly know what she's doing." He bent down and whispered. "I could probably cook. I'm not bad. But, well, you can see I'm sick too."

Mara groaned. "Listen, thanks anyway, but I have to get back to work."

"Are you sure?" The waiter's eyes met hers, and there was desperation in them. Mara was pretty sure he was mostly concerned about losing his tip.

She stood up to leave. "Yes, I'm sure." Reaching into her pocket, she pulled out a few bills and laid them on the table. "Thanks anyway. I appreciate that you won't handle the food directly. Try to keep anyone who is sick from cooking. OK?"

The waiter shrugged. "Sure."

"I'm a doctor. I work at the Ethan Allen Health Care Clinic. If you get worse at all, you come and see me. OK?" Mara said warmly.

He smiled. "Sure. Thanks."

The way he scrambled to retrieve the money as she headed for the door made her wonder about his desperation. But wasn't everyone desperate lately? She walked quickly back to the clinic. The volume of noise seemed to have increased in her absence, and she wondered if it just sounded more frantic because she'd been away for a little while or if there were actually more patients than when she'd left. Lisa, a second-year medical student who helped out in her spare time, pounced on her before she could get out of her coat and answered her question.

"We've had eleven more admissions since you left. Ten of them are showing the same viral symptoms we've been seeing for the past couple of weeks. The other one is just pregnant and wants to be checked out."

"What? Did you say pregnant?" She remembered the young girl.

"Yes, pregnant. She figures she's about six months along. She's complaining about some abdominal pain. I put her in the last cubicle. Who do you want to see first?"

"I'll see the girl," Mara said. She noticed the surprised expression on Lisa's face. "It'll be refreshing to see a patient with a normal condition, Lisa."

She slipped through the curtain that separated the cubicles. In front of her was the same girl she had observed on Church Street. Her pallor contributed to her overall waiflike appearance. She was so thin she looked like a child's drawing of a pregnant stick figure. Her brown hair was chopped into a shag cut that clung in fine wisps to her hollow cheeks. Dark circles ringed her eyes, making them appear almost black. They eyed Mara warily as she picked up the chart and read Lisa's notes.

"Danielle, is it?"

"Dani," the girl replied simply. "Just Dani."

Mara consulted the notes again. "No last name, Dani?"

The girl shook her head stubbornly. "Just Dani."

"Well, Dani, I understand you've been having some abdominal pain." Mara said, trying to sound neutral despite her curiosity about the girl.

Dani's head jerked up and down almost mechanically, and she absently laid a protective hand over her abdomen.

"Where exactly has the pain been?" Mara asked.

The long, thin fingers traced a line along the left side of her belly. "And sometimes it's on the other side, too, but mostly this side."

Mara raised an eyebrow. "And you haven't had this pain before?"

Dani shook her head. "No, just in the last couple of days."

"What does the pain feel like?"

"Shooting," Dani replied, wincing slightly at the sound of the word. "Or stabbing." Again she winced as if she had other associations for those words.

"I see," Mara said. "Does this pain last very long?"

Dani shook her head. "Maybe a minute or two."

"Well, Dani," Mara said after a brief preliminary examination, "I think what you are experiencing is a stretching of the ligaments attached to the uterus. That can cause the type of pain you're describing. It's very unpleasant, to be sure, but also very common."

Relief flooded Dani's face. "Really?"

Mara softened. The girl looked so much like a lost child. "Yes. Of course, if it gets worse or lasts longer, you should seek medical attention right away. But, at this point, I'd say that's what we're dealing with, and there is no cause for alarm. Why don't you hop up on the examining table, and I'll check you out to be sure everything looks OK."

Mara completed the exam quickly and asked a few more questions. "Go ahead and get dressed. I'll be right back."

She stepped out of the room and scribbled some notes in the girl's chart before knocking on the door. Hearing a muffled "OK," she reentered the room. "Well, Dani, you look fine, but as I said, if the pain gets worse, you come back and let me know."

Dani pushed herself carefully off the examining table. Standing fully erect, her head came to just below Mara's chin. She looked up at her, and Mara felt her throat constrict as she tried to control an unexplained ball of emotion. "Thank you, Doctor. I'm afraid I don't have any money. . . ." Her voice trailed off as her eyes dropped to the floor.

Mara laid a hand on her shoulder. "That's OK. There's no charge."

Dani looked up. In her face there was relief and thanks. "Thank you. Thank you so much. Do you, I mean, that is . . . do you know somewhere I can spend the night? A mission or something where I might be able to get some food and a place to sleep?"

Mara had to force herself not to gape at the girl. "You mean you haven't got a place to stay?"

Dani shook her head. "I just got in on a bus two days ago. I don't know anyone here, and I used all the money I had on a motel room for two nights."

Mara thought about the mission in town. It was the only one. All the others had shut down years ago. The city only kept this one open because of the high demand, but even the police wouldn't go near the place. Some local churches tried to help out by staffing it and donating food, but lately even they had become too frightened of the rampant violence and disease of the place to help out much. Mara shuddered to think of what would become of Dani in such a place.

And there was nowhere else she could go either. It was much too cold to sleep outside, even if a park bench was safe and she wasn't pregnant. The next thought that popped into her mind she almost dismissed out of hand. She had a spare room and could easily put the girl up for the weekend at least. She remembered the gang she had watched on the street earlier, and that decided it for her.

She shook her head as if to clear it. *I must be working too hard,* she thought. *I've never thought of doing anything this crazy before. What am I thinking of? I don't even know her!*

Still, looking at Dani's hopeful expression again, she could hardly believe it would be too much trouble to have her around for a couple of days. "There is a mission in town," she said finally. "But you can't go there."

Dani's face fell, and her lower lip quivered. "Why not?"

"It's a horrible place. You wouldn't last five minutes there. It really isn't safe. But, if you'd like, you're welcome to stay with me for a few days."

Dani looked up at her, eyes narrowing suspiciously. "Why would you want me to stay with you?"

Mara shrugged. "Well, you have nowhere else to go, and I do have a spare room. It's not exactly four stars, but I like to call it home. Besides, if you have any more problems with that pain or if it gets worse, I'd be right there to help you out."

Dani seemed to consider this for a minute. "How do I know I can trust you?" she asked finally.

"How do I know I can trust you?" Mara countered.

Dani's lips turned up in what was close to a smile. "OK, I guess we're even. Thank you again."

"You'll have to stay here until my shift is through in a few hours, but in the meantime I'm pretty sure I can find something around here for you to eat and a cot so you can take a nap or at least rest for a little while. Then you can catch a ride home with me." Mara turned and led the way out of the cubicle, butterflies colliding in her stomach. *Oh, Lord,* she thought, *what have I done?*

* * *

Jack wasn't sure why he did it exactly. There was really no point, and he was at a place where it didn't pay to do pointless things. He brooded in the Corolla for about ten minutes before making up his mind and pulling out into traffic, headed right off Virginia Park onto Woodward Ave. He consulted the map with his free hand and kept one eye on traffic.

He took a right onto I-94 and fought the surge of automobiles as he navigated onto Highway 10 and off the ramp to Howard Street. He turned into the bus depot, quickly zipping into a parking spot being vacated.

The air inside the terminal was stale and smelled vaguely sour. There was litter everywhere, despite the man at the opposite end of the terminal pushing a broom around. People milled restlessly, waiting for the next bus, and somewhere in the crowd a child cried irritably, getting ready to really shriek, Jack guessed.

As he headed toward the ticket counter, people began to board a bus. He stepped out of the way and sank gratefully down on one of the benches to rest his leg. Feeling suddenly overwhelmed with helplessness, he covered his face with his hands.

He knew where Dani was going, but he had never imagined a killer following her too. What if Dietrich caught up with her before he did? He couldn't let it happen. "God," he muttered under his breath. "You've got to help me. How am I going to find her?

Please, please keep her safe until I get there."

He thought about questioning the station manager or ticket taker for information about anything peculiar that Dani might have said or done the night she came through, but he remembered what Detective Coleman had said about the setup to arrest whoever asked questions about Dani. There was nothing more he could find out here anyway. His best option was heading straight for Burlington, Vermont, picking up her trail from there. Surely someone had seen her or remembered where she had been headed.

Jack's stomach rumbled with hunger, and he heaved himself off the chair and made his way over to the vending machine. Slipping in a dollar bill, he punched the button for a bag of popcorn and a package of cheese crackers. The machine churned out the popcorn, but the crackers stuck. Jack placed his hands on either side of the vending machine and shook it fiercely. As he did so, he looked down and noticed something glittering at his feet. Without thinking, he bent over to retrieve it.

In his hands he held a broken gold chain. Dangling from the chain was a tiny heart. How many times had he seen that same heart hanging around Dani's neck? How many times had the sight of it made his blood boil? Now he clutched it as though it were a lifeline.

Here was tangible proof that Dani had been there. This was something that had belonged to his little girl. Jack felt new purpose and hope surge through him. God *was* leading him, he knew that now. And God would keep Dani safe until he found her.

In front of him, the vending machine choked out the crackers, and they dropped into the tray. But Jack was no longer thinking about his stomach. He had to find his little girl, and there was no time to waste.

* * *

Dietrich stepped out of the bus depot and spit on the ground.

He surveyed the surrounding area. There was not much activity for what was the largest city in Vermont. A stiff breeze from the nearby lake stabbed through the open front of his leather jacket like a knife. With small, dispassionate eyes, he studied the few people hurrying along the sidewalk.

For someone of his skill, tracking the girl had been easy, although it had consumed nearly two days. He knew she was in town and that she had stayed in a motel. After checking at the depot, he knew also that she had not left Burlington, at least not on a bus. But now it was too late to continue looking for her. There would be time enough in the morning. What he could really use now, he thought, was some exercise to loosen the stiffness in his legs and a good stiff drink.

He left his car near the depot and cut across the park, heading to the greatest concentration of lights a few blocks up. He hadn't even walked a complete block when he was drawn to loud music and smoke spilling out onto the sidewalk from an open door.

Finding little room at the bar, he squeezed into the only space available. "Give me some whiskey," he demanded. The bartender nodded and picked up a glass.

"I haven't seen you here before."

Dietrich turned to look at the speaker and found himself staring into eyes that lacked every emotion but despair. They were like the eyes of a dead man and were sunk into a pock-marked face oozing with sores. Instantly he understood why everyone else had given this man space. He sneered and turned his back on the man.

"Listen. I didn't mean anything by it except conversation. Sorry I said anything. Just grateful you're not afraid to sit next to me."

Dietrich half smiled. "I can't remember the last time I was afraid of anyone, or anything, for that matter." He pointed at the man's face. "Including whatever you've got."

"You aren't afraid of getting sick?"

Dietrich shook his head.

The man stared at his drink for a moment. Dietrich surveyed the room and downed his drink. As he set his glass down, the diseased man said, "That makes me curious. I mean, that you're not afraid of getting whatever this is. It's like a plague or something. The doctors don't even know how it gets caught or what it is. Could be that everyone who gets it will die."

Dietrich shrugged. "Maybe. But I'm not afraid of death."

The man nodded, accepting the explanation. He'd probably heard that line a few times before, Dietrich thought.

"Religious freak, huh?" He didn't realize that *fanatic* probably would have been a better term. He stuck out his hand. "My name's Harry, by the way. So tell me, what is it you do?"

Dietrich thought about this for a moment. Recruiting people had never really been an activity he concerned himself with. There were plenty of other members in the Freedom Society who understood politics much better than he and who brought people into the organization based on the simple ideology that for America to be the greatest nation on earth it had to be continually strengthened through unity and morality. And after listening to Gavin Larson, thousands of people fervently committed themselves to practice strict, pious living. Gavin told his followers that God would certainly protect and richly bless them if they finally began doing what God wanted them to do. It had to be a simple, combined commitment, Gavin preached.

Though he didn't particularly care for the game of chess, he did know how it was played and why it was appealing. And he understood completely why it was such a popular euphemism for what went on in politics. He thought briefly about Stan Shultz. Shultz had threatened to investigate Gavin's use of contributed funds. He had unwittingly underestimated Gavin and had paid for it, but the real irony of his death was that it could be used against the Remnant Church of which he had once been a member. The Coalition had cast a seed of doubt, in connection with Shultz's death, that the Remnant Church was nothing more than a shrinking sect of people who were bitter toward the United Religious Coalition. Dietrich focused on Harry, almost forgetting there was a question to be answered. "I think that the less you know about me, the better off we'll both be, my friend."

Harry looked genuinely let down. Dietrich thought he saw an opportunity. Though he didn't usually recruit people, he did recognize the benefit of having someone feel like they owed him. Harry was probably as ostracized because of his condition as someone who had AIDS. He was sure Harry needed money.

"Listen, Harry, you've heard of those Japanese kamikaze pilots in World War II who sacrificed their lives for their country? Or those Islamic Arabs who drive truck bombs into buildings?"

Harry shook his head ruefully. "Sick. That's what they are."

"True. They are misguided. But soldiers like that are devoted to a cause. You could say I'm the same type of soldier. Only difference is I'm on the winning side. Makes a difference."

One thing about Harry, he was persistent. "Do you know much about Burlington?" he asked Dietrich.

Dietrich shook his head.

"I could help you out, whatever it is you do. Show you around, stuff like that. I need a job real bad."

"All right." Dietrich pulled two one-hundred-dollar bills from his wallet and tossed them on the bar in front of Harry. "I don't make mistakes," he warned.

Harry reached out tentatively then swept the money into his hand, committing himself. "What do I call you?"

Dietrich smiled again. "Dietrich. You meet me here tomorrow morning at eight. And, Harry, don't cross me." He pushed his way through the throng of bodies back out onto the deserted street. After a quick look up and down the street, he returned to his car.

* * *

Later in the evening, Jack wearily pulled his car up in front of a dirty looking motel on the outskirts of Toronto, Canada. He'd spent the last hour lost in the city. Looking up to get his bearings, he saw that the sun had thrown burnt orange shadows on the CN Tower and the 72-story Bank of Montreal building. Under any other circumstances, it would have taken his breath away. Tonight it only made him more frantic.

As he chose streets randomly, driving past provincial parliament buildings, private dwellings, public housing, and high-rise apartments, he was afraid he'd never get out of the city. Every moment he was lost pounded out a rhythm on the imaginary clock that ticked in his head like a time bomb. Finally, spitting a prayer through clenched teeth, he'd made a fortunate turn that led him out of the city, put him back on the main drag, and past this motel where he decided to stop and get a room for the night.

Weary, his leg throbbing with pain, he limped into the reception area and rang the quaint silver bell on the counter. Instantly a man appeared from behind a greasy, polyester curtain in back of the desk. Fat lips poked out from beneath a bushy mustache. They turned upward in a friendly smile.

"Bonsoir, monsieur. Comment allez-vous?"

Jack blinked stupidly for a moment before he remembered that this was, after all, Canada. "Uh—I'm sorry, I don't speak French. Do you speak English? Uh—parlay English?"

The man held up his hands and his smile, if possible, increased. "It is not a problem, monsieur," he assured Jack. "Etienne Gagné speaks also the English."

Jack sighed in relief. "Oh, great. Had me worried there for a minute."

"What is it monsieur desires? A room, perhaps?"

"Yeah, I need a room for the night. Do you have any left?"

"But, of course." Etienne fished around behind the counter for a minute before he found what he was looking for. Drawing out a rusty looking key, he brushed it off apologetically and handed it to Jack with a flourish. "I am sorry. It is the only one that is left. I will have Georgette clean it while you are waiting."

He disappeared behind the curtain, and a few minutes later a surly looking woman in a baggy housedress shuffled past the front window pushing a cleaning cart. Etienne reappeared. "And will monsieur be using a carte de crédit this evening? Or does monsieur prefer to pay in cash?"

"Uh, cash," Jack said, fumbling in his wallet. As he peeled the required amount of bills out, he worried about his money supply.

"C'est bon," Etienne gushed, snatching the bills eagerly and stuffing them into the open cash register drawer. "Georgette should be finished with your room now. If you wish anything further, you will please to let us know. Bonne nuit, monsieur."

"Yeah, you too," Jack muttered as Etienne backed through the curtain and disappeared. He fingered the rusty key and made his way out to his car to get his duffel bag. He passed Georgette as she grumpily pushed the filthy cleaning cart back to the office.

"Thank you," Jack said with forced cheerfulness.

She looked him directly in the eye and spat on the ground by his feet. "Américain," she growled under her breath as she passed him.

Jack swallowed hard and made his way to his room. He let himself in but was hesitant to set his duffel bag down anywhere. Cobwebs decorated every corner of the room, and there were giant, dark red stains covering the carpet. From his position by the front door he could hear the bathroom faucet dripping. His nose alerted him to the cat feces long before he located it behind the television set.

Gingerly, he turned back the sheets on the bed. Once white, they were yellowed and stained also. He opted to sleep on top of the bedspread fully clothed and determined not to let any of his body parts touch anything unnecessarily during his brief stay.

Jack wolfed down a vegetarian hoagie while he glanced at his map to get a general idea of the direction he would be taking in the morning. His plan was to go through New York to get to

Vermont and Dani. Laying aside the map, he flipped on the television, surprised that the tube in the ancient set actually fired up. There was no remote control, so he was forced to turn the channels the old-fashioned way. He passed several French language channels before coming on an American station. Popping some painkillers to calm his leg down, he settled back as comfortably as possible on the bed.

A picture of Pope John Xavier flashed on the screen. The pontiff was saying mass at St. Peter's. That clip was quickly followed by a shot of Gavin Larson waving at an enormous crowd. "Loyal followers and even skeptics everywhere are awaiting with great interest the meeting of these two religious giants scheduled to take place on Friday," reported Lee Jin Shil, a pretty Korean news anchor. She turned to her fellow anchor with a charming smile. "I'm pretty anxious to see the outcome myself."

Jack was keenly disappointed he had missed the story, but his interest was immediately captivated as she continued. "In other news, authorities are urging citizens everywhere to admit themselves at emergency health-care facilities at any sign of a virus that is sweeping the East Coast. Some areas are beginning to make admission mandatory. Several concerned citizens turned their neighbors in, but on the whole, most people are acting responsibly. Medical professionals urge that there is no need for panic but stress the importance of early detection and treatment.

"In related news there is no word on the condition of Vice President Carson, who was taken sick a week ago and hospitalized. White House officials continue to deny rumors that the vice president has been stricken with the virus.

"The body of a white male pulled from a canal in Detroit Thursday afternoon has been positively identified as Shon Cole, who is the suspected murderer of billionaire philanthropist, Stan Shultz. Police are still looking for two other suspects in the case, a man who operates under the name of Gunnar Dietrich and an unidentified pregnant girl. And that's all the news for tonight,

Bob," she concluded.

"Th-th-that's all folks," Jack muttered as he flipped off the set and rolled onto his back on the bed, staring up at the disgusting ceiling above him. "Lord," he prayed, "things are getting pretty complicated. Please help me to find Dani before someone else does. I trust You, and I know You're looking out for her. Thank You for that. And for leading me every step of the way."

He thought momentarily about shutting off the light but fell asleep before he could make himself get up off the bed and do it. Sometime during the night, the electricity flickered several times and then died. Jack groaned in his sleep and rolled over, burying his face unconsciously into the seedy pillow under his head.

Chapter Five

Saturday, November 13

Dani woke up slowly. She found that if she didn't move at all and kept her eyes closed, she could almost imagine she was in her old room at home. Mom would be in the kitchen making breakfast, and Dad would be sprawled out on the couch reading the paper. He would give her a hard time about being a sleepyhead when she finally got up.

A good hard kick chased her daydreams away. The tiny foot of her baby hooked underneath her rib cage, and she squirmed to get away from the uncomfortable pressure. When her eyes opened, she saw Mara watching her from her perch on a stool at the kitchen counter. Dani sat up on the futon couch Mara had pulled down into a bed for her.

"So you're awake," Mara said, one hand cradling a mug of coffee and the other flipping through the newspaper. Her red hair was tied back with a multi-colored scrunchie, and she wore men's boxer shorts and a T-shirt that looked three sizes too big.

Dani ran her fingers through her knotted hair and rubbed

her face. "Dad always said getting me up was like trying to wake the dead," she mumbled, her tongue feeling thick and her brain operating slowly. "I'm not a morning person." She got up and pulled out a stool next to Mara.

Mara smiled warmly and gave her the sections of the paper she'd already read. Dani immediately scanned the national news. The shooting was still a first-page story, telling her, in a way, that Stan Shultz had been a very important man, not just very wealthy. *At least my face isn't staring back at me,* she thought.

"Does the news interest you?" Mara asked.

Dani shrugged. "Sometimes." She set aside the rest of the paper and read the article about Shultz. Brian Willis, of the United Religious Coalition, was quoted as saying that the Coalition was stunned and appalled over the shooting. "There were very few people in this world," Willis said, "who had the means to help so many people. And there were fewer still who had such a giving spirit." Dani secretly wiped her eyes and blinked to clear her vision.

When her eyes focused again, the words "Shultz killer Shon Cole" and "murdered" leapt off the page at her. Panic-stricken, she scanned the rest of the article. Shon was dead! The police suspected Dietrich. Beside the article was Shon's high school picture. Dani closed her eyes and struggled to control herself. She couldn't let go of her emotion in front of Mara.

With extreme determination, she flipped the paper over to refold it and noticed the full-page ad on the back. "I saw something about this on the TV," she forced herself to say.

Mara leaned over. "What is it?"

Dani read it, then paraphrased. "Looks like a big religious rally in Washington, D.C."

"They estimate that there will be over a million people at that rally," Mara agreed.

Dani faked a yawn. "I'm going back to bed."

"Well, you'd better stay up if you're going to go to church with me," Mara said, glancing at her watch.

At the word *church,* Dani felt her skin prickle. "Church?" she asked, not even attempting to keep the hostility out of her voice. "Don't tell me you're one of those Remnant believers."

Mara shook her head. "No. No, I'm not a Remnant believer. I'm Catholic."

"If you're a Catholic, why do you go to church on Saturday?"

"It's easier," Mara replied. "I usually go help out at the clinic on Sundays. Anyway, it's not like it makes a big difference which day you go to church."

Dani snorted. "It does to Remnant believers. They believe that the Bible is the only Word of God and that nothing God said was ever changed by Him or anyone. So they believe there is only one day to worship on, and that's Saturday, the Sabbath."

"Well, Catholics go to church any day of the week they want," Mara informed her. "Most go on Sunday, of course. As long as you go, the Church isn't too particular about when you go. It's not like there's some law saying which day you have to go."

"That's not what Remnant believers say. But that's the whole point. They're so rigid it's unbelievable."

Mara's forehead wrinkled. "Whoa, whoa, what are you talking about? There's no law saying which day you have to worship."

Dani chuckled at Mara's ignorance. "Duh! Sure there is. It's called the Ten Commandments. Even I know that, and I'm no religious freak like my father." Immediately, Dani sensed she'd said too much and clamped her mouth shut. Fortunately, Mara didn't seem interested in pursuing any reference to Dani's family at the moment. Instead, she went across the room and began rummaging in a bookshelf that was nearly bursting its seams with books. A stack of particularly huge medical books piled on top threatened to crash down on her head.

Dani yawned again. "Is there anything for breakfast?"

"It's got to be here somewhere," Mara muttered to herself. "I know I used to keep it in here. Aha! Here it is." Triumphantly, she pulled out a Bible. Dust exploded into the air when she blew on the cover.

Dani laughed. "Looks like you use it a lot."

Mara threw her a dirty look. "My parents gave me this for Christmas the year I left home to go to college. I read it some. All right, I read it a little. But the one I had when I was a kid was practically read to pieces. That's why they gave me this one." She sat down cross-legged on the floor and began thumbing through the Bible.

"Breakfast?" Dani reminded her. "Anything to eat? I'm kinda hungry."

Mara waved absently toward the kitchen. "Sure, help yourself."

Disgusted, Dani heaved herself off the stool and padded into the kitchen to look around. She found some eggs and bread. A little more hunting produced a frying pan and a banana. Her stomach rumbled loudly as she set about cooking breakfast.

"What are you looking for anyway?" Dani asked around a mouthful of banana.

"A text, a word, something. I know there's something in here where Peter, or maybe it was Paul, changed the day of worship to Sunday to celebrate when Jesus rose from the dead. Maybe it's in Acts." She flipped furiously through the book while Dani watched her smugly.

"You aren't going to find it," Dani said.

The certainty in Dani's voice brought Mara's head up.

"It's not there," Dani repeated.

"How do you know?"

"I know a lot about the Bible. I just don't believe it, that's all." Dani finished her breakfast and headed into the bathroom to get washed up. She climbed gingerly into the shower and let the hot water pour over her. It felt so good. She hadn't had a shower since . . . Suddenly the events that had propelled her to flee came back in a rush.

Leaning heavily against the side of the shower, she allowed herself to grieve for Shon's death. She fondly recalled the good times and blocked out the bad ones. Her tears washed away in the warm water.

She wondered where Dietrich was. Was he after her? Did he know where to find her? The thought worried her. Of course he was after her, because the night before Shon had killed Stan Schultz he'd told her something. It was something that she hadn't believed at the time. Now she wasn't so sure.

Before he'd done it, she would have sworn that Shon would never, could never, kill a man. And yet he'd done it as if it were an everyday activity. The last night they were together, he opened up to her in a way he never had before. He told her he was willing to do anything to become a pure member of the Freedom Society. He traced the tattoo on her wrist with his finger and told her that he would soon have his own.

Dani remembered laughing nervously, telling him that she was afraid she had done the wrong thing and that she wasn't sure she wanted to be a "pure" member of the Freedom Society anymore, and she certainly didn't care about the stupid tattoo. But Shon had told her never to say that, and she'd shut up quickly.

Then Shon told her why he had joined the Freedom Society and why he was willing to do anything to help Gavin Larson become the most powerful person in the world. He'd do whatever was necessary, he'd assured her. Even kill the president.

Dani remembered asking him why he would even want to do such a thing and what it would accomplish. He had given her a funny look, as if he wondered if he'd said too much to her. Then he had stopped talking.

She probably would have dismissed the whole conversation if not for the fact that late that night when the baby woke her up with the hiccups and she couldn't get back to sleep, she'd gone wandering around in the kitchen area of their tiny apartment. On the table she found some papers Shon had been looking at before he'd gone to bed. Among them were a map of the White House, road maps for D.C., and an itinerary for the president and a lot of information about bombs, every type you could imagine. She wanted to think it was just coincidence, but deep down she knew it wasn't. Deep down she knew what they were planning to do.

At the same time she realized how deep she was in, she also realized she couldn't leave. That scared her, not only for herself, but for her baby. That was why she had run when she got the chance.

Dani pushed herself away from the wall of the shower. For now she was safe, she reminded herself. They'd never find her here.

Mara pounded on the bathroom door. "Hey! Did you drown in there? We've got to get going, or we'll be late for mass. Hurry up, would you?"

Dani had never seen the inside of a Catholic church and was surprised at how ornate it was. Polished white marble gleamed in the bright fall sunshine, and heavy wooden doors were propped open. Dani watched Mara dip her hand in some water and make the sign of the cross. Then she headed up the aisle to find a seat. Most of the pews were filled, but Mara found them a spot practically in the front row. Dani didn't bother to mimic Mara's genuflection in the aisle.

She sat down beside Mara and immediately dozed off. It was necessary to ignore Mara's elbow to her ribs several times, and she was vaguely aware of people continually standing, sitting, kneeling, and singing all around her. She was finally nudged awake just before the closing hymn, and she stood up with a yawn to join in the singing, giving Mara an apologetic shrug. She had only agreed to come, after all. She never said she'd participate.

On the way out of the church, Mara approached the priest to shake hands. "Father Chevalier," she asked, not releasing his hand. "Could you tell me where in the Bible the day of worship is changed from Saturday to Sunday?"

"Oh, it isn't there, my child," the priest said, smiling, as he attempted to extricate his hand.

"That's what I told her," Dani piped up.

"But," Mara sputtered. "It has to be there somewhere. Most of the major religions worship on Sunday."

The priest nodded, pulling his hand away from her and rubbing it slightly. "That's true, but it wasn't changed in the Bible. The holy Catholic Church, by the authority of our Lord, changed the day of rest to Sunday in remembrance of the resurrection of our Lord."

"You mean there's no scriptural basis for worshiping on Sunday?" Mara asked incredulously.

Father Chevalier shook his head with a benevolent smile. He didn't appear at all disturbed by her line of questioning. "No. We didn't need it."

"Didn't need it?" Mara echoed. "Thank you, Father."

Dani followed closely behind Mara as she made her way down the steps and out to the parking lot where they'd left her car. She was still mumbling to herself when they reached the car and got inside. "You were right," she conceded.

"I know," Dani replied smugly. "I told you I know a lot about the Bible . . ."

"You just don't believe it," Mara finished for her. "Would you mind if I stopped by the clinic on the way home? I want to check up on some of my patients. Then I'll take you sightseeing if you want."

Dani nodded. "That sounds great."

She sat back in her seat and stared out the window as Mara drove them through the city of Winooski and back toward Burlington. On the left they passed the Champlain Mill and crossed over the Winooski River. Mara explained how the river used to be quite impressive but in the last year or so it had dried up to a trickle. The phenomena had local experts stumped.

Mara parked a few spaces down from the clinic, remarking how lucky she had been to find a spot so close. "Do you want to come in with me?"

Dani shook her head. "No, I think I'll just sit here and take a little nap."

Mara nodded and left the keys in the ignition. "I'll only be a minute. But be sure to lock the doors once I get out, and don't open them for anyone except me."

"Yes, Mom," Dani joked.

* * *

The moment Mara entered the clinic, she knew immediately things were much worse. Extra beds were set up on the floor, nearly wall to wall. Nurses, doctors, and interns wove their way around the makeshift beds like overworked androids. The patients who were in the most advanced stages of the disease caught her eye first, because they lay still with detached, expressionless faces. *Almost like they have masks on,* she thought.

Mara grabbed Lisa's arm as the harried intern walked past. It took a few moments before Lisa recognized her.

"Dr. Benneton! Oh, it's been just awful. I was home sleeping, and they called me in. It's a wreck here. The hospitals are the same way. We've run out of room, so we're moving people to the Burlington Auditorium. The mayor requisitioned it as a temporary casualty facility."

"Why didn't anyone call me?" Mara demanded.

"I know they tried," Lisa said. "Dr. Ellis said your pager must be off or broken. I know Jodie's been trying to call you all morning. They thought about sending someone to get you, but no one has been available because it's been such a madhouse."

"I never turn my pager off." Mara's hand flew automatically to her pager. The unit looked fine. She slapped it against her hand, and it let out a series of sick-sounding beeps. She groaned. "I don't believe it."

Lisa shrugged. "Yeah, well, you're here now."

Mara thought of Dani sitting in the car waiting for her. "I can't stay though, Lisa. But I'll come back as soon as I can." She looked around the room. She could taste the fear of the patients and the panic of the medical personnel. Whatever the sickness was, it was letting them know it was serious. *What on earth is this thing?* she wondered.

Lisa was about to turn away when one of the patients by their feet began to thrash around on the floor. Beneath him was a puddle of blood. It was pouring out of every opening in his body. It looked as if everything inside him was coming out . . . intestinal linings, everything. The blood was bright and thin. *No clotting factors,* Mara thought automatically.

Lisa bent down and felt for a pulse. "He's arresting!" she yelled. "Get me a crash cart!"

Mara dropped to her knees and began compressions on the man's chest. From what she could see of his face, he was young— maybe twenty, probably a college student. She leaned on his chest while Lisa tried to work a laryngoscope down his esophagus to open his airway.

He gagged and vomited black noxious material that splattered over Lisa's white coat. The smell was so bad that Mara fought to keep her stomach down. Lisa's face turned sheet white, and she turned her head, throwing up next to him. Doggedly, she continued trying to insert the laryngoscope.

Mara concentrated on maintaining the rhythm of her compressions while her mind searched for a strategy to fight something they didn't understand. *This man is having a massive hemorrhage of some kind. His eyes have rolled back; the pupils are dilated. Brain damage*, Mara thought. The implications were that they could do nothing to save him.

"I need whole blood," Lisa yelled.

"Lisa, I'm going to call it," Mara said, stopping her chest compressions and feeling for a pulse. There was none.

"No, he's dehydrated. He needs a transfusion."

"He's dead, Lisa."

Lisa collapsed on the floor next to the man in the midst of an amazing amount of blood and her own vomit. Her head dropped into her hands, and she sobbed wildly, her tears flowing freely down her arms and mixing with the blood. "I knew him. His name was Steve. He was my best friend's brother. He was a great guy. Always telling me he was going to marry me someday."

Mara laid a hand on Lisa's shoulder. "I'm so sorry. There was nothing more you could have done. It was too late even before we started. Look around you. Look at these people who still need you."

Lisa wiped her eyes and did as she was told. After a few moments of battling her fear of the unknown, Lisa pushed it into the background and focused her mind on helping the others. "I can keep going, Dr. Benneton," she said firmly.

Mara squeezed Lisa's shoulder encouragingly. "Yes, you can. And I'm going to make a few phone calls. We're not the only ones in the country dealing with this thing. Maybe USAMRIID or the CDC know something definite about how to fight it by now. If they don't, I'm afraid we're in a lot of trouble."

Lisa nodded, but her attention wasn't with Mara. "OK." She got to her feet unsteadily. "I'll see about removing Steve's body and cleaning up this mess."

"Lisa," Mara said, "make sure you use plenty of disinfectant. And try to avoid touching any body fluids as much as possible until we know what we're dealing with here."

Mara commandeered the phone at the receptionist's desk and dialed a number she knew from memory. She was on hold for ten minutes before her call was routed to Amy Cooper's desk. When her friend answered, Mara was instantly aware of the strained, guarded voice on the other end.

"Amy? It's Mara. I have a situation here. It's this disease. It's turned deadly. We just had a healthy young man die." She lowered her voice to a whisper. "Do you remember in college when I did that extracurricular work in the labs studying viruses? I never worked on anything higher than Level 2, of course, but I was very intrigued with the filoviruses. I wrote a research paper on them. In some ways this acts like a filovirus."

"It's impossible," Amy replied sternly, but her tone was hardly convincing. "There's no way, and you know it."

"I'd like to believe that."

After a few seconds of silence, Amy said, "OK. What symptoms are you seeing?"

"Right now lesions, a cough, set expressions, and diarrhea. But Amy, this guy just crashed and bled out."

Amy's voice was tight. "Have you done an autopsy?"

"No, but . . ."

Amy cut her off. "Don't. I mean, double bag the body and sterilize the area."

"You know what this is, don't you?" Mara asked suspiciously. But then the frustration that had been building up inside her for days finally broke loose. "What is it, Amy? I want to know! I have a *right* to know! I've gotten nothing from the CDC either! Every time I call I get put off! If no one knows what in the world is going on, then at least admit it!"

"Calm down, Mara." Amy sounded even more tired, and it was this realization that caused Mara to collect herself. Maybe she, too, was as frustrated as Mara. "All I can tell you, officially, is to take strict precautions handling the patients and the bodies. Be religious about using masks and gloves." After a pause, she said, "I know this is scary, Mara. We're doing everything we can. Believe me. I'll talk to you soon." Then she hung up.

Mara was left holding the phone, staring absently at the random texture designs on the wall.

"Dr. Benneton? Are you all right?" Jodie, the receptionist, asked.

Mara nodded.

"There was a man here earlier asking about one of our patients. I didn't know who he was referring to because he said her name was Dani Talbot. But I don't have record of a 'Talbot' receiving treatment."

Mara's head snapped around. "Oh yeah? Where did he go?" She scanned the lobby but saw only patients and medical personnel.

Jodie looked around too. "I don't know now. He was over there just before all the excitement." She pointed to a section of seats in the lobby, but now there were only two elderly women. She shrugged.

"Well, if you see him again," Mara said, "see if you can get more information out of him. I'd like to know what he wants. Ask around. See if he talked to anyone else. I have to run home for a few minutes, but I plan to be here throughout the night."

Jodie nodded, and Mara made her way out the door.

* * *

Colonel Amy Cooper, M.D., ran clammy hands absently up and down the black stripe on the leg of her green Army slacks as if trying to rub it off. The nervous motion of her hands reflected the panic she felt inside. She couldn't remember a time when she had been this scared. Even when she had started working in a spacesuit in Level 4 areas with viruses like Ebola and Marburg, she hadn't felt so defenseless.

This was just the sort of recurring nightmare her husband, Ray, had had since she started working with the hot viruses at the United States Army Medical Research Institute of Infectious Diseases—USAMRIID (you Sam rid), or the Institute, most people called it. In fact, Amy could pinpoint the beginning of their marital strife to almost the moment she'd been assigned to Fort Detrick. Only the fact that she knew Ray was afraid something would happen to her prevented their problems from escalating. She had practically been on the verge of requesting a transfer when "It" happened.

The Institute, as well as the Center for Disease Control in Atlanta, had been receiving scores of calls from the entire eastern coastal region. Patients with lesions and sores, coughs, and mild dysentery were showing up in droves at hospitals. Specialists had been sent out to collect blood samples, taking only normal precautions, and they'd found nothing significant. Initially, their collective opinion had been that it was some wild, virulent strain of the flu. There were new ones every year. At least no one had died so far.

That was until one of the cases crashed and bled out with symptoms chillingly like one of the four known filoviruses—Ebola Zaire, Ebola Sudan, Ebola Reston, or Marburg. Except that this first case, the index case, did not test positive for any one of the three viruses which were lethal to humans—Ebola Reston so far had only proved fatal to monkeys, though it had proven to jump from one host to another much easier than its deadlier kin had. Ebola Reston traveled easily in the minute particles of air, which seemed to be happening with the current illness.

Could it finally have happened? Amy asked herself. *Had Ebola or Marburg finally evolved and become sophisticated enough to wipe out the human race? Maybe Reston had finally mutated like the experts feared it could. One mutated gene could be the switch that turned Ebola Reston into the deadliest virus known to man.*

The virus, like a predator, had stalked mankind from ancient times. However, it was so destructive to its host that humans did not live long enough to be able to infect large portions of the population. It was ironic that a virus as lethal as Ebola could actually be too deadly to kill a large amount of people.

Amy reviewed the facts. The index patient, Pierre Cartier, a ship captain from Nova Scotia, had been traveling in Africa on vacation. He broke out with lesions a full week after he returned home. The lesions grew worse until he finally sought medical help about a week later. He was treated and sent home and by every report had tried to get on with his life.

He continued operating his ship and roaming around Halifax, Nova Scotia's capital and largest city. About two weeks later, he suddenly crashed, bleeding through every orifice in his body. His terrified crew put him in a life raft and set him adrift while they notified the authorities to have him picked up. Before the rescue crew got to him, however, he was spotted by a fishing vessel and hauled aboard. They made a mad dash for shore, but Cartier died before reaching a hospital. That was four weeks between contracting the virus and death—plenty of time to infect more people and ensure that the virus would survive.

Who knew how many people Cartier had been in contact with and how many people *they* had been in contact with. Every person on the two trawlers who had been in contact with Cartier had died horrible, gruesome deaths, which the governments of Canada and the United States had gone to great lengths to suppress from the media.

And now reports from along the coast indicated an epidemic of disastrous proportions that was impossible to keep secret much longer. She herself had admitted twenty workers at USAMRIID to the Slammer—the Level 4 bio-containment hospital where doctors and nurses wearing spacesuits treat highly infectious patients. One of them was the vice president of the United States, who had died just before Mara's phone call. Amy wondered how long it would be before the others crashed as well.

Amy sank into the chair at her desk, her legs shaking weakly. Her head throbbed too. A headache was the first sign of Ebola. She pushed the thought out of her mind. So far, everyone had broken with lesions first, and she had no lesions.

There probably was no way to contain this because the incubation period of the virus was turning out to be longer than Ebola and Marburg. She feared it eventually could be just as deadly, but since it did not destroy the bodies' cells and organs as aggressively as Ebola or Marburg, people were living plenty long enough to spread it.

It was going to go global. She couldn't see any way around it. Right now it seemed as if the East Coast was primarily affected, but she knew it was only a matter of time before they started receiving reports that it had spread toward the Midwest, as well as to other countries. It was most certainly spreading on the warmer coasts and was probably on every flight to every major city in the world. She had learned that the disease was raging in Africa.

What she must concentrate on most right now was to try and defuse the national panic it would create when people began to find out that you could die from this virus. And if what Mara had told her on the phone was true, she had better move quickly. Delaying the news of the vice president's death a few days would buy them some time to gain control of the public. It could be done. . . .

Almost in answer to Amy's thoughts, the phone rang. Its two short bursts told her that Private Derek Grosse was on the line. Wearily, she reached for the receiver. "Yes?"

"Colonel Cooper, there's a call for you from a Greg Harrison."

"Thank you." She punched the blinking light on the phone. "Hello? Mr. Harrison?" Amy visualized the serious rugged look of the CNN reporter anxiously returning her call. "Yes, USAMRIID is ready to make a statement on the virus."

After she made a date to speak with the reporter in front of the cameras, Amy sat in her office staring into space for a long time. Deceiving the American public would be easy; it wouldn't be the first time. Keeping her own fear under control so she could pull it off—that would be the hard part. She picked up the phone.

"Derek? Get me the White House."

* * *

Harry gestured wildly as Dietrich joined him in the bushes on the campus of the University of Vermont across the street from the Ethan Allen Health Care Clinic. "That's her!" he said, pointing toward a woman emerging from the clinic. "Look in the red car. Is that the girl you've been looking for?" Dani's dark head could be seen through the window. It bobbed rhythmically as if she were listening to music, and her fingers drummed on the dashboard.

Dietrich nodded silently as he pulled out a Sig P229. It came with a mate, a silencer the German fitted onto the end of the barrel. "What did you find out?"

"She came to the clinic alone yesterday," Harry said. "Apparently she left with the doc who saw her. Now they're back again, together."

"What's the doctor's name? Did you find out where she lives?"

"Mara Benneton." Harry shook his head. "Nobody would give me her address, and I stopped askin' right away. They were starting to get suspicious."

That morning Dietrich had put Harry out on the street looking for information about the pregnant girl, and the arrangement had paid off quickly—Dietrich smiled to himself—in more ways than one.

"Hey, can I have my coat back?" Harry asked, eyeing the gun. For some reason, it made him jumpy. Yet only an idiot would not have expected it. Dietrich ignored the question about the coat. Harry swallowed hard. "What are you going to do?"

Dietrich laughed gutturally. "What needs to be done." He coldly turned his back on Harry and aimed at the doctor.

A split-second later, Harry's shoulder drove into Dietrich's side, throwing him off balance and sending his shot wild. The killer staggered a few paces before regaining his balance. He was out from behind the cover of the bushes now and when he looked up to sight again, he saw that his first shot had narrowly missed the doctor as she returned to her car.

Harry tackled Dietrich around the knees. As Dietrich went down, he brought the barrel of his gun down on the back of Harry's head.

* * *

Mara was mentally packing her overnight bag when she heard a peculiar sound. It was neither loud nor scary, at first. It was simply a *poof!* and then a metallic *ping!* She jumped and looked around.

In the next few moments everything happened in slow motion.

Across the street, a man in a heavy silver parka moved quickly toward her. Both hands were stuffed into the large pockets of his coat. Quite abruptly, he pulled out his right hand. Sunlight glinted on his fist, causing Mara to wince at the reflection before realizing the barrel of a gun was causing the glare. He was so deliberate she could hardly accept that he intended to shoot her. That's when it registered that the muted *ping* had been a bullet striking her car just inches from where she would have been had she kept walking.

She instantly dove for the driver's door. Another *ping!* slapped the rear fender, and then she remembered that she'd had Dani lock all the doors. She spun away from the door and ducked in front of the Accord. In the peripheral of her vision, she saw the silver parka moving toward the rear of the car about three parking meters away. Instinctively, she bolted around to Dani's side of the car.

Mara pounded frantically on the door, which Dani threw open in a panic, bowling Mara backwards. Dani fell out of the car.

"Dani! Stay in that car!"

"I can't! We've gotta get away!"

"Dani!" Mara yelled at the top of her lungs. "Stay!" The order would have frozen a platoon of Marines in its tracks. Mara lunged into the car and pulled Dani after her.

"Stay down," Mara hissed. Then another bullet struck the passenger's side window, blasting the interior of the car with a cloud of glass shards and dust. Dani screamed as Mara turned the key in the ignition and the car roared to life.

Mara stomped on the gas, spinning out into the street, tires smoking. In the rearview mirror she could see the man in the parka aiming again. As she raced away, the Accord fishtailed a couple of times, and two small puffs of white smoke came from the gun.

Mara kept one eye on the figure in the silver parka in her rearview mirror and one eye on the traffic ahead of her as her car surged forward. Dani was crumpled in a heap on the floor of the passenger side, sobbing incoherent words. Mara rode the bumper of the guy in front of her before honking her horn in panic and attempting to squeeze past.

Dani looked up for a moment, terror in her eyes. "Don't let him catch me," she begged. "Don't let him hurt me."

"What are you talking about?" Mara shouted. "You know that guy? He was after you? Talk to me! I want to know why we were just shot at!"

"Oh," Dani moaned, clutching her stomach.

Alarm bells sounded. "What?" Mara asked in panic. "What is it?"

"Pain," Dani whimpered. "I've got pain in my stomach."

Seeing the fear in Dani's face, Mara felt a rush of guilt. "Where in your stomach? Are you having contractions?"

"I don't know," Dani moaned. "It just hurts!"

Mara's foot increased pressure on the gas pedal until the car took the next corner nearly on two wheels. "Hold on," she commanded. "We'll be at my apartment in a minute."

"We can't go there!" Dani protested weakly. "He probably knows where I'm staying."

"Who knows? Who is after you?" The only reply she received was more groaning.

With a concerned eye on Dani, Mara contemplated her options. "What am I going to do?" she muttered to herself. Someone was after Dani, obviously. And they didn't seem to mind if she got caught in the crossfire either. Whoever it was must be pretty dangerous. And Dani was worried that they might have tracked her to Mara's apartment.

Mara hoped the pain Dani felt was false labor contractions brought on by stress and nothing more serious. She approached her apartment and slowed down, glanced at the brick front of the stately building, and considered a quick stop. Then she nailed the gas pedal, shooting them past the only available parking space to the intersection, where she made a left and continued around the block to give herself some extra time to think. She realized suddenly that if she wanted anything out of the apartment, she must act right now. Any more time and whoever was after Dani would certainly show up. *A few minutes at the most. That's all I have. It wouldn't take a genius to find us now.*

Mara made another sharp left and was on the opposite side of the block from her apartment. Pulling into the parking lot of a small market, she parked as far off the street as possible and hoped her car was well hidden. "How are you holding up?" she asked Dani.

The girl looked up at her with tortured eyes. "It hurts," she whimpered.

"Look, I'm going to go into my apartment and get some stuff. I'll be right back. Don't you move. Understand? I'll grab your stuff too."

"Don't leave me," Dani begged.

"You'll be OK," Mara promised. "He didn't follow us. But he will probably come to my place sooner or later, and I'd prefer to be somewhere else. I'll just be a minute. Stay down. I'll be right back."

Not giving Dani a chance to argue, she jumped out of the car, sprinted across the street, and hurried around her block. Everyone on the street seemed suspect, and she tensed up, on the verge of ducking and running if someone so much as pointed a finger at her. When she finally reached the door, she fumbled with her keys and quickly let herself in, half running, half falling up the stairs to her apartment.

* * *

Though Dietrich had failed his first attempt to capture Dani Talbot, he remained philosophical. He would have another chance. It should have been so easy. Kill the doctor, force Dani into his car, and drive away. He cursed Harry vigorously.

At the sound of sirens, Dietrich turned around and walked briskly back toward the bushes. Harry was trying to sit up, trembling from the November cold. "I'm finished," Harry spat. Then he seemed to remember the gun and what Dietrich had said about crossing him.

Dietrich peeled off Harry's silver parka and threw it brusquely on the ground, then stripped his leather jacket from the man's back. Harry gave him an ugly look, pulling the parka around him and hugging it as if trying to absorb Dietrich's warmth. He watched Dietrich with wide, frightened eyes, but Dietrich simply ignored him, slipping the gun under his jacket and walking off down St. Paul's street, leaving Harry to the police, who would be looking for someone in a silver parka.

* * *

All Mara's instincts warned her the killer could show up at any moment. Each time she thought about it, she had to force back guttural sounds of hysteria. Every scary movie or story she had ever seen, heard, or read came back to her with the rush of a tsunami as she stood in the entryway to her apartment trying to think of what to do next. The fear sucked her rationale away in the undertow.

The radiator pipes hissed and popped as the heater kicked in. The floorboards creaked under her feet as the old wood adjusted to the change in temperature. Mara held her breath, half-expecting the once familiar noises to be the footsteps of the killer. She was ready to scream from the tension alone.

Dani's things were already neatly stored inside her only duffel bag. Mara snatched it up and threw it over her shoulder. She mentally ran over the list of things she had packed for herself and tried to think of anything she was forgetting. Some food went into a canvas tote bag, and she threw that over her shoulder too. As she passed silently through each room, she grabbed things she would need. A plan had begun to form in her mind, but she hadn't completely decided what she was going to do.

Her medical bag was in the trunk of the car, she remembered. She hastily scanned the apartment looking for anything she might have missed. At the last instant, she grabbed her Bible off the shelf where she'd left it and tucked it into her own bag. As her fingers reached out and closed around the doorknob, a shrill ring stopped her cold.

In the second that her heart stopped, she realized the sound was coming from her phone. Her own voice cut off the ring as her answering machine picked up. Mara hastily strode to the door, not waiting to hear the message, no doubt from the clinic, but before she could gain the door, a cold, menacing voice stopped her.

"I know you're there," the voice said, and Mara felt a chill chase down her spine. "Make sure you pack your toothbrush." There was a rough laugh. "All I want is the girl. You give her to me, and I'll let you go. It's that simple. If I have to come after her, I'll kill you."

Icy fingers of fear closed around Mara's heart. "If you want to live, here's what you do. You call me at 555-1324 and tell me where you want to drop her off. If you don't call, I'll come after you."

The line went dead, and Mara stood frozen by her own fear as the answering machine hung up the phone and readjusted the tape. What had Dani done to make someone want to kill her? What if. . .

Mara walked over to the window and looked down at her car parked across the street. She could see Dani's small form hunched over in the passenger side, right where she'd left her. Who knew where the killer had called from? Mara assumed a pay phone, probably nearby. It would have to at least be in the vicinity, so he would be there if she did decide to give Dani up.

Sprinting, she dashed down the stairs and out of the building. There was something she had to do before she returned to the car, but she didn't want to stay like a sitting duck in her apartment. Walking in what she hoped was a nonchalant manner, she ducked swiftly into an open garage door.

Her conscience twinged as she opened Dani's bag. Maybe there would be a clue about what Dani was involved in. Mara bit her lip nervously. She wasn't used to prying, but then she wasn't used to being shot at either. If she was going to protect Dani, she had a right to know what she was involved in.

She pulled out some clothes first, large baggy maternity clothes that had seen better days. Dani had probably picked them up from some mission somewhere. There were very few toiletries: some cheap hotel shampoo, a brush, a cracked hand mirror, and a nearly used up bottle of lotion. She was surprised to find a bottle of expensive prenatal vitamins and some dried fruit. Next, she pulled out a packet of papers tied with a string.

Carefully she loosened the string and slid some of the papers out. Most were newspaper clippings. Mara scanned the contents. The name United Religious Coalition stood out in each, but other than that she could see no valuable information in them. She laid them aside and pulled out some pictures next. One was of a nice looking man in a policeman's uniform in front of a modern blue and gray building. He was holding an award up for the camera, but Mara couldn't make out the award or the location.

The next photo took her breath away. It was of an angry looking young man with an arm casually draped over Dani's shoulders. Dani wasn't pregnant in the photo, and Mara wondered if this could be the father of her baby. His cruel eyes were set in a hard face. A cigarette dangled from his fingers.

But the figure in the background scowling at the couple was the one who made Mara's blood run cold. Even though she'd had only a glimpse of him, she recognized the man in the photo as the same one who had shot at them earlier. Instead of replacing the photo, she placed it in her pocket.

The rest of the images were of a laughing woman who looked very much like Dani but older. Mara suspected it was Dani's mother. A few love letters from someone named Shon were the only other things in the stack. Mara was tempted to scan them, but then she remembered Dani and her labor contractions. They could talk about this later.

She carefully put everything back the way she'd found it and grabbed all the bags again. As she made her way back out of the garage and over to her car, she felt as though unseen eyes were marking her progress. She wondered how long it would take the man who was after Dani to figure out she wasn't going to turn her over to him.

It was odd, she mused as she got in the car, that even with the threat on her life she hadn't even considered the possibility. She thought of the oath she had taken as a doctor: Do no harm. No, there was no way she could drop Dani off as the man had suggested. Even to save her own life.

But now the question of what to do next was vital. It could mean the difference between life and death. Mara's first instinct had been to go to the police. But even if they listened to her, she doubted very much they could keep her and Dani safe. In recent years they had become so ineffective as to be non-existent. And if the police weren't going to help them, then there was no sense remaining in Burlington. It was better they run.

Except that Mara couldn't think of anywhere to run to. She had no relatives nearby. She had no friends. Suddenly the image of Amy Cooper popped into her head. What if she and Dani made their way down to Washington, D.C., and paid Colonel Cooper a visit? Maybe she could get some straight answers about this virus while she was there. She certainly couldn't do much more at the clinic, even if she had been able to stay.

"What took you so long?" Dani moaned.

Mara looked down and felt a surge of pity. Dani was kneeling in the middle of all the glass from the window. There were small cuts on her face and hands as she rocked back and forth, clutching her abdomen.

"Sorry," she said kindly. "How are you doing?"

"The pains have gone away," Dani said.

"Good. I think it's just false labor, but we'll pull in somewhere, and I'll check you out as soon as we can." Mara pulled out onto the street. An icy breeze streamed in the open window.

"We'll put something over that window too," she said. "Now, just suppose you start at the beginning and tell me what you know."

"I don't know anything," Dani said stubbornly.

Mara glanced at her quickly and then pulled the picture out of her pocket. "Then maybe you would be so kind as to explain why this man was trying to kill us. Obviously you know him. It may interest you to know that he called my apartment and left a message on my machine."

"He did?" Dani looked up sharply, fear in her eyes. "What did he want?" she croaked.

"He wants me to drop you off somewhere for him. Otherwise, he says he'll kill me."

Dani's voice was dull, resigned. "Are you going to?"

"No," Mara said. "But I want to know why he wants to kill me. I have a stake in this too. It's not just you anymore. And if you want me to help you, then I have to know what's going on." Mara waited patiently for Dani to respond. It was going to be a long trip.

* * *

As Dietrich blended with the homeless people in Battery Park, he smiled despite his frustration. A cold wind whistled off the lake with teeth like needles, but he barely noticed it. He'd just hung up from a call placed to a government official in Washington, D.C., who gave him the home phone number of Mara Benneton. Unfortunately, Dr. Benneton's home address was unlisted in the local directory.

He quickly dialed the number and got her machine. It was probably useless, but he decided to leave the message anyway just in case it might work. There was no telling what people might do when they were afraid. He didn't know too much about the doctor, but based on what he did know—that she had taken in a stranger and was in the healing profession—he doubted very much that she would just drop Dani off somewhere with a cool, "See ya around." It was much more likely she would try to protect Dani at all costs.

Striding briskly, he returned to the black Mazda 626 he was driving and roared out of the parking space. Mingling with traffic, he slumped against the door and brooded. There was no sense chasing Dani now. No telling where she might have gone, and expending the effort it would take to find her now would be wasted effort. If she was going to try to foil the Freedom Society's plot to assassinate the president, then he would run into her later, in D.C.

If not, well, let her disappear into the woodwork. There was always time to look for her later, after things settled down and she thought she was safe at last. And he *would* look for her. She had something that belonged to the Freedom Society. For right now, when he weighed her as a potential threat against the ticking of the clock as they counted down to Friday's rally, it just didn't make sense to keep after her.

Now that he had put the matter behind him, Dietrich turned his attention to the task at hand. He would drive straight through to Washington, D.C. He estimated arriving in about ten hours.

He thought briefly about Randy Burton and felt an unpleasant sensation in the pit of his stomach at the thought of the risk they were taking by using him. Burton had been Gavin's choice, and he mentally castigated himself for allowing Gavin to make decisions he had no business making. While Dietrich was completely loyal to Gavin and his cause, he did believe that Gavin was becoming too involved in matters that would best be left directly to those who were most intimately acquainted with them.

After all, how could Gavin judge between Burton and any other candidate? He had no expertise in such matters. A man was a man to him. Now to men like Dietrich, there was plenty of difference. Take Shon Cole, for example. He was Dietrich's choice, and he'd done well. At this very moment he was dead, but he had died to further the cause of the Freedom Society.

Shon's only mistake had been involving his girlfriend. For a while she had been so zealous that Dietrich had mistakenly thought he might be able to train her personally as a "soldier." There were plenty of women in the Freedom Society. But when she'd gotten pregnant, Dietrich saw a soft spot in her grow until he was positive she couldn't be counted on to be strong, to be firm, to resist.

He had thought the Shultz job might straighten her up a little, empower her and give her a new sense of purpose for their cause. In the end, of course, he'd been wrong.

He laughed harshly. So they were all fallible, it seemed. But how much easier it was to deal with his own fallacies than to deal with Gavin's. He expected his. After all, he was only human. But, Gavin—he was supposed to be like God. He wasn't supposed to make mistakes.

But then, that only proved to Dietrich what he had known all along—that God did not really exist. There was only Gavin, and he was just as human as the rest of them. The only difference was that Gavin had it straight. He understood that there was a difference between the "clean" and the "unclean," the "pure" and the "impure." And Gavin wasn't afraid to make the distinction or use whatever means available—namely the Freedom Society—to clean up the country and make it a decent place in which to live.

But maybe in the end there was some ultimate purpose Burton could serve, some whipping post he could fill. Maybe Burton's "assets" outweighed his liabilities. After all, they would need a fall guy, and Burton was so available.

Dietrich found a good station on the radio and settled down to endure the long drive to D.C.

Saturday, November 13

Alice Nolan brushed several loose strands of hair into place as she took a deep, calming breath. For a fleeting moment, she contemplated walking back down the driveway and going home. But she'd had that same feeling a thousand times before.

"I wonder if the apostle Paul ever felt this way?" she asked herself. Certainly he had.

Alice depressed the button and clearly heard the doorbell ring inside the little house. Seconds passed without so much as a whisper of movement, so she pressed the button again, twice in quick succession, immediately feeling guilty that she might be waking someone up. She was just about to leave when the deadbolt clicked. Alice quickly composed herself.

The door opened a crack, allowing Alice a look at just a slice of humanity peeking out at her.

"Hello?"

"Hello. You're Lynn, right? My name is Alice. You called me this morning?"

"Oh yes!" Lynn paused. "I'm glad you could come over." She unlatched the safety chain and opened the door. "Come in."

Alice tentatively stepped inside. She was curious about something that had happened the day before and decided to ask right up front. "Who was that man you were with yesterday? You must have known him."

"That was my brother, Randy."

"Your brother? Why, I didn't know that. He never mentioned that he knew you."

Lynn looked puzzled, so Alice skipped it and went on. "It's nice to have family nearby. I have a brother and a sister, but they live in California. I haven't seen them in five years. And my children live out of state."

"Sometimes I think that would be nice," Lynn muttered. Self-consciously she brushed a few strands of dirty blond hair out of her eyes.

Alice sat down on the couch and put her bag of Bibles on the floor.

"Why do you give out Bibles?" Lynn asked.

Alice smiled warmly. "It's very simple, actually. I wanted to help people find Jesus Christ, but I couldn't think of any way to do it that I was comfortable with. I get flustered so easily; I have a hard time just talking to folks, much less telling them about Jesus. So, I guess you might say I hide behind the Bible."

"But you're here talking to me."

Alice nodded. "True enough. But what you don't know is that I almost ran away before you answered the door. It really is tough, Lynn. I feel like I can't breathe when I meet people." Lynn smiled. She was warming up. *Thank You, Jesus,* Alice thought.

Alice had never seen anyone as open to the Message as Lynn appeared to be. It actually scared her, and she wondered how she should proceed, afraid that if she made any mistakes, she risked losing this fragile soul. Again, she offered up a silent prayer.

Dear Jesus, I feel you have literally placed this young woman's life in my hands, and I'm scared now. Please guide the words that come out of my mouth so that I don't crush her spirit.

Lynn placed a hand on the older woman's arm. "I'm glad you're here. I can see you really care about me. Last night I had a weird dream. I have weird dreams lots of times," Lynn said hastily, "but this was different." She was admitting to her problem with drugs without coming right out and saying it, but Alice understood. Lynn lowered her eyes, ashamed. "I guess that's why I called you."

Alice reached out and squeezed Lynn's arm reassuringly.

"You think I'm crazy, don't you?" Lynn said.

"No, Lynn, I don't. Dreams *can* be a way for God to talk to us. All of a sudden, Daniel pops into my head as an example."

"Daniel who?"

"Daniel from the Bible. Daniel was a Jewish prisoner in Babylon. He had been a young man when he was taken from

Jerusalem by the Babylonians, but he always remained faithful to God. God often used Daniel to witness even in the hostile nation of Babylon. Eventually, Daniel came to hold important positions in Babylon. One time, the king had a dream that troubled him, and with God's help, Daniel was the only one able to provide the king with an answer."

"I've never heard that story before," Lynn replied. "It sounds interesting."

"Do you have your Bible?"

"Oh yes." Lynn left for a back room. She returned with the paperback Bible. "I've tried to read it, but I've only gotten as far as chapter 2 in Genesis."

"That's all right. The Bible is a big book, and sometimes it's very hard to understand," Alice said.

Lynn sighed. "Then how will I ever understand it if it's so hard?"

"Good question." Alice smiled to comfort Lynn, but inside she trembled, wondering if she was skirting the edge of disaster and hoping beyond hope that she didn't accidentally discourage this fledgling Bible student. "Try thinking of the Bible as a storybook. And think of God as a gentle father or grandfather who is sitting in His favorite chair, with you at His knees listening to Him tell stories. The Bible doesn't have to be any more difficult to understand than a good story. All God wants us to do is help us learn who He is and how much He loves us."

"Seems easy, I guess."

"It can be," Alice agreed. "But the devil doesn't like it to be, so he does what he can to discourage us."

"He's done a good job with me. I probably never would have opened the Bible again if you hadn't come when I called."

"Well, I'm certainly glad I came by then. May I keep coming to visit you?"

"Oh yes, please come and visit me again," Lynn insisted. "But—you're not leaving already, are you?"

"No, I'll stay for a while. And there is one thing I want us to do before I leave, Lynn. And that is pray. Do you feel comfortable praying?"

Lynn lowered her eyes. The silence that followed was long enough that Alice felt it reach beyond that moment in the living room to somewhere deep within Lynn's life, a depressing, uncharted land Alice was afraid she was unqualified to learn about. "I'd like for you to pray. I don't know how," Lynn finally said.

Alice took Lynn's hand and squeezed it tight. "I would be happy to pray."

In silence, Lynn slipped off the couch onto her knees, dragging Alice along with her. She clasped her hands and rested her elbows on the coffee table, bowing her head and closing her eyes. Alice watched, barely breathing, wondering if she had ever seen such sincerity before. Just before she closed her own eyes, she saw Lynn's sleeve fall open to her elbow, revealing what might be the most difficult of the devil's traps Lynn would have to face.

Alice Nolan prayed mostly for God to be especially close to Lynn, letting her know at all times that He was near to her. At the conclusion of her simple prayer, Alice sent one of her own heavenward, one that pleaded with God for an extra measure of love and help for Lynn. She knew Lynn faced an uphill battle trying to quit using drugs.

For two more hours, the two women sat in the stuffy little house reading the Bible and learning about God. Alice told her own story about finding God and finally realizing she not only needed Him in her life but wanted Him there too. Lynn often nodded as she soaked up every word. It wasn't until they both heard the car door slam that the warmth in Lynn's face turned to fright.

"What is it?" Alice asked, her heartbeat accelerating like an Indy car at a green flag.

"Randy's home. I can't let him see you. He'd flip if he knew that I was getting religion." Lynn didn't waste time with long explanations. Quickly, she helped Alice gather her belongings together, nearly pulled her to her feet, and ushered her through the kitchen to the back door. "You've got to leave before Randy comes in!" Lynn hissed in a frightened whisper.

"OK, OK, I'm going," Alice replied, also in a whisper. She suddenly decided she didn't want to experience what might happen should Randy discover her. At least for Lynn's sake.

Lynn reached for the doorknob. Then her hand froze an inch away. "Oh no! He's coming in the back door!"

"Your brother?"

"Yes! Yes!" Lynn spun Alice around and pushed her back through the kitchen, into the living room, and out the front door. "Goodbye. Thank you for coming, Alice."

* * *

Dani hugged the velour upholstery of the passenger side seat and debated what to do. The flecks of blood on the seat blurred, and she could feel tears slip down her cheeks. Just hours ago she'd felt so *safe,* and now the whole nightmare had crashed in on her again. Not only that, but she'd managed to involve the one person who had tried to help her. The thought made her sick. If Mara died, it would be her fault.

"I'm sorry," she sobbed. "I didn't want to involve you."

"I appreciate your concern," Mara said gently. "But I think we're past that now. For better or worse, I'm involved. So why don't you tell me what it is I'm involved in?"

Dani tried to explain. As she talked, she feared she was confusing Mara more than enlightening her. The Coalition was rather vague to her, but she knew the Freedom Society openly supported the Coalition. She herself was part of the Freedom Society, which, until recently, she believed in with her whole heart and soul. The Freedom Society had made her feel accepted and a vital part of a cause that would change the world so it wouldn't be so cruel, so life would be easier.

All she knew was that the Freedom Society believed Gavin Larson could turn the country around and strengthen its moral foundation. They wanted him to lead the country closer to God. They believed God had stopped blessing America because its people had become too divergent, immoral, and disobedient. It all seemed so exciting to be on the righteous side of God, at least until the day of Stan Shultz's assassination. Then she had gotten squeamish and confused about her involvement. The Freedom Society was going too far. Now she felt they were trying to kill her, because she knew what was going to happen.

"They're going to assassinate the president?" Mara was incredulous. "That can't be done. It just can't. How on earth do they plan to get past all the security? And what on earth for?"

"All I'm telling you is what I saw," Dani insisted. "He had her itinerary, maps of the streets, and some sort of bus schedule or something. I don't know. And he talked about it in more than a casual way. Even that doesn't scare me as much as Dietrich. Shon was sincere. He was compassionate." Dani felt sadness wash over her. "At least I thought he was. But Dietrich is just a cold-blooded killer. He does what he's told. Period. And he's good at it. He was Shon's teacher." She turned her arm over. "See this tattoo? I earned this. It means that I have a high place in the Freedom Society. Shon didn't have one, but he was willing to do anything Dietrich told him to get one."

"Even kill?"

Dani lowered her eyes. "Yes."

"What did you do to get yours?"

"I—I can't talk about it." She looked up. "Not now. It doesn't matter."

Mara arched an eyebrow, curious, but she didn't pursue it. "OK. But tell me about Dietrich."

"When Shon and I joined the Freedom Society, it was like Dietrich singled us out. He seemed especially pleased with Shon and convinced him that he could have a high place in the Freedom Society if he proved himself worthy." She gave a little shrug. "I think he sensed when I started to become disillusioned, and he didn't trust me."

Mara bit her lip and concentrated on the road ahead of them. Dani heaved a sigh. She'd done what Mara asked. She'd explained the situation. If Mara didn't want to believe her, that was her problem. Carefully, she attempted to heave herself into the seat. Her legs had fallen asleep; she'd been on the floor of the car so long.

"Let's say I believe what you're saying," Mara said tentatively. "What were you planning on doing about it?"

"Doing? The only thing I was planning on doing was getting away. And I was doing that just fine until Dietrich caught up with me. I don't know how he found me," she muttered under her breath. "I'm no expert, but I was very careful."

"You make a pretty conspicuous target," Mara said bluntly. "I don't expect you were that hard to find. We'll have to be more careful. What do you think about going to the police?"

"What?" Dani's eyes were wide, filled with fear. "No! I don't trust anyone! The Freedom Society has members everywhere, even in the police."

Mara reached over and squeezed Dani's hand. "Don't worry. If you don't want me to go to the police, I won't. Not until you're comfortable. We'll think about what we want to do while we're on the road."

"Where are we going anyway?" Dani asked in a small voice. It occurred to her how much danger she had put Mara in. Mara had no idea. Maybe it would be better for her to slip off on her own. At least then she wouldn't be endangering Mara as well as herself.

"We're going to Washington, D.C."

"Washington?" Dani echoed. She could feel the now familiar feeling of panic crush her chest. "We can't go there! What about the Freedom Society? I just want to go someplace safe."

"For the moment, let's say the president *is* in danger," Mara said patiently. "I can understand if you don't feel some sort of responsibility to do something about it, but I feel just the opposite. I can't let terrorists kill the president when I know about it.

I have to warn somebody.

"Besides," she continued, "there's someone in Washington I have to see. She's an old friend of mine, and she knows something about this virus that's infecting people."

"You mean all those sores people have? What is that?" Dani asked.

"That's what I'm hoping to find out."

"Well, I don't want any part of it," Dani said firmly. If there was one thing she knew, it was that she planned to run *away* from the Freedom Society, not *toward* it. She owed her growing baby that much. She rubbed her abdomen thoughtfully. "Do you think the baby is OK?"

Mara glanced at her. "I think so, but I won't know for sure until I check you out. We'll be in Rutland soon. According to this map, we need to cut across into New York there to head for Washington. If your Dietrich is following us and figures out where we've headed—though I don't see how—he will think that's what we did. But instead, we'll keep going south to Bennington and stop there. It's another couple of hours, but it will be safer. We can cut over to Albany from there."

Dani felt her skin crawl when Mara referred to Dietrich as being "hers," but she passed over it. "Don't you think that will give him time to catch up to us if he does know where we're going?" she asked.

"If he does know where we're going or if he finds out, we'll still all end up at the same place. I haven't been there in a long time, but Washington is a big city. Even if he knows where to look, he'll have a hard time finding us," Mara said confidently. Dani wondered if she felt all that confidence or if it was just an act.

She shifted uncomfortably in the seat, turning her face to the window and letting the wind blow her hair back. "When can we stop?" she asked, trying to keep the weariness out of her voice.

"We'll stop in Rutland," Mara promised. "I know a doctor

there, Grad. Gene will let me use his office without any questions. I'll examine you there. We'll find something to eat, fix the window, and then we'll push on to Bennington. Does that sound OK?"

"Everything except going to Washington," Dani said sullenly. It was the last thing she wanted. Why couldn't they go in the opposite direction? She felt a hearty kick against her ribs, and she started with joy. "The baby kicked me!" she exclaimed.

Mara's eyebrows shot up. "That sounds good."

Dani settled back in the seat and closed her eyes, letting the cool air rush over her face. That kick felt like the baby's way of telling her he or she was all right. It was such a relief. As the contractions had gripped her body and she'd been afraid that she might have a miscarriage, she realized as she hadn't before just how much this little life meant to her. The prospect of losing it was more than she could bear.

She had to stay alive for the baby's sake, if for no other reason. If Mara wanted to walk into the lions' den, then so be it. Somehow she had to figure out how to get away from Mara. But first she wanted to make sure that her baby was OK.

She eyed the bulge in Mara's pocket where she'd stashed all the cash she'd taken from her savings account on their way out of Burlington. Mara had reasoned that Dietrich might be able to track them if she used her Universal Bank Card, so she'd decided to take cash. Lots of cash, to Dani's mind. Would it be so wrong to steal some of it to save herself and her baby?

Thou shalt not steal. It was like the commandment was written on her soul. She wasn't at all sure she could break it, even to save their lives. But then, she reasoned, it wouldn't be the first one of God's laws she'd broken. All she had to do was look down to see another one. She poked exploratory fingers into her abdomen, searching for her baby's foot. She determined to be on the lookout for an opportunity to present itself. She would protect her unborn baby no matter what it cost.

* * *

Jack tried to check the map again while he was driving. He didn't want to waste time by pulling over. Already he'd lost several hours by stopping in Middlebury to sleep. He figured he'd waste a lot more time getting into an accident if he didn't. He rubbed one hand over the stubble on his chin and longed for a hot shower and a shave.

Route 7 was about to go through a tangle of streets in Burlington, and Jack wasn't sure where to turn off. At the last moment he realized he'd gotten off 7 when it veered sharply to the right. Swift calculations indicated that if he simply stayed on the main drag, he'd end up by the waterfront and just west of the downtown area. He decided to go with that.

A large body of water, Lake Champlain, according to the map, spread out to his left. A brisk wind had whipped the dark water into frothy whitecaps. Despite this, several sailboats were braving the rough water.

Jack slowed as he neared an intersection and on impulse turned right. He passed a bus station on his left and prepared to make a left turn, but the street was blocked off. Frantically he looked for a place to park. Nothing was available on the street, so he followed signs for a parking garage. He had to drive to the fifth story before he found anything open, and the conditions of the garage made him hesitant to get out and leave his car. In the space directly next to the one he edged the Corolla into was the skeletal frame of a vehicle picked over as if by metal vultures.

Jack got out and made his way quickly to the stairway. Someone had attempted to beautify the dismal walls of the stairway by painting bright scenes of whales, dolphins, swordfish, and other sea life. These had been graffitied over with bold black paint. The spray-painted symbols looked to Jack like the work of inner-city gangs.

He held his breath in the tight space until he made it to the bottom of the stairwell and pushed the door open, escaping into the frigid outside air. Shrugging his shoulders up to burrow deeper into his coat, he faced into the wind and headed back in the direction of the lake. He stepped onto a street, the one that was blocked off except by intersecting streets. It was paved in brick and appeared to be some sort of outdoor mall. He hung a sharp left and headed to the bus station.

He hadn't planned on stopping anywhere, but as he passed one store, the music, piped out onto the street and the smell of hot coffee arrested him. He hesitated, looking up at the sign. Java Jive Cybercafe, it read. Jack glanced down the street, took a few tentative steps, and stopped again. A cold blast from the lake blew down the street and made him shiver. Impulsively he yanked open the door and went inside.

The interior was dimly lighted, and Jack was uneasy. Mostly college students and young businesspeople were drinking coffee and reading or were seated in front of computer screens surfing the Web. Jack stood uncertainly for a moment, allowing his eyes to adjust to the dim lighting.

A young woman, who reminded him slightly of Dani, approached the counter and gave him a questioning look. She drummed her fingers on the counter. "What can I get for you?" she asked impatiently.

Jack stepped up to the counter. "Uh, I'll have a steamed milk with Tiramasu," he replied.

She turned to get it for him. Her movements were quick, and Jack wondered how much caffeine she'd had. Too much, he decided. In moments she whirled with the cup of milk, spilling some of the white liquid on the counter. "That'll be three dollars."

Jack counted out the money and found a seat near three college students who were engrossed in the computer in front of them. Jack sipped his milk in morose silence, deep in thought.

"We're in!" The excitement of the hushed voice behind him made him turn curiously to watch. One of the college students, the one who was at the keyboard, gave his friends a jubilant look. "I told you I could do it."

Jack studied him. Tall and lean, he wore the baggy jeans that were practically the uniform of the day. His longish blond hair was twisted into a French knot and held in place by a Bic pen. A few days' growth of beard shaded his chin area in a goatee. He wore a silver band on his thumb, and Jack was almost mesmerized by its quick movements as he typed.

"I can't believe it, Savon," one of his friends was saying. "You actually got in?"

"Don't sound so surprised," Savon muttered. He continued to apply himself to the keyboard, and Jack watched as pages of information swept by. Curious, Jack rose from his seat and edged nearer to the computer.

The guy on Savon's left with long brown ringlets past his shoulders saw Jack and tapped Savon on the shoulder. Jack felt a rush of embarrassment, realizing that not only was he openly staring but he was also crowding Savon's personal space.

"What's up, man?" Savon asked. "What's your problem?"

Jack threw up his hands. "No problem, no problem," he assured them. Then an idea occurred to him. "Can I ask you a question? What are you doing? Are you a computer hacker?"

Savon jumped out of his seat so fast it propelled his chair backward. "You've got a lot of nerve, mister," he exclaimed. One of his friends made a lame attempt to block the computer screen from Jack's vision; the other advanced on him threateningly.

"Wait, wait, fellas, look, I'm not going to turn you in or anything," Jack protested, dropping his voice and glancing around nervously. "Thing is, I was wondering if you could help me? I need some information."

Savon eyed him coolly, sizing him up, Jack guessed. Wondering, he supposed, what was in it for him. "It's worth money to me," he added.

"I'll pay you. A hundred bucks?"

"Two hundred," Savon countered, grabbing his chair and setting it upright. "What kind of information?"

"I'm trying to locate my daughter," Jack explained. "Can you get into the medical records of the city and see if she was admitted anywhere in the last week?"

The guy with the ringlets laughed. He scrubbed one hand over his scruffy face and then folded his arms across his chest. "Are you kidding? Savon was doing medical records when he was a baby. That's child's play. Don't you have anything harder?"

"Shut up, Kenny," Savon snapped. Jack edged in closer to watch the computer screen. Savon held out his hand. "Money first, man."

Jack took out two hundred in twenties. He was going to have to call Dan Reiss soon and get some money wired. But if this lead paid off, it would be well worth the money.

Savon leaned over the keyboard as Jack watched, hardly daring to breathe. In what seemed like mere seconds, the computer beeped and Savon asked, "So what's her name?"

Jack half-expected someone to come running up and arrest them. "Dani," he replied in a whisper. "Try both Dani and Danielle. Her last name is Talbot."

Savon's fingers flew over the keyboard, but he came up empty. "Nothing under those names. Sorry."

"Wait, wait," Jack said, his brain spun searching for possibilities. "If she did go to the doctors, she wouldn't use her real name."

"Then how are we going to find her?" Savon asked in exasperation. "I can't very well look at the files of every person who was admitted to the hospital or the clinic. Especially with so many people getting sick lately."

Jack picked up the stray word like a radar signal. "Clinic?" he asked.

"Yeah," Kenny said. "There's the one big hospital and a welfare clinic, the Ethan Allen Health Care Clinic, down around the corner."

"Check that," Jack urged. "Only check under Dani Doe."

"Doe?" Savon mumbled. "Yeah, that makes sense. Like Jane Doe. You think she'd use her real first name though?"

"I don't know."

"I can look for all Does," Savon said, more to himself than Jack. His eyes stared intently on the screen, and Jack felt excluded from the search, helpless and frustrated as usual. *"But, I'm not helpless,"* he reminded himself. *"I can pray."* While he waited impatiently for Savon to find something, he prayed silently as hard as he knew how.

"Got something," Savon reported. "Two Does. The first one is a Jane. DOA. Isn't that 'dead on arrival'? Cause of death undetermined. There's an investigation. You want me to check it out?"

"What's the other one?" Jack said. His mind screamed, *Dear God, please don't let that Jane be Dani!*

"Bingo," Savon said. "This one's a Dani. Admitted to Ethan Allen Health Care Clinic for abdominal pains. She was treated and released the same day. There's no further information."

"Treated and released," Jack echoed. "Must be it wasn't anything serious." He felt his entire body go limp from the news. Dani *had* been here. She'd gone to a doctor and been treated, but she'd been released. "But, now where is she?" Jack muttered under his breath.

"Why don't you go ask at the clinic?" Kenny suggested. "Maybe they'll remember her."

"A Dani Doe? Not likely," Savon snorted, then he seemed to remember Jack was her father. "Sorry, man. That's all I got. You should do what he said. Check out the clinic. Kenny's right. Maybe someone will know something. Can't hurt."

"Yeah," Jack said. "Can't hurt. Where is it?"

Jack barely waited for Savon to finish the directions. As soon as he had a clear idea of which way to head, he tore out of the cafe and up the street. The edges of his thin coat flapped in the wind, and he clutched them around himself, trying to stay warm. His leg ached worse with the cold than usual, his limp so pronounced now that he staggered every time he put weight onto it.

Still, he pushed himself. Reaching the top of Church Street, he made a right and tried to walk even faster, convinced he was not far behind Dani now.

Chimes from a nearby church split the air. Jack glanced at his watch in dismay. Lunchtime. Chances were good that half of the people he needed to talk to would be on their lunch breaks.

"Forget it. If they're gone, I'll come back or I'll wait. I couldn't eat now even if I were starving to death. I've *got* to find Dani," he said out loud.

He wrenched open the door of the Ethan Allen Health Care Clinic and stared in dismay. It had the look of a place that had bugged out. He recognized it from his short stay in a M.A.S.H. unit in the Gulf War. Used medical supplies littered the floor, but every bed, cot, and piece of equipment was gone. What had happened here? What on earth could cause an entire medical facility to close down?

Before his mind had time to process the information it was receiving, he was startled by a young woman who came out of one of the rooms. She gasped when she saw him, and her face went white. She was so short her large blue woolen coat swept the floor. On her head was a French beret several sizes too large. It slipped rakishly down over one ear. Curly brown hair poked out at frantic angles from beneath the hat.

"Who are you? What do you want?" she asked in a trembling voice.

"I'm looking for my daughter. What happened here?" Jack asked, still too bewildered to think straight.

The woman looked at him as though she were trying to decide if she could sprint past him and make it to the door before he could tackle her. "Everything has been moved to the Burlington Auditorium," she said slowly, edging around him. "If you need assistance, you should go there."

"I don't need medical help," Jack said. "I'm trying to find my daughter. Can you help me?"

"Sir, like I said, everything has been moved. I'm just the receptionist. I only came back because one of the doctors forgot something. Everything, even the computers, has been moved to the Auditorium. I suggest you go there, and we'll try to help you find your daughter."

"But you must remember something," Jack said, desperation making his voice sound harsh. He lurched forward and grabbed onto the woman's arm. "Please, please help me. Someone is trying to kill her. I have to find her before they kill her!"

The woman flailed her arms, trying to get away from him, but Jack hung on tight. She was no match for him. Finally she stopped struggling and regarded him with eyes filled with terror. "Sir, let me go," she pleaded. "I don't know anything about your daughter."

"Try to remember," Jack begged. "She's just a kid. Seventeen years old and pregnant." A light flickered in the woman's eyes, and Jack shook her. "You remember her!"

The woman cringed away from him. "Yes," she admitted slowly. "I remember her."

"Then you have to help me. Someone is trying to kill her."

"They caught him," the woman said reluctantly. Jack felt like he was pulling the information out of cement.

"What do you mean? Caught who?"

"That guy that tried to shoot her and Dr. Benneton," the woman said. "He tried to shoot them right outside the door there, just this morning. One of the bullets shattered that window, but the police said it was unlikely he meant to hurt anyone in here. His target seemed to be Dr. Benneton and the girl."

Jack saw that the window off to one side of the entrance had been broken and hastily repaired with tape and Plexiglass. "Did he hit them?" he asked hoarsely.

"No," the woman replied. "No, at least I don't think so. The police came right after it happened. The man was just walking down the street. They arrested him on the spot. We couldn't find Dr. Benneton, but she called. . . ." The woman broke off and snapped her mouth shut.

Jack's eyes narrowed. "What did she say?"

"I'm not going to tell you that," the woman said stubbornly. "I'm not supposed to tell anyone. She only called us to let us know that she was all right. How am I supposed to know you aren't in cahoots with that killer? I'm not going to tell you where she is."

"Yes," Jack said. "You are. What's your name?"

The woman glared sullenly at him. "Jodie," she finally said.

"Well, Jodie, my little girl's life is at stake here, and I have to find her. Tell me where they're going."

Jodie stared at him belligerently. "No."

Jack bowed his head in defeat. "Dear God," he prayed. "Please help me. What do I do now?"

"Are you . . . praying?" Jodie asked in disbelief.

Jack let go of her arm and stepped away from her. Jodie rubbed the spot where his fingers had gripped and watched him suspiciously. He pulled out the wanted poster of Dietrich that Coleman had given him. "Is this the man they arrested for trying to shoot Dani?"

Jodie looked at the picture. "No. That doesn't look anything like the guy they arrested. He was much thinner, and he had sores all over his face. But when I talked to Mara, she confirmed his identity. He was wearing a big silver parka. That's kind of hard to miss."

Jack felt fear course through his veins like ice water. "This is the man who is after my daughter. If she is still with Dr. Benneton, then they're both in danger. Will you please tell me where they are? I'm only trying to help. I want my daughter back."

Jodie sized him up, and he watched her struggle with herself. Finally she seemed to make up her mind. "Mara said they were headed to Washington, D.C. She knows someone there at USAMRIID. She was going to try to get some answers for us about this epidemic."

"Epidemic?"

"Yeah, haven't you noticed? People are breaking out with sores and stuff." Jodie lowered her voice. "We've had people die really horrible deaths. I've been thinking of quitting and getting out of here. You know? It's scary. I mean, I'm just a receptionist. I can do that anywhere. I hear the West hasn't been affected that much yet."

"No," Jack said hollowly. His mind jumped ahead. Washington? She was headed to Washington? "No, there's no epidemic there yet."

Jodie seemed to sense Jack wasn't a threat, and she began babbling about the epidemic and how it gave her the creeps. "You know what I think it is?" she was saying when he managed to focus his attention on her again. "I think God is angry with us, and He's punishing us. Don't you think so? I mean, you said a prayer just then. Are you a religious person? Not that I used to be, you understand, but with all this stuff happening, it makes you wonder. Doesn't it?"

"Look at all those earthquakes. In Hawaii, no less. Who'd expect earthquakes there? Practically wiped them out. And the typhoons that did so much damage to those islands, which ones were they now? And this last year I heard on the news they set a record for tornadoes. I think God's trying to wake us up, get our attention, you know? Don't you think?"

She'd paused to take a breath and was looking at him with her head tipped to one side. "I think," Jack began and then stopped. What exactly *did* he think? Since all this stuff had happened with Dani, he'd thought of little else. "I think," he finished finally, "that we're coming up on the end of the world. That's what I think. I think we're living in the last days."

Jodie blinked at him. "Last days? Like what? You think God's going to wipe us out or something?"

Jack felt his insides coil up like a spring. Some killer was after his daughter, and all this woman wanted to do was stand around talking about plagues and disasters. The last thing he had time for was a discussion on end-time events. On the other hand, what if God had thrown Jodie into his path so that she could help him find Dani and he could help her find God? Did he dare brush her off?

"Do you have a Bible?" he asked softly.

"A Bible? Sure I do." She began to rummage around in the large purse slung over her shoulder. "I've got a bigger one at home, but I carry this one around to read on my lunch hour." She pulled a slim leather New International Version from her bag and handed it to him. Jack limped over and sat down on the windowsill. He flipped the Bible open to Revelation.

"Let's start here," he said. Jodie sat down hesitantly beside him. Her clear brown eyes widened as she waited for him to speak. Jack sent up a prayer for guidance and began his first impromptu Bible study.

* * *

Randy's entrance through the back door had coincided exactly with the closing of the front door as Alice left. He probably didn't hear the door shut or anything, but Lynn's heart was still racing about a million miles a second. She took a deep, calming breath. Randy had never talked about anything remotely connected to religion after he got out of academy, at least that she could remember, so she didn't know what he would say if he found out she wanted to learn more.

Randy put his sports bag on the counter near the back door and met her as she was entering the kitchen.

"This kitchen is a disaster," Randy said, as if she couldn't tell.

"I know. It's exactly the way you left it," Lynn responded tartly. "I'm going to clean it up right now."

"I suppose the whole house is the same way."

"No, it's not. I've done some laundry, and the bathroom is clean."

Randy's mind had obviously been prepared for either a long

list of excuses or for her to ignore him altogether. He pinched his lips together as he brushed past her into the living room. A few seconds later the television warmed up, and Lynn could hear the evening national news.

She stayed in the kitchen and began clearing dishes and wiping the table and countertops. Once in a while she checked on Randy. Then something came on the news that made him sit up. She came out of the kitchen and listened too.

"Have you heard much about this disease?" Randy asked.

"Huh-uh," Lynn said. "I never turned the TV on this afternoon." She brought him a glass of water and sat down next to him. She didn't know anything about what he was talking about, but she noticed that it made her feel good that he was talking *to* her instead of *at* her. She watched the news clip. "What's the disease like?"

Randy shrugged. "I don't really know, actually. There doesn't seem to be a lot of information." He took a swallow from his glass and set it down. "I'm not saying nobody knows anything, but I do think the government is downplaying it."

"Aren't reporters usually eager to report a story like that?"

"Yeah."

"Maybe there's a cover-up then."

Randy nodded. The CNN broadcast flashed a woman in an army uniform poised to talk to a reporter. The caption on the screen read "Colonel Amy Cooper, M.D., USAMRIID."

Lynn stayed with Randy and watched the clip.

"Good evening. I'm Greg Harrison." The reporter looked behind him, motioning with his free hand toward the foremost building. "I'm in front of Fort Detrick with Dr. Amy Cooper. Dr. Cooper is a colonel with the United States Army Medical Research Institute of Infectious Disease. Doctor?"

The camera zoomed in on Dr. Cooper.

"Thank you, Greg. We have been receiving reports from the eastern part of the country and eastern Canada of a viral disease, which we suspect at this time to be extremely contagious.

However, we have instigated plans to contain persons infected with the virus so the chances of contact will be lessened. The known symptoms are lesions, a cough, masklike expressions, and diarrhea. If you have any of these symptoms, we urge you to admit yourself to the nearest medical facility for evaluation. Emergency facilities will be in place to handle any overflow from hospitals and clinics. As long as you get proper medical treatment, there is nothing to be concerned about."

"Did you see her bite her lower lip?"

Lynn shrugged. "No. Besides, what if she did? Everyone has funny quirks."

Randy stared thoughtfully at the screen as the picture flipped back to Greg Harrison. "I think she was lying about something. Or not telling everything she knows. Probably not telling the whole truth. I'll bet this is a lot worse than anyone wants to admit."

* * *

Dani rolled over onto her back and poked absently at her abdomen, hoping to make her baby kick her. Mara sat cross-legged on her own bed across the motel room. She had the phone cradled in her lap, and she was talking to someone named Jodie. This was the third or fourth time she'd called Jodie, and it was making Dani nervous. She didn't have any of Mara's reasons to trust this Jodie, but she was every bit as vested in Jodie's trustworthiness.

"Hello, Baby," she crooned to her stomach, which rose up like a mountain and undulated as the baby squirmed into a more comfortable position.

Their first stop in Rutland had been to Mara's doctor friend's office. Mara had examined her and dressed her umpteen little cuts from the glass. She had performed an ultrasound, and Dani got to watch her baby materialize on the black-and-white screen. After what seemed like an eternity, she'd been pronounced fit and the baby healthy. Then Mara shamelessly loaded up on medical supplies and, to her credit, disclosed very little about their situation despite Dr. Grad's rather obnoxious curiosity.

Dani glanced nervously at Mara and then whispered to her stomach. "Don't worry, Baby. I'll take care of you."

Mara hung up and looked at Dani with a triumphant smile. "They caught him," she said.

"Who?" Dani asked stupidly.

"Your Dietrich," Mara said. "He was such an idiot that they found him wandering down the street."

"It wasn't Dietrich. He wouldn't let himself get caught so easily. And he's not *my* Dietrich," she added belligerently.

"But he was wearing the same silver parka, and there were witnesses who identified him."

"It's not true! They just *think* they caught him. Dietrich is still free! He's probably right behind us!"

Mara pressed her lips firmly together and stared up at the ceiling as though it held some direction. Moments later, she began punching the keypad of the phone again, this time trying to get through to her friend Amy. Dani rolled over and studied Mara, who was unaware of everything but the voice on the other end of the phone.

"Look, Amy, I need to see you," Mara said, her voice high and strident. Dani was beginning to recognize that look of determination in her eyes. "I can be there tomorrow. Late probably. Can you meet me somewhere? Monday?" There was bitter disappointment in Mara's voice. "OK, I guess I can wait until then."

Dani knew she had to slip away from Mara before they left the next morning. Doing so without detection was the problem. Mara wanted to leave early, so she had to make her move that night some time. She flexed the muscles of her legs, testing their soreness. Physically, she wasn't really prepared to do something like this, but for the sake of the baby, she would do whatever she had to.

It was hard for her to imagine that just that morning they'd been shot at by Dietrich. She wondered where he was now. Surely he had figured out where they were headed. That was his job, and he was good at his job. But would he figure out the detour? Or would he assume that they had taken the straightest route possible in their headlong flight?

Mara had ended her conversation and leaned back against the headboard, eyes closed. Dani felt a pang of sympathy for her. She'd gotten involved in something she could never have imagined. It wasn't right that Mara now suffer for Dani's mistake.

My leaving will make things better for her, Dani thought. *Maybe once I'm gone she'll change her mind about Washington and go back home. Dietrich really only wants me. He won't bother with her if she's alone.*

Mara was rummaging in her suitcase for something, and Dani watched as she pulled out her Bible. She opened it hesitantly, as though she wasn't sure where to start. Flipping back and forth, she couldn't seem to settle down and read anything in particular. Finally, she looked up with a sigh. "So how come you know so much about the Bible?" she asked.

Dani groaned. Not this topic again. "I read it a lot, that's why."

"Why did you read it if you don't believe it?"

"I didn't always not believe it," Dani explained impatiently. "I mean, I used to believe it. That's when I read it. Now I know better."

"What was it that changed your mind?" Mara slid down on the bed and cupped her chin in her hands. She looked as though she really was interested in the conversation. Dani struggled to be polite.

She shrugged. "I don't know, exactly. I guess it was about the time that mother fed her kids sleeping pills and killed them because she thought the world was too evil for them to grow up in. She said she wanted to protect them from that. She didn't want anyone to hurt them. Do you remember that?" Dani struggled to keep her voice even, to keep it from cracking, but she could feel the same anguish she remembered feeling when she'd seen the news that night. She waited for Mara's silent nod before she continued. "I had just found out I was pregnant, see? And then this woman comes on the television and says those things after killing her babies. Her babies! How could she do something like that? How could God allow it?"

Dani wiped her eyes, and Mara passed her a tissue from the box on the nightstand between them. "I don't know if it was just that I was listening harder or if things just got worse all of a sudden, but after that all I seemed to hear about was the terrible things people were doing to each other. The murders, the crimes, the torture; it was awful. I couldn't take it.

"I'd been going with Shon long enough to know that the Freedom Society wanted everyone to have a better life in the United States. They were fed up with all the horrible things that were happening in the world too. They want America to become a morally strong nation. They want a moral leader, a godly man who will be accountable to God and make us accountable to God too. If we all did what God wanted, He'd bless us, and the bad things would stop happening."

She paused for a moment.

"And is that what you found?" Mara asked.

"I don't know," Dani replied. "I thought I had. I remember telling my father just before I left that I was going to be with Shon and the Freedom Society because at least they were going to make a difference. I wanted to *do* something to stop all the suffering in the world. But then Shon murdered that bank president, and I felt confused and . . ."

"Betrayed?" Mara said.

"Yeah, I guess so. Now, I'm just not sure anymore. I don't care about anything but my unborn baby."

"But you can't not care about everyone else. Not now. Look, we've got Dietrich chasing us. He's after you, and he's not going to give up just because you did," Mara said. "What about that man, the banker, who was killed? There is no justification for taking another life, and if you just pretend it never happened, if you 'don't care,' then you are just as guilty. Right?"

Abruptly Dani shut up. It felt as though a steel door inside had closed with a slam. She'd felt really good opening up to someone, but now she wished she hadn't. There was no way Mara would understand. Besides, Dani recognized a judgmental tone sounding suspiciously like her father.

She rolled over. "I'm tired," she said. "I'm going sleep."

"Good idea," Mara agreed. "We've got to get an early start tomorrow morning. You might want to make sure you have everything in one place so it won't be so hard to find when you're half-asleep."

Since this suited Dani's purposes anyway, she pushed herself off the bed and placed all her things in her bag. She set the bag near the door and laid back down on her bed.

"Aren't you going to change your clothes?" Mara asked curiously.

"No," Dani said. "If I don't get changed, it'll be easier to get out of here in the morning. Besides, it's too cold in here for my nightgown. I'd freeze."

Mara seemed content with this explanation. Dani stared into the darkness long after Mara shut off the light and her breathing became regular. Her whole body throbbed with fatigue. She had no intention of falling asleep, but she was sucked into an exhausted sleep as her mind spun in crazy circles that made her think she was still awake.

* * *

Lynn awoke in the cold sweat of death. Her body trembled uncontrollably. Her heart, which felt as cold and heavy as iron, was pumping so fast it scared her. *Oh no! I'm going to die!* This was the first thought that entered her mind. Her second thought was that she needed something to calm down, something to help her breathe. Her chest felt as if it were being crushed, as if she were being buried alive.

But her mind told her something entirely different. She could see the darkness of the ceiling hovering over her and the walls of her room and the closet doors that stood open and the shadowy forms of her clothes. For a startling moment, she saw one of the shapes pick itself up and walk toward her.

And then it sank back into the shadows so quickly that she blinked in disbelief. Knowing she had not been imagining things, she stared at the closet while she sat up in bed and swung her legs to the floor. She wanted to be prepared to defend herself.

For several minutes, Lynn sat on the edge of her bed and stared into the closet as if in a trance. Suddenly, her body gave an involuntary jerk, and she shook her head and looked around. She felt a little more alert than she did when she first woke up, but now the tremors were worse. She raised her hands and stared at them. They trembled so badly in the dim light filtering through her bedroom window that she could no longer make out the solid forms of her palms and long fingers.

Lynn put her hands down. When they continued to tremble, she reached out and gripped her knees to minimize the shaking. It worked. The tighter she squeezed with her hands, the less they shook. Then she turned her attention to the four walls of her room. The room had now become a dense, confining prison. It wasn't just her chest anymore that felt crushed by an invisible weight; her whole body was beginning to feel the pressure.

One part of Lynn's mind knew all of this was not real. Yes, in fact, it was real, it was all happening to her, but there was something wrong with parts of it that made it not right. Maybe it was the way she was interpreting things. She knew she shouldn't be scared or anxious, but because she was, she was causing herself even more anxiety. The shadows in the closet were not real; they were only images she was convincing herself were real bodies. She had always been afraid of nighttime shadows.

She knew, for instance, that her heart was racing because

she was in withdrawal and that the sweat turning cool on her body was also because of the heroin. She was so messed up. Could she die if this went on? She didn't know for sure. *Maybe,* she thought. She thought she should give herself a small dose just to calm down and stop some of the pressure.

After Alice Nolan came by to visit, Lynn had felt impressed to throw away her remaining supply of drugs. She did her best to get rid of everything, but she had also been afraid that her withdrawals might be too bad to deal with. She knew people who'd had bad experiences with withdrawal, and she herself had tried to quit on several occasions, so she knew it was tough. She kept a small stash just in case. It was a safe choice and a prudent one, she decided. Her drug kit was hidden in the right shoe of a pair of rotten old tennis shoes in her closet.

She slid down to the floor and stared for a long while at the closet.

"God, please help me," she whispered.

Silence.

She'd prayed a lot since she started reading her Bible. It seemed to help. She'd made a decision to give God a fair try. He was all that she had. Well, except for Alice Nolan. Maybe she should call Alice. That was an idea. Maybe Alice could help.

Where was the card she left, the card with her phone number? Lynn narrowed her eyes though it was too dark to see anything. But it was a thinking mechanism. It was no use; she couldn't think clearly and couldn't remember where she had put the card.

"Why don't You help me, God?" Tears began to flow freely, dumping in a nearly steady stream onto her bare legs. She crossed her legs and began to rock. She rocked for some time.

The symptoms didn't get any better. In fact, they seemed to get progressively worse. The tremors were constant. Lynn felt cold and ran her hands up and down her arms, but mostly she felt the goose bumps and an ensuing cool, ticklish feeling.

"I can't live through the night like this," Lynn murmured,

feeling scared, sick, and alone, even though Randy was in a room not too far away.

It feels so awful to be alone, she thought. This was more a rebuke toward God than a particular revelation to her. She'd felt this way before, lots of times.

That's what prompted her to make a final decision about the hypodermic needle and heroin in the closet.

Chapter Six

Sunday, November 14

When Dani jerked fully awake, dawn had already softened the night sky outside her motel window. She began to push herself up with alarm but then realized Mara might already be awake. She strained to hear her breathing. It sounded even and deep.

Mara slept with abandon, one arm thrown up over her eyes and her red hair fanned out over the pillowcase, which in the predawn light seemed eerily like blood beneath her head. Dani felt her spine shiver at the thought.

She eased herself from the bed as quietly as she could. Her feet searched for her cheap imitation Birkenstocks on the floor by her bed. She slipped them on without having to bend over and ever so quietly began walking to the door, rolling each foot from heel to front to minimize any sound she might make.

At the door, she reached for the handle of her duffel bag while the fingers of her other hand closed around the doorknob. A slick film of sweat coated her palm and made the door hard to open.

As she gripped it tighter, Mara stirred in her sleep and rolled onto her side.

Dani swore under her breath and desperately yanked open the door. She shut it carefully behind her, realizing she didn't have much time, knowing Mara had requested a wake-up call at five thirty and it was nearly five o'clock now.

In the car, she had looked at Mara's map and decided the safest thing for her to do was to head west. It didn't matter so much where she ended up, as long as it wasn't Washington, D.C. Ignoring the stretching pains in her abdomen, she slung her duffel bag over her shoulder and began hiking as fast as she could along Route 9. There wasn't much traffic in the early hours, and before a car came along, she guessed she had walked nearly a mile.

The beat-up old red pickup truck slowed as it approached, and Dani wearily stuck out her thumb, begging silently that it would stop and offer her a ride. For a second she thought perhaps it would continue on its way, but at the last instant it slowed and swerved onto the side of the road ahead of her. Gratefully, she jogged as quickly as she was able up to the truck.

She opened the door and hoisted herself onto the seat before turning toward the driver. Immediately she wished she had declined the ride after all. The man who put the truck in gear and eased back out onto the road grinned balefully at her. Dani's stomach lurched in fear.

He was dressed in the dirtiest overalls she'd ever seen, and she quickly judged that they accounted for at least part of the horrible stench filling the interior of the cab. A greasy baseball cap was pulled down so that the visor partially obscured his face. Large, rough hands gripped the steering wheel.

"Howdy, there," the man said. "Ya ain't in great shape to be traveling, now are ya? How fer ya goin'?"

Dani swallowed hard. "Not far," she said. "Maybe Glens Falls or Albany."

"Wal, this here's yer lucky day. I happen to be headed all the way to Buffaler with this here loada chickens."

Dani craned her neck and saw that indeed dead chickens were jammed into a large crate and lashed to the bed of the truck with frayed rope.

"Isn't that a long way to go for just a few chickens?" she asked.

"Yeah, maybe, but I got me some other business out in Buffaler, too, ifn' you know what I mean." He winked at her in an exaggerated fashion, and Dani thought she might throw up all over the cracked vinyl seat of the truck. "You from around here, girlie?"

"No," Dani replied shortly. If he thought she was about to volunteer information to him, he was a few eggs short of a dozen. She stared resolutely out the dirty window.

"Ha! Me neither. Came up from Virginny long about, oh, I dunno, maybe six years ago. Done left the missus number two down there. Up here they call us flatlanders, ya know."

"No," Dani said politely. "I didn't know that."

"Why, shoot, yes. Figure they got claim to the only mountains in the world, I guess. Sure, some of 'em's big, but I seen bigger." Dani could feel his eyes on her. "You put me in mind of missus number five. She was a purty young thing like you. Gonna have a baby herself last time I seen her. Never did see that young 'un. She run out on me."

He rubbed his chin ruefully. "Come to consider it, she was the only one what left me. I done left all the others myself." He added the last part as though it was something to be proud of. Dani grunted.

"My name's Roy," the man said. "Whatcha want me ta call you?"

Dani bit back a smart-alecky reply. "Mrs. Talbot," she said stonily.

The scenery rolled by as Roy's scratchy voice kept pace. After awhile he seemed to be repeating himself in a hillbilly monotone. Dani felt her eyelids getting heavy, and she slumped against the door of the pickup.

When she woke up, the truck was no longer moving, and Roy was shaking her shoulder roughly. "I said, give it here, missy," he growled.

"Wha—" Dani blinked in confusion. "What's going on?"

"I knowed ya got money in that bag. Now give it here."

"But I don't," Dani began.

Roy produced a pistol and aimed it at her face. "I don't want ta hear no excuses. Give the money here."

Dani's brain spun frantically. She *did* have half of Mara's money. Mara had insisted that they split it up in case something happened to either one of them. Dani had meant to leave it all with Mara that morning, but in her haste to get out before Mara woke up, she had forgotten it. The barrel of the gun pointing between her eyes jogged her memory, but there was no way she was going to let him take that money. It was all she had to get her and her baby somewhere safe, if there was such a place left on earth.

"Give it here," Roy growled. "I kin smell money a mile away, and I says yer loaded."

Dani knew the instant she tried the stunt, it would never work, but her desperation didn't allow for rational thought. Ducking, she lifted the handle and jammed her shoulder against the door. It stuck, and that was all the time Roy needed to backhand her across the face with the gun.

Reeling from the blow, Dani again threw herself against the door. This time it gave way, and she tumbled out onto the pavement, falling directly onto her bag. Cars whizzed by on the highway. Dani groaned from the force of her fall. It felt like she'd broken every rib, but she forced herself to crawl away, dragging the duffel bag behind her.

She heard the sound of Roy's door open and close and the click of his boot heels on the pavement as he came around the backside of the truck, swearing under his breath. It was useless to flee. Dani sank into a heap and waited.

"God," she whispered. "If You really are there and You really do care about what happens to us, please help me. Not for my sake. I don't deserve it. For my baby. Please."

Dani heard the blood pounding in her eardrums as she waited for Roy to shoot her. She wondered if she would hear the report of the gun before she died. Then, squealing tires and Roy's loud curses and receding footsteps prompted her to lift her head tentatively.

Roy's pickup truck peeled back out onto the highway, nearly causing an accident. The smoke from his exhaust drifted over her, and Dani couldn't see at first who or what had saved her. When it cleared, she thought she must be seeing a vision.

* * *

Randy knocked on Lynn's door. At first, he used a gentle tap, but when there was no answer, he knocked harder. Still, there was no answer. When he came through the door, he found his sister lying on the floor in a fetal position. She didn't move. Her blond hair looked dirty and stiff with dried perspiration. She was wearing a tank top and a pair of wrinkled jogging shorts. He could see from the paraphernalia on the floor that at some point during the night she had injected herself with heroin.

Randy lifted Lynn off the floor and put her into bed, covered her, and gently tucked her in. He took one-hundred percent responsibility for her drug use. He swore as he looked at Lynn that there was something terribly wrong with him to allow his kid sister to get so lost, and he knew he could probably have done something to stop it had he only cared enough soon enough.

* * *

The shrill ring of the phone interrupted Mara's dream. It was a nightmare really, in which a giant silver marshmallow was chasing her. She ran around and around a fiery pit while the marshmallow laughed and pointed a gun at her, and Father

Chevalier kept trying to pull her into the white marble church in Winooski.

Mara groped for the phone. "Hello?" she said groggily.

"Good morning," wheezed an old man's voice. "This is your five-thirty wake-up call."

"Oh, yeah, thank you." Mara said, bolting up in bed and replacing the phone in its cradle. "Dani, it's time to . . ."

She never finished her sentence. Dani's bed was empty. The light wasn't on in the bathroom either. Mara felt a cold shiver run down her back like the icy feet of tiny mice. She looked around, and looked thoroughly, but the whole time she knew it was no use. Dani had left.

Why did she leave? Mara asked herself as she brushed her teeth with much more vigor than the task required. *I can't believe she'd take off. I don't understand. Why would she do something like that?*

It took less than twenty minutes to take a shower and get on the road. Her damp, red hair clung to the back of her neck, and she brushed it back. Turning the heater on full blast, she let it air dry while her mind played with her options.

"I've got to get to Amy," she said out loud. "That's first and foremost. Once I tell her what's happening, maybe she will know the best way to contact the president. She is in the army, after all. Keeping the president safe is part of their job."

Now that Dani wasn't around, Mara wished she had asked more questions. Why was the Freedom Society going to assassinate the president? She tried to piece together her conversations with Dani. What had the girl said exactly?

Panic jabbed her fiercely in the stomach, and she suddenly wondered what to do.

"Our Father who art in heaven," Mara began, as much to steady her nerves as to actually pray. She said three Our Fathers, five Hail Marys, and threw in a Twenty-third Psalm for good measure, but she didn't feel any comfort from God.

"Look, God," she said finally, cringing, almost expecting a

bolt of lightning as punishment for addressing God directly. "I need help. I don't have time to find a priest to talk to, and going through the saints seems to me like asking a nurse to fix a gunshot wound instead of going right to the doctor. So I'm going to go right to the Doctor. I thought I knew a lot about You at one time, but now I'm seeing that I really didn't know You at all.

"I'm sorry about that. I'm sorry for a lot of things. And I'm willing to do just as much penance as necessary to make it up to You. But right now I need some help. First of all, I need you to keep Dani safe and if possible to help me find her. Second, I need You to smooth the way for me in Washington. I have no idea what I'm doing, but I know what needs to be done. I'm just going to follow. You lead. I'll do whatever I have to do. But if You aren't in this with me, let me know now, and I'll just turn around and go back home. I'm not about to do this alone."

Mara paused and waited what she considered an appropriate amount of time. Nothing happened. "I'll take that as a Yes, then," she said, wishing she felt the confidence she expressed. "Thank You. Amen."

She shrugged her shoulders, squirming to get comfortable in the seat. She had a long trip ahead of her.

* * *

"But I had faith, and I asked God to help me. He let me down when I needed Him." Lynn said this even though it was hard to get the words out. It was like admitting God didn't really exist, or if He did, He really didn't care about people with problems. At least with her kinds of problems.

Alice's eyes were moist now. She shook her head slightly in a gesture that showed she felt Lynn's pain and then reached out and embraced Lynn. Into the young woman's ear, she whispered, "God is closer than I am at this moment to you. He's inside your heart, dear girl, and since you have invited Him, He will never leave you nor forsake you."

"But I couldn't help myself. I sinned. Jesus must have left when I put drugs into my body. Maybe you're wrong."

"No, no, Lynn. That's not true."

"But He didn't even help me when I asked Him to." Lynn took a sharp, deep breath. She wasn't making excuses, but she remembered this vividly: She'd called on the Lord in her time of need, and He wasn't there. Her eyes, still dreamy from the drugs, were trying to look adamant. The incongruity seemed to define her helplessness.

Alice had come right over when Lynn called her. From what Lynn had said and the way she sounded, she must have had a hard and lonely night. Alice set her purse on the coffee table and clutched Lynn's hands. She led Lynn to the couch, and a little shakily, the girl sat down. She watched while Lynn wiped tears out of her eyes with the backs of her hands.

"I'm not good enough," Lynn said a few moments later, and then she paused, as if this belief were sealed for eternity. "Have you seen that man on television? He's always talking about God and that if we all live better lives, we'll be able to see God, and He'll bless us if we're good."

Alice smiled because Lynn had managed to cut out all Gavin Larson's flowery words and condense his hour-long messages into one sentence. "I know I'm no great religious leader, Lynn, but I hope you won't be offended if I say that Gavin Larson is full of hogwash."

"Why?"

Why? Hmm . . . Well, mostly because Alice just didn't like the guy. Alice couldn't figure out why people couldn't see that there was not an ounce of sincerity in him. But she couldn't say this to Lynn. Lynn was searching for truth, not Alice's personal commentary. "First of all, Mr. Larson and you have a different definition of the word *good* than God does. It doesn't matter to God that you used some drugs last night. He knows, probably even better than you do, why you ended up losing that fight. Maybe God doesn't even expect you to quit all at once, because maybe

He knows it's impossible for most people to do. I guess what I'm trying to tell you, Lynn, is that God already considers you 'good.' Unlike what Gavin Larson preaches everywhere he goes, God already loves us without the strings."

"Strings?" Lynn asked.

"All God wants from you is that you get to know Him and love Him. He'll work out the rest in His time. The more you get to know Him, the more you'll naturally want to do to please Him. You'll begin to live a Christlike life but not because you *have* to. Because you want to."

"I still don't understand why God didn't just help me keep from shooting up last night. I didn't want to do it."

"He knows the hairs on your head, Lynn, and He knows that you couldn't handle things last night. But most of all, He knows you didn't want to use drugs last night. The drugs are bad, all right, just like sin. God hates sin and how it hurts us, but He doesn't hate us. He knows He's the only One who can overcome sin, so He doesn't expect you to do it on your own. You feel like you lost last night, but God doesn't. I think He's smiling right now because you are still faithful to Him.

"Lynn?" Alice gently reached out for Lynn's delicate chin and turned her head until her downcast eyes met with Alice's. "Lynn, I want you to remember one very, very important thing. You stay honest with God. Talk to Him, even demand His help when you feel you need it. He will always treat you with respect and immeasurable love. Just never let go of your faith, and He will answer. OK?"

Lynn nodded, heaving a sigh that meant she was afraid she would never understand, but she was willing to try.

Alice smiled. She saw Lynn's yearning to know God. She was surprised—or maybe not so surprised after all—that even after Lynn had ended up using heroin last night, her faith in God seemed to have grown out of it. Could this be part of God's plan? She didn't know, and certainly she could never guess, but it was something to wonder about. Could be that she was exercising her faith some too.

* * *

Jack's chin snapped off his chest with such force that it popped a vertebrae in his neck. Panic gripped him as he realized he'd been asleep at the wheel. Not good at any time but particularly bad as he headed into a very congested area of Albany, New York. Sleep clouded his mind, and he fought to remember which exit he was supposed to take as they all converged on him at once.

"Lord," he breathed. "Which way? Which way?"

He watched helplessly as the flow of traffic forced him into the wrong lane. Too late he realized that he was headed west toward Buffalo, New York, rather than south toward Washington, D.C.

He slammed his fist onto his bad leg and yelped in pain. "Lord, I asked You for direction," he said angrily. "Why didn't You help me? I can't afford to waste time here." Fuming, he studied the side of the road ahead for a good place to turn around. Pulled over ahead was a beat-up old red pickup truck. Probably a flat tire, Jack mused. Any other time he might have stopped to help. Today the thought never crossed his mind.

As he watched, a body tumbled out of the passenger side door and scrambled away from the truck. The brown hair was short, ragged really, but there was no mistaking the protruding abdomen. That girl was Dani!

Tires squealing, Jack cut off the car in the right-hand lane and swerved over onto the side of the road. A man coming around the driver's side of the pickup with a gun changed his mind suddenly and jumped back into the vehicle. The pickup roared to life and peeled back into traffic. Dani lay in a heap on the pavement, and Jack hesitated a moment before he trusted himself to get out of the car.

"Dani?" he asked tentatively, as he walked up to the girl. In the back of his mind he was afraid he had been hallucinating.

Surely there were many pregnant teenagers who looked like his daughter. "Dani?"

"Daddy?" a small voice answered him. Dani's frightened and amazed eyes peered out of the tangle of hair as she gingerly picked herself up from the ground. "Daddy? Is that you?"

"Oh, baby!" Jack sobbed, running to her and helping her to stand up. "Baby, what happened? Are you all right?"

"I—I think so," Dani said. Her arms and legs quivered, and she leaned heavily against Jack. He could feel every rib beneath his hands as he supported her and helped her walk the few steps back to his car. Opening the door, he gently helped her inside. Clucking nervously, he lifted her legs and swung them into the car and carefully shut the door.

Racing around to the driver's side, he hopped in the car and sat looking at his daughter, suddenly at a loss for something to say. Dani filled in the gap.

"What are you doing here, Daddy?" she asked. She folded her arms across her chest, resting them on her stomach.

"I am—I was looking for you," Jack replied. "I read in the paper about the—" Jack swallowed hard—"murder. I knew you were in trouble, so I came looking for you. I'm so glad I found you before Dietrich did."

"Actually, you didn't," Dani said quietly. "Dietrich found me first, but I was with a lady doctor, and she protected me."

"Where is she now?" Jack asked. "She isn't . . ."

"Dead?" Dani finished tiredly. "No, she isn't dead. She's on her way to Washington because . . . well, just because. And I didn't want to go to Washington. Besides, she'll be safer without me. Dietrich only wants me."

"Because you witnessed the murder?" Jack asked.

"No, because . . ." Dani looked up suddenly. "Why are you asking me these questions?" she asked suspiciously.

"Danielle," Jack began. He heard the authoritative tone creep into his voice, but he felt powerless to stop it. "Now look here. I've been halfway across the country looking for you, racing with a cold-blooded killer to get to you first. I have a right to know what you're involved in."

"Do you?" Dani spat. "And why is that, exactly? Because you felt so loyal, so *parental*, that you came looking for me? Is that supposed to impress me? And just because you showed up at the right moment and saved me, you feel you have some claim on my life. Is that it? Well, it doesn't work that way."

"And how does it work, Dani?" Jack asked wearily. "I don't know what to say to you anymore. Everything seems wrong. You don't want to hear about God. You don't want to tell me anything about yourself and why you're in trouble. I keep trying to open the door, and you keep slamming it in my face. I don't know what to do any more."

"Then don't *do* anything, Daddy," Dani said. "Leave me in peace."

"On the side of the road?"

"If that's where I want to be," Dani replied sullenly.

"And where *do* you want to be?"

"You want to know what I know, Daddy?" she asked suddenly, fiercely. "I'll tell you. I was there when Shon killed Stan Shultz. Shon did it, Daddy, not Dietrich. Oh, Dietrich trained him, and he watched. He did nothing to stop him. Neither did I. But it was Shon who pulled the trigger."

Dani stopped and bowed her head, seeming to struggle to gain control of herself. "I ran away from Shon, Daddy, because I got scared. I have something they want, and I know something they probably want to kill me for. Something so awful . . ."

"What?" Jack coaxed her. "What can be so awful?"

When Dani looked up, her eyes were dry and hard. "I believed in the Freedom Society once. They weren't afraid to do things to make this world a better place. But, now . . . they're going to assassinate the president. They want to unite the world under Gavin Larson," she said bitterly.

"Assassinate?" Jack repeated in a whisper. "It's not possible . . ."

"Believe me, it is," Dani said. "I saw the plans, the routes, the maps, the schedules, everything. I don't know exactly how, but I know they're going to do it. And I'm sure it has something to do with the big rally coming up in Washington, D.C. That's why I'm getting as far away from that place as possible."

"Have you told anyone this?" Jack asked.

"Only Mara," Dani said. "She made me tell her everything. Even after I told her, she insisted on going to Washington. That's when I knew I had to get away from her."

"She's headed to Washington?" Jack asked incredulously.

"Can you believe it?" Dani scoffed. "She thinks she can stop the assassination. I told her she has a death wish, but she wouldn't listen to me. She wants to be the big hero. Let her. I've got more important things to do."

Jack felt rage fill him at Dani's ungrateful, flippant attitude. He grabbed her arm and gripped it hard. "You listen to me! That woman saved your life, and now she's trying to save the life of the president from *your* friends."

"I'm not taking this from you!" Dani screamed, as tears sprang up in her eyes. She yanked her arm free and pushed open the door. Jack followed right behind her. "I'd rather have Dietrich find me than to spend one more minute with you!" she shrieked.

"Dani, get back in the car!" Jack yelled.

"I will not!" she screamed.

Jack stopped. "Dani, I will hogtie you if necessary. Get in the car." His voice dropped to a deadly calm, and Dani stopped in her tracks, stamping on the ground in frustration. Jack returned to the car, and Dani followed in protest.

Jack buckled his seat belt and then buckled Dani's when she made no move to do it herself. She turned her face stonily toward the window and refused to speak to him. Resolutely, he put on his blinker and pulled out into traffic, confident that sooner or later she would be sorry for the way she behaved.

Three hours later when they pulled into a gas station, Dani had still not spoken. Jack stretched gratefully as he got out of the car. His leg throbbed dully. He pumped the gas and made his way into the cramped station. An attendant sat behind the counter chewing gum and reading a paperback. Jack handed him a twenty-dollar bill for the gas, pulled a couple of Gatorades out of the cooler, and set them on the counter. The attendant stared stupidly at the money.

"Don't you have a card?" he asked, taking the money reluctantly.

"You mean a credit card?" Jack asked.

"No. A Universal Bank Card."

"I didn't think businesses were going to go to that cashless system so soon. Do I need one?" He remembered, back before Dani had left home, that the government and banks were planning a universal cashless system. Later, he had learned that everyone would eventually have a Universal Bank Card to use instead of cash. He hadn't given it much thought, because it seemed it would take quite a while to fully implement the system.

"The banks are really pushing the program," the attendant said apologetically. "They're not charging businesses that get on line before the end of the year transaction fees for another two years. We haven't been accepting cash. But since you're not a regular customer, I guess I can make an exception." He took the money and counted Jack out the change, mostly in ones because he didn't have a lot of cash in the drawer.

"I tell you, it's been a whole lot easier since they started the switch, man," the attendant was saying. "Used to be a 7-11 was the riskiest job in America. Most of the quick stops switched over completely in one month. Nobody's robbed one since." He glanced around uneasily. "I know I feel kinda jumpy sometimes late at night. Every time some redneck comes in, I'm afraid I'll be squinting down the barrel of a gun next thing."

"Yeah, I know what you mean," Jack said politely. He folded the wad of ones and placed them in his wallet.

"If it hadn't been for Gavin Larson and the United Religious Coalition putting pressure on the government, they'd still be doing studies on it to see if it was the best kind of system. That Gavin Larson's got some power. It's the best thing he's done for this country so far. If he ran for president, he'd get my vote, and I'm not even a religious person." The attendant smiled broadly and gave a friendly wave as Jack stepped out the door and got into his car. Dani had fallen asleep. He started the engine and pulled out on the road again without waking her. The attendant's words repeated themselves in his ear. *He'd get my vote. He'd get my vote. My vote.* But, Gavin Larson wasn't running for any office. Or was he?

Jack began to consider that Gavin Larson might indeed have aspirations for the presidency. He would certainly be a wildly popular candidate. Pair his current popularity with the fact that in less than a week he was meeting with the pope, presumably to cement a religious alliance, and you are suddenly looking at someone with the potential to become the most powerful man on earth.

* * *

As Dan Reiss listened to the undulating chant of the auctioneer, he stared out over the flat landscape in the direction of the mountains. He found himself looking toward the mountains a lot these days. And when he did, he felt a pull he was incapable of explaining. It was a drawing almost, an incessant tug.

It was easy for him to believe that it was the prompting of the Holy Spirit and not the workings of an overactive imagination; but like Abraham who sought to stay the hand of the Lord, Dan pleaded daily for more time or more wisdom. He had to have one or the other unless he was to be the only one to take refuge in the mountains.

Most of the people in his congregation didn't want to hear anything about it. Scores had left in search of more permissive doctrines found at other churches or because they believed the majority couldn't be wrong. Dan certainly wasn't the majority. A few had stayed, though, and others straggled in, coming *from* other religions. These were the ones Dan had the most hope for. They had begun to bond together, to spend time on their knees seeking God's will, to repent of their sins, and ask for an out-pouring of the Holy Spirit.

Presently, most were unconvinced they were living in the end times. The older members especially were convinced there was little more wrong with the world than there had ever been and that things would get better. They had seen bad times before. Life just seemed to cycle that way. Dan felt as though he were exhorting a brick wall when he pleaded for them to open their eyes. "Either You're going to have to make me more persuasive, or You're going to have to tell them Yourself," Dan muttered under his breath.

That was another thing.

He had always prayed fervently and often, but now he found himself talking to God not just as a friend but as a constant companion. Time and again he found himself carrying on a con-versation with God, out loud, as he walked, did his chores, or ate dinner. It didn't bother *him*, but his parishioners were be-ginning to think him a little odd.

One of the runners for the auction approached him. "Excuse me, sir, but they're finishing up now. Would you like to come and begin to settle up?"

"Certainly." Dan followed the stocky man to the table where two women sat keeping the records of who bought what. Around him, on the grass and at the feet of the people attending the auction, were Jack's possessions. Before he had left, Jack had asked Dan to have an auction house sell everything. He needed the money.

As he walked up to the table, Dan heard the auctioneer say, "I thank you all for coming, and I hope to see you at my next auction." Unclipping his microphone, he stretched and walked up to Dan.

He put out his hand. "It was a good auction. I hope you're as pleased as I am. Mr. Talbot has good taste. Quite a number of remarkable antiques."

Dan shrugged apologetically. "I can't say as I know much about antiques."

"No matter," the auctioneer said pleasantly. "Everything was appraised fairly, and we got very good prices for it all. And an amazing turnout considering the short notice. But I called several high-end buyers myself when I saw the quality of the antiques."

"So what now? Can I get a check?" Dan asked.

"Uh, no, sorry, we don't do checks anymore, but I can have the funds transferred to Mr. Talbot's UBC. All I need you to do is sign here stating that we agreed to do that and give me his UBC number."

"I'm afraid he doesn't have a UBC," Dan said fretfully. "Can you use mine, and I can get the money to him?"

"Makes no difference to me," the auctioneer said cheerfully. "So long as you sign, releasing me of responsibility in the event that you should decide not to give him his money. You're the one with the power of attorney."

"Oh, I would never steal his money!" Dan said, aghast that anyone would even consider such a thing.

"Somehow I believe that," the auctioneer said, studying Dan.

Dan smiled faintly. "That's not me you trust, that's He who dwells in me."

"Huh?"

"I-I was referring to God," Dan elaborated clumsily. "God lives in me, and He is completely trustworthy."

"Don't I know it," the auctioneer agreed emphatically. "I like what I see of Gavin Larson's United Religious Coalition. He's going to make this a God-fearing country, and that's what we need. He's the most clear-minded religious leader I've ever heard. He talks about stronger moral standards and stiffer penalties for people who break the law. Why, it's gotten so a man continually fears for his family, while criminals go free. I've had trusted employees steal from me and best friends betray me. Where does it stop? That's what I want to know."

"I don't think Gavin Larson is the answer," Dan began, but the auctioneer cut him off.

"And now that he's meeting with the pope, Protestants and Catholics can find some common ground. You know, united like that, this country will be a whole lot better off. And it's about time too!"

Dan stepped back from the force of the man's words. His zeal was written on his face, but Dan could see the fear that prompted it lurking in the depths of his eyes. He was afraid to disagree with him outright and struggled to think of another way to reach this searching soul.

"Ahem." He quietly cleared his throat and waited for the flush on the man's face to abate. "You know, you seem to be a godly fellow. I would dearly love to see your face in my congregation this Sabbath. Please consider this a personal invitation from me. What did you say your name was?"

The auctioneer sized him up again with a long, drawn out, appraising look. "I'm Mark," he said finally. "Mark Bradford. I'm the owner of Mark Bradford Antiques and Auctioneering."

Dan blushed with embarrassment. "Of course," he said. "How stupid of me."

"No," Mark held up a hand to stop him. "I like a man who isn't afraid of making mistakes and owning up to them. And I like your honesty. I'll go to your church, sir, if you'll give me directions."

Dan drew out a quick map on the back of an unused auction number and handed it to Mark, promising to watch for him that Sabbath.

Mark's brow furrowed. "Sabbath? Sunday, of course."

"No," Dan corrected him. "Saturday is the Sabbath."

"Well, I guess you can explain that to me then," Mark said cheerfully, "because right now I've got to get this auction tied up so my help can go home. It was nice meeting you, Preacher, and a pleasure doing business with you."

"Likewise," Dan agreed, shaking Mark's hand again.

As Dan returned to his car, his feet felt as though they were barely touching the ground. "Who would have thought, Lord," he whispered under his breath. "Here, of all places?" Just went to prove, he decided, that God was at work no matter where they were or what they were doing at the time.

And really, it seemed like that was happening more and more often lately and in the most diverse places too. One of the most exciting things that had happened in his congregation was the weekly prayer meetings. At one time they consisted of the same faithful few members who met, warbled through a few moldy hymns, offered long-winded, stale prayers, and then went home with the smug satisfaction of getting one up on those members who attended prayer meeting irregularly or not at all.

Now, prayer meetings were packed. Joy and excitement rippled over the room like exhalations of the Spirit. Prayers were fervent and effectual. The consuming power of love melted every heart and was the salve of every wound. In addition to the weekly prayer meetings, members met in small groups at each other's homes during the week as well. His church had become like an exuberant, trusting child who was obedient, curious, and faithful, peeking expectantly into the future.

"Thank You for trusting them to my care, Father," Dan said, as he opened the door of Jack's car, which squeaked in protest. "I *am* grateful for them, Lord, but call me greedy. I want more. The more souls You send me, the more I want. The time is so short. So very short. I can feel it."

Chapter Seven

Monday, November 15

When Brian returned to headquarters for the United Religious Coalition located in downtown Chicago, it was the first time he had been back to the office since returning from Boise, Idaho. He had spent the entire weekend with his family, and he enjoyed every minute of it, but Gavin was eager to have him in Washington. Before his flight, he had a few things to attend to. He paused after stepping through the door of his office and collected his thoughts.

After a few moments, he set his attaché case on his desk then went back out and roamed the halls. He took note of who was in the office at this early hour. He dropped in on a few of his colleagues and said Hello. His good friend, Tyler Brownell, occupied the last office he stopped in. Brownell had been an accountant with the firm for six years, and there were some things Brian wanted to understand. His friend was laboring over some figures on a sheet of paper in front of him, his palm resting in front on a calculator to his right.

"Tyler?" Brian spoke softly.

Brownell looked up, saw Brian, and smiled. "Brian, you're back." He stood up, and the two shook hands. "You must have a lot of work to catch up on."

Brian nodded and smiled tiredly. "You're right about that. But then I leave for Washington this afternoon."

"Are you all right, Brian? You seem a million miles away."

"I guess I am thinking about other things. Stan Shultz, specifically."

Brownell shook his head sadly. "What a tragedy."

"Could you tell me how we, the Coalition, distributed the money Shultz gave?"

Brownell's face wrinkled into a thoughtful frown. "Well, I don't know for sure. I'd have to look up some of our records. Why?"

Brian ignored Tyler's question and went on. "Shultz was a regular contributor of charity funds, wasn't he? His charity kept pace with his growing net worth?"

"Of course." Brownell had quit smiling. "Like many businessmen who are able to amass such fortunes, Stan Shultz's fortune continued to grow. Tax write-offs persuaded him to increase his charitable contributions, of course, but Shultz enjoyed giving to people who needed it."

"Lucky for us."

"Lucky for thousands of homeless," Brownell said.

"Could you give me a rundown on how much Shultz donated through us and where the funds were distributed? I'm going to hold a press conference at noon. Several stations would like to have a follow-up to the funeral from the Coalition, something that will give an idea how Shultz's death will hurt the nation's homeless and affect the hunger situation."

Brownell nodded. He'd been nodding all along as if he were agreeing, but Brian knew it was mostly out of habit, a learned behavior to show you were listening when you weren't. When Brownell quit nodding, it became evident his gesturing was completely artificial.

"I'd like to help you out right now, Brian, but—"

"Didn't you say you had the records?"

Brownell grinned lavishly. "No, I said I'd have to look up the records."

"Then could you do that?"

A frown instantly replaced the expansive grin. "Right now? No, I can't do it right now."

"Why not? I've got a deadline for this press conference. I need them even sooner than now."

"But the records aren't here."

"They're in the building, aren't they?"

"Yes, yes, of course. It'll take some time to get the information you need together."

Brian nodded as if he understood when really he didn't. Brownell had an expensive computer sitting like a trophy on the corner of his highly polished oak desk. Like Brian's own computer, it was hardwired into the Coalition's network. If the Coalition generated a record, the network stored it. Only problem was, Brian didn't have access to the financial records. Brownell did. He had every record available at his fingertips. "Why don't you have an assistant round them up?"

Brownell snapped his fingers. "Excellent idea. I'll get on it right away and bring the files to you myself." He made some serious calculations on his watch and then glanced at Brian. "What do you say, oh, about nine o'clock."

Brian stayed rooted in the chair for a few moments longer, causing Brownell some discomfort. They seemed to have lost the potential for small talk, so after lingering a few moments longer, Brian stood and leaned on the desk. Brownell understood full well that Brian knew he was avoiding the issue, but he seemed compelled to stick to his story.

"Yes, right," Brian said. He thanked Brownell and shook his hand again.

Brownell looked frustrated. "Well, welcome back, Brian."

"Thanks, Tyler."

Back in his office, Brian flipped on his own computer. He had twenty-seven e-mail messages. Many were outdated. The senders had questions that would have been answered by now or were obsolete. He forwarded a few, deleted the messages he didn't need to respond to, and then fired up his word processor to begin working on Stan Shultz's memorial.

At nine o'clock Brian quit working and waited for his secretary, Joleen, to tell him over the comline that the financial records he had requested had been delivered. Fifteen minutes later, surprisingly enough, they did arrive, and he went out to retrieve them. For the next hour, he read them at his desk.

The records were a mixed bag, and Brian was left to wonder how much of it was accurate. Tyler Brownell seemed to know he shouldn't just give Brian the itemized statements the Coalition sent to Shultz. Brian had met Shultz a few times, and he knew the Coalition ran out these statements only because Shultz wanted them. Shultz genuinely cared. Those statements might have made Shultz happy, telling him what his millions of dollars were going to, but other than for his personal interest, they were of little importance. Brian placed them in a pile to the side and began reading the important information.

Tyler had also sent records of deposit into the Coalition's charitable donations account from Stan Shultz. As Brian read, he began to realize that the dollar figures from Shultz's statements and the funds distributed to various homeless shelters and soup kitchens across the country matched almost cent for cent.

But comparing the dollar amounts to the figures at the shelters was confusing. He chose one at random and examined it. The M Street Shelter in Washington, D.C., had received $400,000 in each of the preceding five years from the Coalition, courtesy of Stan Shultz's generosity. However, that same shelter only serviced forty to fifty regulars, according to their reports, and of those only about fifteen or less stayed overnight.

The statements filed by Desmond Krane, the shelter manager, reported a zero balance at the end of each year, meaning that all the funds were used. Brian had a hard time seeing how the shelter could possibly soak up an entire $400,000, servicing so few people. His thoughts wandered to Krane, whom he remembered meeting at Gavin's annual Coalition fund-raising convention.

He could recall nothing peculiar about the man besides his tacky clothes and the penchant for retro fashion: the gaudy, wide, tooled belt, the engraved wristbands that had gone out in the 70s, and the unbuttoned shirt look that exposed a rather hairy chest. The man seemed harmless enough. He could remember only one conversation with Krane and had received the impression he was sincere almost to the point of being militant. He had a real zealous fervor for the Coalition and its work.

Brian focused again on the papers in his hand. As a nonprofit organization, Brian understood the Coalition did not have to report charitable donations to the Federal government. But sometimes records were merely tools to help hide the fact that money wasn't really going where it was supposed to go. Was that what was happening with the M Street Shelter? But what was the money funding if not the homeless?

Although Gavin was proving daily to be more of an enigma, it *was* possible to read him. Brian had spent several years with the man in which, almost by osmosis, he'd learned to anticipate Gavin. If Gavin wanted to hide something, he'd do it by muddying the waters as much as possible.

What Brian wanted was evidence of Stan Shultz's contributions. He searched through his own files but could not find the information he was looking for. Gavin, however, kept a folder of correspondence from Stan Shultz in his office, a folder Brian had once left several copies of Shultz's rather large checks in after writing an article about the philanthropist.

"Joleen," Brian said through the comline. "Please tell Trudy I need to talk to her. I'm coming right over." He halfheartedly straightened the stack of records before abandoning it on his desk. There were three statements he was particularly interested in, and he slid them inside his attaché case under a *Newsweek*.

Trudy was Gavin's secretary. She was efficient, plump, and unless you knew her, appeared as perpetually austere as a nineteenth-century portrait. Brian liked her and her meandering wit.

When he got to Trudy's office, he saw that Gavin's office door was still closed, probably locked, although he knew Trudy often opened it to enjoy the view and the warm sunlight when Gavin was gone. Trudy had a cubicle for an office, and Gavin had a view of Lake Michigan and the morning sun on modern high-rises that glistened like diamond-studded crowns. On the street, it was different, he remembered. It was easy to forget that, when you weren't down in it.

"Trudy." Brian nodded, smiling infectiously. "Been holding things together?"

"Always," she said, without returning his smile.

"I'd like to look at some information in Gavin's office, if it's all right."

"I don't know Gavin's password."

Actually, she probably did. Brian always let Joleen know his new passwords, based on the assumption he would call in some-time needing information that was tucked away in his system. Brian didn't argue, and actually, it gave him some leverage. "That's fine, Trudy, I don't need to get into his computer." He pulled up a chair, sat down, and leaned forward a few degrees with folded hands, good eye contact—the kind of stuff great communication is made of. "The networks want me to say some things about Stan Shultz this afternoon. Gavin keeps a folder of memos from Shultz, and I thought something there might be useful. I was hoping you could help me."

Trudy's eyes flicked from Brian to Gavin's door then back again. Indecision. Brian decided he might be sounding too mellifluous, like a child hoping his good behavior will pay off big in the toy store.

"I-I don't know," Trudy said, nervously. She was usually quite relaxed. This wasn't like Trudy.

"I won't be but a minute. I've been in Gavin's office dozens of times when he's been on the road. We both know Gavin doesn't keep confidential files where they can be gotten to easily. If Gavin were concerned about some private files, he'd have them encrypted and password protected in hidden directories. I'm not even going near the computer."

To someone who loved computers, as Trudy certainly did—Brian had learned this when she began working for the Coalition—it all sounded reasonable. Brian was serious, just wanting to do his job, and it showed plainly on his face. If there were other reasons for her hesitation earlier, she couldn't seem to think of them now.

"Oh, I'm not worried," Trudy said. "They—I mean, *we*—*we* just have to be careful about computer policy, you know." She said this as she wiggled out of her chair and pulled open a top drawer on her desk until Brian thought she would pull it completely out, spilling an entire office-supply catalog worth of inventory on the floor.

Way at the back, in a small metal box with a lock on it, she retrieved a key ring with two keys. The key she used to open the lock went back into her purse. She led him to Gavin's door and let him inside. She even looked at him with a cocked eyebrow and wrinkled forehead, as if she were saying, *You're sure you won't go near the computer?* At least Brian took it that way, and he nodded. This seemed to appease her, and she left him standing on a sky-blue plush carpet with the smell of wealth in the air. It was the smell of new furniture, new wood paneling, and new carpet, of course. He looked behind him as he walked to a set of oak filing cabinets and saw that his feet didn't leave tracks. The carpet bounced back like the Dallas Cowboys football team, and he mused that there was no way to camouflage money.

As he walked across the spacious office, Trudy left and closed the door, which surprised him because he didn't think she would leave him alone.

He quickly thumbed through several file drawers for the Schultz folder, but it was gone.

He searched more carefully through numerous files alphabetized under the United Religious Coalition and struck out again.

Brian knelt on one knee, prayed a quick prayer for God's help, and began searching through the W files for his own articles, which he often made copies of for Gavin's information. He pulled out a folder marked *Willis, Brian—Articles* and opened it. Near the back of the folder in what were the most recent weeks of the current year, he found several copies of Stan Shultz's checks. Apparently he'd misplaced them when he filed the copy of his article. He removed the photocopies and slid them into the inside pocket of his jacket, returned the file folder, and closed the file drawer. It banged loudly, echoing in the spacious office. Brian grimaced.

He moved quickly and quietly to the door. He was about to grab the handle when he heard voices on the other side. Gavin's door was solid wood and well insulated against noise, yet Brian could still make out Tyler Brownell's voice as he talked to Trudy. He caught only an occasional word. ". . . you . . . what Brian . . . doing?"

Brian could imagine Trudy's blank response. She wouldn't tell Brownell that he was in Gavin's office, and the way Tyler had phrased the question gave her an easy out. *How could I know what Brian is doing? He's in Gavin's office with the door closed.* Brian could imagine her thinking this.

"Did . . . try . . . office?" Trudy said, as if Tyler were brain dead.

Tyler didn't respond, so Brian guessed he had nodded, probably completely missing the gist of the question altogether. Trudy could run circles around Tyler in an IQ obstacle course.

After a few moments, it seemed Tyler Brownell had gone. Brian cracked the door and peered out. Trudy's curly, reddish strands of hair were visible just under Brian's nose. Her fist was raised, presumably to knock on the door and not on his chin.

Brian slipped out and quickly pulled the door closed behind him. Apparently, Trudy was having a hard time recovering from the excitement, because she raced back to her desk and plopped down in her chair. The hem of her dress trembled.

"You—you—you! I won't let you in Gavin's office again. You almost gave me a heart attack!"

"Sounded like you handled Tyler well."

Trudy glared. "Why all the sneaky stuff?"

"I'm sorry, I'm not trying to be sneaky."

"I'm not talking just about you."

"What's been going on?" Brian asked, curious, thinking Trudy might have noticed some clues that would reassure him he wasn't just imagining some kind of fantastic conspiracy.

"That's what I would like to know. Tyler didn't look happy. In fact, he acted nervous and angry that he couldn't find you."

"Maybe I should go see what he wants," Brian said.

Trudy tilted her head and lifted her eyebrows, like he was second place in the IQ race. Trudy, Brian assumed, still figured she was in the lead, which was all right, considering she'd just saved his hide.

"Has anyone else been in Gavin's office?" Brian asked.

Trudy shook her head. "No. I haven't let anyone in, except you . . . for the last time," she added firmly.

"Don't worry."

"Why, is something missing?" Trudy read the frown on Brian's face.

"I couldn't find a folder I thought should have been there."

"Maybe Gavin took it."

Brian shrugged. "Maybe. Any other keys lying around? Could someone get into his office without you knowing about it? Maybe there are some old keys hanging on key chains you and Gavin don't know about."

Again, Trudy shook her head. "No. Definitely not. In fact,

last week while you were in Boise, Gavin called me and said he was having the lock changed on his office. He said he would make the arrangements. The next day, the locksmith came just like Gavin said. He left two keys. They're locked inside my desk." It seemed to dawn on Trudy just then that if Gavin wanted the lock changed to his office while he was gone, she probably shouldn't have let Brian in until she checked with him. Well, it was their secret now.

"You didn't go near Gavin's computer, did you?" Trudy asked.

Brian shook his head.

She looked relieved. "I guess I know you were at the filing cabinets, anyway."

"How?"

"Because you slammed a drawer shut. I could hear it all the way out here."

Brian remembered. It had sounded loud in the office, but he never imagined the sound would carry all the way to Trudy's cubicle. "Tyler didn't notice it, did he?"

"No, he didn't. How could he know what it was? Could've been the heating ducts, the elevator doors down the hall, me ungracefully hitting my knee on the corner of my desk." Trudy's face wasn't so austere anymore.

"Thank you, Trudy," Brian said. He smiled at her and left.

* * *

When Brian returned from Trudy's cubicle, Joleen wasn't at her desk. He walked through the open door of his office.

"Excuse me," he said. "Tyler, what are you doing in my office?"

"Uh, hello, Brian." Tyler jogged a handful of papers together, then placed them on the front right corner of Brian's desk as he walked around. It appeared he was going to ignore Brian's question.

Brian strode across to his desk, purposely brushing Tyler's

arm as they passed. He glanced at the papers. They were the statements he had had delivered earlier. He wondered if Tyler had time to leaf through them and decided that it didn't matter much because Tyler was planning to take them with him.

Apparently he had changed his mind about letting Brian examine them after all. Brian thought about the copies he had in his jacket pocket and wished he'd had the presence of mind to make copies of all the statements Tyler was holding.

"What are you doing? You're way out of bounds, Tyler," he said pointedly, at the same time noting his ability to sound completely self-righteous in the face of an obvious double standard.

"I thought that if you were finished with these records, I would take them off your hands."

"They were no bother. As a matter of fact, I wasn't finished with them quite yet."

Looking uncomfortable, Tyler cleared his throat.

Brian gave a sharp nod toward the door, and Tyler quickly exited, still with enough presence of mind to pick up the stack of statements he'd laid on the corner of Brian's desk.

* * *

Dietrich sat hunched over, a slim IBM Thinkpad balanced on his knees. Long, cruel fingers were poised over the keys like cobras, striking with lightning swiftness as he entered information, his eyes narrow and calculating as he watched the screen. His fingers twitched impatiently while the modem connected to the Internet and the home page loaded. He entered a password and after a short pause encrypted information scrolled onto the monitor. A faint smile crossed his face. The staccato click of the keys soon filled the room.

Over a secure line, he left e-mail for Gavin, alerting him of the recent events and their coinciding problems. It rankled him to admit his failure. It was the first time in his association with the Freedom Society that he had even come close to failure. Now he was on a first-name basis with it.

He blamed the doctor. If she hadn't meddled, he would have accomplished his task by now. Dani wasn't smart enough or agile enough to avoid him on her own. Now with the doctor, an unknown dynamic thrown into the mix, everything was much more complicated. Who knew where she was going to go or what she was going to do next?

Anticipating Dani was not difficult. He had tracked her to Vermont as easily as he could have tracked a deer through wet snow. But the doctor he didn't know. He grinned with satisfaction as he downloaded the information he had been waiting for. The Freedom Society had a multitude of skilled investigators as well as inside "plants" in every imaginable institution in the United States. The moment Dietrich had found out about Mara Benneton, he had entered a request for immediate information about her to the head of Ops who was in charge of coordinating all the gathered data. Now the mystery would be unlocked.

Everything about Mara Rosamunde Benneton, every minute detail of her life, scrolled onto the screen. Every credit card or UBC purchase, every bank deposit, every record ever entered or written about her from the parking ticket she got in Wichita on vacation in 1983 to the order of recycled toilet paper she bought from a Save The Earth catalog was listed. There was a record of the vaccinations she received before joining the Peace Corps and going to Bolivia, as well as a copy of the research she had done on filoviruses in college. And every detail told something about her life and what she believed and what she cared about. But the most important information for him to be able to keep track of her was knowing which bank she used.

She was a Catholic. Good. That might help them later on down the road. Because there *would* be a later. Dietrich was not about to let this failure become permanent. He would track them down, and he would finish what he had set out to do. One did not just "leave" the Freedom Society. Particularly when one owed something to the Freedom Society. One paid one's debt first, and then it was possible one might be accepted back into the fold if the proper noises were made and the proper apologies extended. If not, well, there were other methods that could deal with a deserter. Permanently.

Somehow Dietrich couldn't see Dani taking flight again. Not once had they collected what she owed them. That would be tie enough to keep her there forever. In time, she would see things their way. If not for her sake, then for the sake of her child. The Freedom Society's child.

Dietrich mulled over Mara's information, making notes and generally getting a feel for the woman. Under other circumstances, he might have admired her. She had a strong personality. As an enemy, she earned his grudging respect. He found himself strangely pleased that they would meet again. And they *would* meet again.

* * *

On Friday, Randy had finished the first phase of his mission for the Freedom Society, and he was glad it was over. But it also meant the Society was that much closer to pulling off an act of terrorism that he still knew little or nothing about. He remembered the Oklahoma Federal Building bombing, thinking that none of the victims knew what had happened. Those involved had no warning. He was afraid of the same type of terrorism all over again, but he had no proof. He knew nothing, and the agent in charge of the investigation, special agent Dave Watters, was becoming more and more anxious for results.

Although he was raring to do more now that he was finally finished with following buses and timing their routes, he really didn't know what he was supposed to do next. He had waited the entire weekend hoping for some contact, but Monday morning had dawned and still nothing.

He paused for a moment as he passed Lynn's room and put his ear to the door. There was no sound. Lynn was fast asleep.

He stepped outside and grabbed the *Washington Post*. There was only one story he was particularly interested in: the disease he'd been hearing about lately. For some reason, it peaked his interest, although he didn't know anyone who was sick.

The headlines felt like a dash of cold water in the face.

The vice president of the United States was dead. He scanned the story in fascinated horror. After a long struggle against the unknown flu epidemic, the vice president had passed away. Funeral arrangements were being made, but due to the nature of the illness, it would be a closed-casket service.

After thirty minutes of filtering through the *Washington Post* and reading reports of a few more scattered outbreaks of the disease and a recap of the Army doctor's "sterilized" account from the night before, Randy felt numb.

He sank into a kitchen chair and tried to settle his mind. And then he realized that the house was too quiet. He pushed himself up from the table and headed for Lynn's room after realizing she should have been up at least an hour ago. He had a quick vision of finding her accidentally overdosed in her bed. The last time he found her passed out had scared him to death. He felt a sudden eerie sensation as he rapped on the door. Nothing. He knocked again, louder. Nothing but silence. His heart sped up, thundering against his chest.

When Randy opened the door, what he saw surprised him even more than what he'd prepared himself for. Lynn's bed was made, and she was gone. She must have left while he was out running.

To Randy's surprise, the doorbell rang. No one had purposely come to the house since they'd been living in it, and he was suddenly wary. He returned to the living room, hugged the wall, and peered between the curtains and the windowsill to see two muscle-bound young men, one with a severe haircut, one whose head was shaved. Both wore sunglasses though the day was overcast.

Randy got a semiautomatic from the drawer beside the couch.

The doorbell rang again, twice, impatient fingers stabbing it now. He shoved the gun in his pants at the small of his back and unlocked the door.

"Randy Burton?"

Randy half-shrugged. "Yeah."

"Good," the taller, blond man said. As if this were some kind of invitation, they stepped around Randy into the house.

Randy glanced up and down the street before closing the door. He watched them walk up and down the hallway and through the bedrooms, inspecting it all. Nervous, he sat down on the couch and tried to appear calm and patient.

The blonde was the leader, Randy decided. When they returned, each took a seat, the blonde sinking into the recliner.

"My name's Scarpetti," the blonde said. "That's Leaman."

Leaman cracked a grin and stuck out his hand. He'd chosen to sit next to Randy. They shook, and Randy looked at the wristbands Leaman wore.

"You guys are here to . . . what?" Randy spread his hands as he looked from Leaman back to Scarpetti.

Scarpetti studied Randy as if he were trying to decide what he was good at. "We're here to initiate the second phase of the operation and to help you however you need it."

Randy kept a straight face through the anxiety he suddenly felt. Working alone as he had this past month had been comfortable for him. He had been both eager and anxious for this day, and now it had come. The threatening demeanor of Dietrich's men did not help him feel any better, and he wondered if their purpose here was dual in nature. First, to help him do his job. Second, to make sure he was sufficiently intimidated enough to follow through.

Randy glanced from Scarpetti to Leaman and back again. Then Scarpetti pushed himself out of the chair and opened the door. Leaman fell in right behind him.

"We're moving in. All right if we park in the garage?"

"I'll have to move the 4Runner."

"Leaman will do it," Scarpetti said.

Leaman held out his hand for Randy to toss him the keys. When they left, Randy jumped up and watched them. Scarpetti drove a Ford Ranger with a shell on it into the garage. Scarpetti worried him.

For a while, Randy had forgotten about Lynn leaving. But after Scarpetti and Leaman brought their gear in and made themselves at home, Randy began to worry how they would react when they found out about her. Surely they had noticed there were two rooms occupied and that one of those rooms belonged to a female. He decided not to bring it up himself and just play it by ear, supposing, after some thought, that the Freedom Society, and Scarpetti in particular, already knew about her.

Scarpetti rummaged through the refrigerator, pulling out a package of deli meat, lettuce from the crisper, a tomato, cheese, and the mayo. "We'll have to do some shopping," he observed.

Randy watched in taciturn silence as the two men wolfed down three sandwiches apiece. Then they motioned him to join them at the table. Scarpetti wanted to see what Randy had accomplished. Randy pulled a round tube out of the coat closet near the back door and removed the laminated map he had been marking routes and times on.

Chairs were scooted away as the three of them leaned over the table. After several minutes, Scarpetti made eye contact with Randy. "It looks like we're ready. This is good work."

"It's a go?"

Scarpetti nodded, the muscles in his massive neck rippling. "Yep. You were able to get a job in the bus depot with no problem?"

"Yeah. I start tomorrow. Seemed awfully easy, but I expect strings were pulled." Scarpetti didn't bother to confirm Randy's suspicions. Finally, Randy looked away. He'd been over the map a million times, knew each route by heart. He worried about Lynn. Wandering to the sink, he stared out the window. If anyone knew the juggling act he was doing to protect Lynn *and* himself, they'd be discussing therapy for him. He expected to be reprimanded by the Bureau for letting Lynn stay with him. He would feel lucky if he only received a letter of censure.

"Question for you, Randy."

Randy looked at Scarpetti.

"You think you can handle this operation?"

Randy nodded. "No problem. I'll hold up my end. So far, piece of cake." He just wished he had some idea what the Freedom Society was planning.

"Good." Scarpetti smiled faintly. "Say, who's living here with you?" The question sounded harmless, coming out as if it were an afterthought.

"My sister, Lynn."

"We assumed you'd be alone while working on this operation."

Randy propped himself against the kitchen counter, thinking that Scarpetti was too casual with his questions not to have already known about Lynn. They had probably known from the beginning. "I am working alone. She's not involved, but she's safe, otherwise she wouldn't be here. She needed a place to stay, and I'm a good . . ." His voice trailed off when he realized that saying he was a "good" brother might have been pushing it. *Nothing like being on the defensive to know how much you've been offensive,* he thought.

* * *

While Randy was actually *defending* his sister, from Scarpetti and oddly enough, from himself, Lynn Burton was learning more about a God she had never known. Alice was reading from the Bible. Lynn felt as if she were resting beside a pristine mountain lake while a soothing breeze whispered through the trees and tickled meadow flowers.

At least that was the vision she had built in her mind while Alice Nolan read the Twenty-third Psalm. "That was beautiful."

Lynn's breathless comment was hardly an understatement to Alice, who thought she had never before encountered someone as eager as Lynn to learn about God. It frightened her to a degree. Was it genuine? "It really is," she said. "It's a wonderful promise."

Lynn turned her head to look at Alice. She had been peering out the window at Alice's apartment-building parking lot. Her blue eyes, recessed in their dark sockets as if they were lost in deep wells, blinked with mist. Alice moved from her recliner to the couch and wrapped an arm around the young woman.

"Tell me what you're feeling, Lynn. Are you worried about what your brother will do?"

Lynn shook her head. "No, it's not that. I-I-I'm not sure what it is exactly. It's like this unbelievable feeling of acceptance . . . well, of being loved no matter what I've done. I've never felt anything like it before. Not from my parents . . . not from Randy . . . not from anyone."

"I understand," Alice said simply. She rocked Lynn in her arms for some time, wondering if all Christians felt this way, or at least most of them. She vaguely remembered times in her life when such emotions had come upon her, but lately, at least since her husband had died, she had not felt such intense passion for God. Was she even the person to lead this poor young woman to Christ? How could she if Lynn's relationship with God far and away eclipsed hers?

Alice found herself holding on even tighter than Lynn had grasped her. Maybe it was some subconscious attempt to siphon some of what Lynn was feeling. *Oh, God, help me do and say the right things for this poor girl. Help me not to get in the way of her relationship with You.*

When they broke their embrace, Lynn dried her eyes with a tissue. "I knew there was something different about you that first day you gave me the Bible. You know, in front of Club Rio." Alice lifted an eyebrow, but she was immediately prevented from saying anything when Lynn glanced at the living-room clock and caught her breath.

"Is it really that late? Randy's going to . . ." She stopped herself and forced a counterfeit smile. "Randy's going to be worried."

Alice worried about the girl's situation. "That's all right, Lynn, I'll hurry you home." Alice hastily retrieved their coats and found her keys. Lynn was already halfway out the door before Alice could get into her coat.

In the car, Lynn's feet tapped continually on the floorboard. Alice glanced at her often. Finally, halfway home, she said, "Lynn, let's pray about it. I think it will help you feel better. God's always on our side, but He likes to be asked too." She gave Lynn a comforting grin.

Lynn glanced over, expression completely ingenuous. "But you're driving. You can't pray." Lynn's childlike sincerity caused Alice to laugh, which in turn made Lynn's face turn crimson. "Did-did I say something wrong?"

"No, no, Lynn. You said something perfectly right."

"What?"

"Let me see if I can explain it." Alice pulled up to a red traffic light, affording her a chance to make eye contact. "It was your sincerity just then. We can pray at any time, eyes open or closed, hands working or still. Doesn't matter. But I think it's the sincerity that does matter. Many Christians pray with the same habitual nature they have while getting dressed or walking or any other routine chore." The light changed, and Alice accelerated. "I'll have to tell you about the publican in the closet sometime."

Lynn shrugged and sank back in her seat.

"Lynn, you can pray anytime. God knows what's in your heart. You can't fool Him, you know. Don't lose the reverence and wonder you have for Him right now, and most of all, the faith." Alice reached over and patted her young friend's hand.

"But I'm a drug user and a wh—"

"Don't say that," Alice ordered gently.

"Well, I'm a lot of things. None of them are respectable."

"You're God's kind of people." Alice felt Lynn was depressing herself by comparing herself to what she believed to be God's impossible standards of holiness. What could she say to swing the pendulum the other way?

"It's hard to believe. Impossible," Lynn muttered.

Alice concentrated on the road; she could not seem to find the words with which to reply. Deathly silence flooded the car with pressure. After several minutes, Lynn said something simple that deeply touched Alice's heart.

"I wouldn't even believe there was a God if it weren't for you, Alice. I can't see Him. I can't touch Him. Sometimes maybe I think He's speaking to me, but I can't even be sure of that. I've heard voices before, lots of times. So I don't believe in a whole lot."

Alice's eyes began to water. She reached over and clasped Lynn's hand. She was getting rid of a little of that doubt she had earlier. "Thank you. You're helping me, too, Lynn. You're helping me a lot."

* * *

After four hours of intense debriefing, Randy went for a walk around the block. As he rounded the last corner, his pace slowed. He didn't care to spend any more time with Scarpetti and Leaman than absolutely necessary. As he neared the house, he looked for Lynn, wondering if she had returned while he had been gone.

The house felt empty when he entered through the front door. He walked down the hall, checked the rooms and bathrooms, then wandered through the kitchen. No one was home. The 4Runner was gone, he noticed. Scarpetti or Leaman must have taken it. He hoped they didn't search it.

He went out the back door of the house and opened the door to the garage, stepped in, and shut it quickly. Light filtered through the one window located at midpoint between the front and the back of the garage, illuminating the pickup.

The Ranger sat in utter silence, without the usual creaks and groans of engine metal contracting as it cooled. He touched the hood, and it was cool to the touch. He searched the pickup's interior through its front and side windows. There was certainly nothing he could learn from outside the cab.

Taking a deep breath, Randy pulled open the passenger-side door and slid inside the pickup. He opened the glove box and thumbed through its contents: The owner's manual with no name inside anywhere and no entries in the maintenance log. A pack of gum, sugarless, of course. Sunglasses case. Trial size bottle of Bain de Soleil. A small package of tissues. There were no registration papers or proof of insurance in the glove box, nothing attached to the visors either.

He became so absorbed in the process of looking for clues that the moment when he returned to his senses actually scared him into a cold sweat. *You could get yourself in a lot of trouble, Randy, if you don't pay attention.*

After a few minutes, he jumped out of the pickup and checked for Scarpetti and Leaman through the garage window. Everything seemed as it had been before he entered the garage. He returned to the pickup and reached under the driver's seat, sweeping his hand around. Sliding out onto his knees, he searched under the passenger's seat. Considering the size of Scarpetti and Leaman, it was small wonder the seats were shoved against the rear window. He looked behind them anyway and between the seats. He was sure when he had finished that new cars rarely rolled off the assembly line as clean.

Although he had not planned this little excursion, he had known he must do it as soon as possible. He removed what appeared to be a laminated business card from his wallet. The clear plastic material detached from around the card fairly easily, and he carefully unfolded it. Also in his wallet was a small packet of silver powder.

* * *

No one saw Alice Nolan drop Lynn off. Lynn was prepared to see Randy as soon as she walked inside, so it came as a surprise when she discovered the house empty. But then, she had not seen the 4Runner parked in the driveway, either, now that she thought about it.

Lynn put her Bible in her room and walked through the rest of the house, practically retracing the very steps her brother had taken when he was looking for Scarpetti and Leaman. When she got to the back door, she buttoned her jacket again and stepped outside. A breath of chill air flushed her cheeks. The sky had progressively transformed into a dreary slate gray from the time she left Alice's apartment, and the late fall air trapped under the clouds leached into her body. She felt cold to her core.

As cold as her bones felt, she wondered if she was destined to get the flu. She sincerely hoped not. How in the world would she know, anyway? She was probably feeling more symptoms of withdrawal. And how was that supposed to feel? She didn't know for sure all the symptoms she might have and how they would affect her.

When Lynn turned, her gaze swept across the kitchen-sink window. The illuminated light from the clouds against the dark window caused a reflection of the garage, and her peripheral vision picked up some movement.

Lynn immediately swung back around.

Her impulsive reaction caused her right foot to slip down a step, and her arms flailed wildly for balance. She managed to keep from crashing onto the concrete but felt ridiculous for her clumsiness. Whatever she thought she saw had apparently been a figment of her imagination. Lynn shook her head, attributing her reaction to paranoia. That's when she saw the shadow again. *Definitely something in the garage,* she thought, suddenly chilled even more from fear. A shadow passed the window.

* * *

Randy finished taking fingerprint samples from the door handles and the steering wheel of the Ranger. He set the plastic strip down on the hood of the pickup and took out his wallet again. When he had extracted the item he wanted, he took a few moments in complete silence to listen. He was aware he had spent far too much time out here. Certainly it had been time spent dangerously, no matter how opportune.

Amazingly, his fingers were not trembling. He erected the small container that he had carried folded up in his wallet. The container was about the size of a cigarette carton. Carefully, he slid the plastic inside. The edges of two thin pieces of cardboard inside the box kept the plastic from sticking to anything. That would be a problem, should it happen.

He put the box in his jacket and stuffed his hands in his jeans while he searched the garage for evidence he had been there. After visualizing every move he had made, he was positive he had left no indication of his activities. Reaching for the doorknob, he cracked the door and peered out. His heart stopped cold. Scarpetti's solid form blocked his line of sight.

Randy hoped he had replaced the look of culpable shock on his face quickly enough with one of simple surprise. He thought he'd been quick, but Scarpetti eyed him suspiciously.

"I wondered what had happened to you, Burton."

Randy's mind kicked into overdrive in a search for a credible answer. Then he knew that he was caught. His mouth opened but wouldn't generate anything sounding reasonable. And then another voice spoke from outside.

"Randy, are you in there?" Lynn's voice sounded tentative, a little frightened. Randy thought he had imagined it at first.

Scarpetti's thick neck twisted as he glanced to his right. "Who are you?"

"I think I should be asking *you* that question," Randy heard his sister say. Now she sounded more bold. "This is where I live."

Scarpetti's head rocked back. "Ah, so you're the sister." His cool eyes fell back on Randy, as if he'd drawn a trump card. He grinned. "We're friends of your brother."

"Randy?"

Randy drew a deep breath. "Yeah, Lynn. It's all right."

Leaman appeared behind Scarpetti, and the two of them shoved their way past Randy into the garage. They stared at the pickup then glanced around the garage much as Randy had done not five minutes earlier. During the extended period of awkwardness, Randy expected something like a TV monitor to materialize and replay his activities of the past fifteen minutes. Scarpetti gave a narrow look, the kind Randy had known from his childhood days—the look parents give their children when truth and reality don't appear to intersect.

Lynn came in and stood beside Randy. "Did you look at my bike like I asked you to?"

Randy felt a soft kick on his foot and realized Lynn perceived the position he was in and was trying to help. The bike she was referring to, an inexpensive Huffy mountain bike, hung upside-down on hooks screwed into the rafters. "Uh, yeah. The rear tire will need to be fixed, but I can do that as soon as I run to the store for patch material."

Scarpetti moved toward the bike, presumably to have a look for himself. Randy felt Lynn's hand reach up and anxiously crunch his forearm. Her grip got tighter as Scarpetti inspected the bike, ran his hand along the frame, reached out for the rear tire. If Scarpetti hesitated any longer, Randy thought he'd lose the circulation in his arm.

Scarpetti squeezed the rubber and rim, and it easily gave way. Randy felt the dramatic release of tension throughout Lynn's body and was afraid she might have fainted. He felt a little weak himself. She gave him a thin, trembling smile, and he felt like winking. If there had not been any chance of getting caught, he would have.

* * *

Jack looked at the mechanic, dismay draining all expressions of hope from his face. "What do you mean, you don't take cash?"

The mechanic, who towered over Jack, hooked his thumbs behind an oversized silver belt buckle that proclaimed "The Eagle Has Landed" and repeated, "No cash. We've gone to UBC."

"But, but," sputtered Jack, glaring at the mechanic. "I don't have a UBC."

"Well, now, that's a problem." the mechanic replied.

"Give it up, Daddy," Dani snapped, breaking her silence finally.

Jack scowled.

"So, we're stuck here," Dani stated. Her voice was a dreary monotone, her eyes were full of accusation.

"No, we're not stuck here," Jack contradicted her. "I can get some money. I can get one of those ridiculous cards. Come on, Dani. Where's the nearest bank?" Jack asked the mechanic.

"Right at the end of the block," the man said, indicating a left out the door of his autobody shop. "You can't miss it."

Dani's hands massaged her lower back, and she whined as she followed him out the door. "Aw, Daddy, I told you we should have stopped when that light first came on. But, no, you were in an all-fired rush to get us killed so you could save the president. Ha. Now look at us."

"Danielle, you are entitled to your opinion," Jack said. "Just keep it to yourself."

The bank was easy to find, which, Jack reflected, was good because that turned out to be the least of his problems.

"I'm sorry, sir," a customer service representative repeated, very patiently under the circumstances, Jack thought. "I can process your UBC application, certainly, and we'll do everything we can to speed things along, but it will be at least some time late Thursday before I will have your card ready."

"Thursday?" Jack reeled away from the counter. "But that may be too late. You don't understand how important this is."

"I understand, sir, that it takes at least three business days to get a card from the time you apply. It's late already today, and if you actually get the card by Thursday afternoon, it will be nothing short of a miracle." She tapped long, polished, red nails on the counter top, and Jack suddenly realized she was irritated at him and trying not to show it.

That brought him up short. She had every right. He'd been a jerk. He took a long cleansing breath. "Look, I'm sorry," he apologized. "I know you're doing everything possible. It's just that—well you wouldn't believe me anyway. It's just very important for me to get on my way as quickly as possible."

The woman appeared to relax. "I'll do my very best, sir," she assured him.

Jack endured Dani's sulking as they finished up at the bank and found a cheap hotel room across the street that would still accept cash.

"I'm tired," Dani complained as she sat down heavily on the bed, which squeaked beneath her weight. "Can I take a nap?"

"You can do anything but leave," Jack replied as he hunted around the room for the phone. He found it stuffed inside the drawer of the bedside stand.

"I wouldn't dream of it," Dani replied sarcastically. "Then I'd miss out on whatever Dietrich has planned for me when he catches up. But, hey, at least the president will be safe."

Jack ignored her sarcasm as she curled up on the bed and threw him dirty looks. He dialed Dan Reiss's number and counted the rings before he picked up the phone.

"Pastor Reiss? It's Jack. Yes, we're fine. That is, we had some car trouble. No, it's fixed, but we're stuck here until we get some money. I have enough cash, but they'll only accept a Universal Bank Card. I've applied for one, but they tell me I'll be lucky to get it before Friday."

Jack's features softened as he listened to the reassuring voice of his pastor. "I know, luck has nothing to do with it. Listen, Pastor Reiss, I need you to transfer the money you got from selling my stuff into my new UBC account. Here's the number they gave me."

Jack fumbled in his wallet for the slip of paper the woman at the bank had given him. As he read the numbers to Dan, he was vaguely aware of Dani's eyes on him, not glaring now, but curious. "Thanks, Pastor Reiss. I'll be seeing you real soon. When this business with the president is over, I'm bringing Dani back with me."

Jack hung up the phone and sat staring, wondering what on earth they were going to do for the next few days.

"What did you sell?" Dani's voice was soft.

Jack started in surprise and turned around. "Everything," he replied simply. "Except the house. I wanted someplace to bring you back to."

"Everything?" Dani squeaked.

Jack shrugged. "I needed to find you. My stuff was worth money. It was an easy choice." That it was his choice, of his own free will, maybe she believed that much, but not that it had been easy. Her face said as much.

"You loved those antiques," she said quietly. "They meant more to you than anything."

Jack nodded. "Yup, they meant a lot to me, but you mean more." Out of the corner of his eye Jack saw Dani swallow thoughtfully. "Dani, I know we don't get along very well, never have. But—"

"Don't, Daddy," Dani pleaded. "Let me have this one moment. Please? Don't spoil it."

Jack started to say something and then changed his mind. It would wait. He would tell her later. Let this sink in first.

* * *

Scarpetti sat at the kitchen table. Randy sat across from him, the map spread before them with empty coffee mugs holding down the corners.

"Are you ready for work tomorrow?"

Randy nodded. "I'll be there at eight o'clock."

"Good." Scarpetti gazed at the map. Minutes passed. "I want to choose some targets. One will be confirmed but not by us. Then Leaman and I will do more legwork on the final choice."

Scarpetti had studied the map at least ten times already. He asked numerous questions. He wanted to know the drivers, their approximate ages, and how attentive they were to their surroundings. He wanted to know the approximate ages of the children; he was more interested in buses that carried the largest proportion of fifth- and sixth- and seventh-graders. Randy assumed this was because the older kids would be too hard to handle and the younger kids would need too much baby-sitting. Although he wasn't totally sure what was going to go down, he could draw reasonable conclusions from the information he had. Though it had been one boring job, he had not been lax while taking notes, and he was able to give Scarpetti all the information he asked for.

The afternoon light faded away into a raven night without moon or stars. Randy got up and peered through the kitchen-sink window. All he saw was his own face reflected back and the kitchen light blazing behind him. Even in the poor reflection, he could see the dark circles under his eyes.

"Burton," Scarpetti said. Leaman jumped out of his nap and nearly crashed on the floor. He'd been snoozing for the past hour. Randy chuckled.

He went back to the table. "Yeah? What do you want?"

"I've looked these routes over several times. I've got my picks, but it isn't up to me which bus we use. All I can do is narrow them down, and that's what I've done."

"Who makes the final call?"

"There's no need for you to know," Scarpetti said. He slid his chair back and put an empty water bottle under the faucet. Randy shrugged to show it was no big deal. "Tomorrow while you're learning the school bus maintenance business, I'll find out for sure which bus route we're going to use."

Leaman, like a good underling, rolled up the map and returned it to its tube and stood around waiting for more instructions.

"I'm going to bed," Randy said.

Scarpetti nodded and lifted his water bottle in a minor salute. "See you tomorrow afternoon. Keep your eyes open in the bus yard."

Randy ignored him as he walked off. At Lynn's door, he paused, half ready to knock but decided against it. Her room was quiet, and he couldn't see any lights. She was asleep, so he went on to his own room. He sat on the edge of his bed for ten minutes or so, not thinking of anything in particular yet thinking about everything. It wasn't until he got up to undress and turn on the lamp by his bed that he noticed the book lying on the nightstand. He crawled into bed and took the book. It was a paperback Bible. He hadn't touched a Bible in years, not since attending Sunday School when he was ten years old.

Randy thumbed through the first few pages. He found Genesis and read the first verse. It was as far as he got. A warm feeling swept over him, and the world seemed to shut itself off, as if he were back in that safe little Sunday-School room from long ago. He tried to remember what had happened to cause him to stop going to the little church. And then he remembered.

The church he remembered had not been exactly a church home for his family. They had bounced around, trying different churches. His parents were looking for a church home, something of a desperate attempt to save their marriage, though at the time he didn't know what it was about. That particular church had been his favorite. They tried it for a month or two, and he had wanted to keep going back. He told his mom this. He remembered the kind woman who put felts on a felt board as she told children Bible stories. He remembered the huge painting of heaven, hanging on the wall directly across from the door, so you saw it when you came into the room.

But then something happened.

One Sunday driving home after church, the atmosphere in

the car suddenly exploded. His parents had been talking in the front; Lynn and Randy had been quietly watching the roadside go by. Mom's voice attained a high-pitched tone. Dad's return barrage rocked the car. Someone had mentioned to Mom that she must quit smoking to be a part of the church family. Dad did not take Mom's side against the church member either.

By the time they had reached home, what was left of their extremely tenuous marriage was gone. It was their mother who got custody of them. They saw their father only occasionally until their mother died of lung cancer when Randy was seventeen.

* * *

I'll meet you, Amy had said. *But not at Fort Detrick. There are too many eyes and ears. Meet me at the Lincoln Memorial. Late at night. Ten, let's say.*

Mara drove the streets of Washington until they became a confusing tangle. The monuments seemed to be off to the left somewhere, but every time she turned left, she seemed to get no closer. Finally, when she thought they must surely be near, she had parked the car and set out on foot. Dressed in a charcoal gray cable sweater, jeans, and an LL Bean storm coat, she wondered why she felt that people were watching her. Zipping up her coat, she tried to blend in.

She glanced at her watch. There was a lot of time to kill. It was only seven now. The whole clandestine feeling of the meeting made her uneasy. And that didn't take into account her fears about being alone in a very large, strange, crime-infested city late at night.

As she stepped off a curb she looked up, and she caught sight of the Lincoln Memorial across the street. The view made her catch her breath. She hurried her steps until she was standing at the bottom of the long flight of white marble stairs. Slowly she climbed, each time planting her foot a little quicker until she was nearly running.

As she approached the magnificent white statue she suddenly slowed, awed by the presence of it. The pictures she'd seen of it had not done it justice. Around her were crowds of people, belying the lateness of the day. An entire group of uniformed school children hedged in behind her, and she heard a teacher begin discussing the late president's life.

Mara simply stood and studied the statue, feeling small. Some school boys jostled her in their attempts to get closer, and Mara backed up, took one last breath, and turned to leave. It was then that the opposing view became all-engrossing. Across the Reflecting Pool and mirrored in its still waters was the Washington Monument, pointing like a beacon up at the now darkening sky. At the end of the Reflecting Pool fountains sprayed geysers of water gracefully into the air.

Mara felt herself drawn by the sight, and she descended the steps to walk by the Reflecting Pool while she had time. A path led her through a park and right by the Vietnam Memorial. The black wall seemed endless with names of the dead. She followed it for a few yards and then turned to make her way to the Reflecting Pool. At the end of the Pool was a walkway that separated the Pool into one large and one small pool.

Mara stepped out onto the walkway and looked back as night fell all around her. At ten-minute intervals, a jet shot out from behind the Lincoln Memorial. Such a feeling of patriotic pride welled up in her breast as she had never felt before. And there was more. It was as if a still, small voice whispered that the God who made this country great was there, right there, to lead her as well.

"I thought I said the Lincoln Memorial," a voice behind her said.

Mara whirled. "I thought you said ten o'clock."

"I figured you'd be early," Amy replied, grinning. Fatigue lined her face, and her eyes were expressionless. "Hi, Mara. It's been a long time."

"Yes, it has," Mara agreed.

"It would have been even longer if I had had my way," Amy said. "Come on. Walk with me." Without waiting, she began to walk leisurely back toward the park Mara had just left.

Mara followed, warily eyeing the bushes, half expecting to see U.S. military personnel jump out and arrest them. "I don't understand. What do you mean it would have been longer. I thought we were friends."

Amy turned abruptly. "Are friends. We are friends," she stressed. "That's why I was hoping it would be longer. I don't want you to get involved with this, Mara. Any of it. I don't want anyone I know to get involved. If I had my way, I'd ship them all somewhere safe until it was all over. If it ever is," she added under her breath.

"What are you talking about? What do you mean? Amy, if you know anything, please tell me. I have to be prepared for what is coming."

"That's just it," Amy said. "There is no preparing for something like this. Of course, we're setting up emergency shelters, and we have experts examining this thing twenty-four hours a day, but we can't *do* anything besides making people as comfortable as possible before they crash. And all of this is off the record, you understand."

"Amy, the last thing I want to do is inform the media of what is happening," Mara assured her. "It's been hard enough controlling the local panic in a small city like Burlington. I can't imagine the mass hysteria it would create in big cities like Washington or New York or Boston."

Amy nodded gratefully. "Good. That's what we're trying to avoid as well. I know it looks as if we're trying to cover this up. We're not. We're trying to manage the situation quietly. Hopefully we can get a handle on this disease soon."

They reached the Vietnam Women's Memorial. Someone had framed a poem to the unknown women who died, and Amy picked it up reverently and read it before replacing it gently and continuing in her seemingly aimless walk, her hands clasped tightly behind her. "So, Mara, what exactly do you want from me?"

Mara looked at her friend. "I don't know exactly. Confirmation, I suppose. Is this thing really a filovirus?"

Amy stopped and stared intently into Mara's eyes. The scrutiny made Mara flinch. "We don't know what it is," she admitted finally. "But it is very much *like* a filovirus. It could be that one of the sisters finally mutated into this deadly strain. Right now we just don't know. I wish we did. I wish we could say exactly what this is. I wish we could point to it and say, here's what to do about it too, but we can't. We've determined that it acts in the body much the same way a filovirus does, with the exception of its length of stay. A person ill with this epidemic peaks at around three weeks or so, lives one week longer, and then crashes.

"One thing we have noticed is that the time between infection and death is getting shorter. This could be a good sign. It could be getting hotter. The hotter it gets, the shorter lived it will be. People simply won't have the time to infect enough other people to worry about a global threat. However, right now that's not the case. At the rate it's traveling now, the entire population, unless a segment proves resistant, will be wiped out."

Mara tried to absorb what Amy was saying, but the implications were mind boggling. "Are you saying we are all going to die of this virus?"

The lines around Amy's eyes deepened. "Unless something happens, I'm afraid so."

"You said a segment of the population might prove resistant. What about all the people who have been around people with the virus but haven't caught it themselves. Might they be resistant?"

"Like I said," Amy repeated, "we just don't know for sure. It's possible, yes. It is definitely possible. Or we may come up with a cure before everyone dies. Or maybe we'll decide to put a part of the population in a biosphere before it's too late. At this point I don't know. Those are decisions we will have to make later. Not that later is too far in the future at this point, but right now we still have some options available to us."

Mara reeled away from Amy and sank onto the grass. She held her head in her hands and knew, more by instinct than sight, that Amy had come and sat down beside her. She felt the same way she'd heard people describe how they felt after learning they had cancer. She wondered how long she had left. And just as suddenly, she realized that the pressing need she'd had to save the president had suddenly become a moot point.

It started as a nervous giggle, but soon she was laughing so hard that tears were running down her face. Amy stared at her as though she'd never seen her before and was taking stock of her sanity. "What is so funny?" she asked curiously.

Mara swallowed several peals of laughter. "Life, I guess. I rushed here to tell you there is a plot to assassinate the president, and now it doesn't matter. She's going to die regardless."

Amy straightened up. "Assassinate the president? It can't be done anyway," she said, dismissing the idea. "But no, you're probably right. It doesn't much matter. From what I've seen of this virus, they'd be doing her a favor." Amy stood and brushed her slacks off. "No, I wouldn't worry about that, Mara. I'm sure a lot of people want to assassinate the president. She's done a lot of good, but that in turn has made a lot of people angry. Still, when haven't people been angry at the president? And in the scheme of things, there have been very few presidents assassinated."

Mara stood slowly and studied her friend. "I *am* glad I got to see you again, Amy. You were my best friend in college. I'm really sorry we lost touch."

Amy smiled sadly. "Me too. Funny, isn't it how we spend so much time and energy pursuing the wrong things in life and it isn't until we get to the end of it that we realize that? Ray and I have never been closer than we have in the last week or so. Suddenly we've been able to cut through the petty differences that had become major hang-ups in our marriage. We're like newlyweds. We've even started going to church. We think that maybe God is trying to tell the country something. I don't have any real medical hope that we'll be able to stop this thing, but I know God can stop it if He wants to."

* * *

From the window seat of his United flight, Brian tried to pierce the heavy fog that had swallowed Washington National Airport. Finding no lights, he frowned and returned to the *Time* magazine in his lap.

While waiting to board his flight in Chicago, he had been browsing the racks of a magazine kiosk when he discovered the article in *Time* about Speaker of the House Donald Thurgood. Now, after reading it through twice, he simply gazed at the photos of the man, one taken ten years or so ago, the other taken during his last few days on the hill. Brian read the article from a different perspective than he might have just a few weeks ago. This new perspective, he understood, had been afforded him because he no longer felt part of Gavin's United Religious Coalition machine.

When Gavin had hired him as part of Thurgood's staff all those years ago, he had really begun working for Gavin. As long as Gavin did not ask him to do anything not in line with the Speaker's agenda, this had certainly been OK with Brian. Gavin was the Speaker's confidant as well as one of his most trusted advisors. Brian had been in many policy-making sessions with both men and had been to the Speaker's Washington, D.C., home in less formal settings with Gavin.

The relationship between the Speaker and Gavin was something to be admired. Their political discussions, extending far into the tender hours of morning while secluded in Thurgood's den, helped him to conceive of the kinds of discussions rich with idealism that Thomas Jefferson and James Madison might have pursued. The ambiance—the den's colonial design with its rich craftmanship—was already quite enough to lose oneself in a timeless daydream, but the Speaker's sage discernment and Gavin's passionate deliberation seemed also to echo America's forefathers. Brian soaked it up.

What had changed, Brian had come to realize through the years, was that Gavin could be rather self-absorbed. Oddly, the more confidence in himself Gavin portrayed, the better able he was to attract people. This was sobering to Brian because a person who exhibited the Christian attributes of love and charity would naturally attract people to Christ. Gavin attracted people to *himself*. The implications were not at all comforting.

He was quite sure of one thing from all the history he had ever studied: Humans did not have a proclivity for following the meek and selfless, or those who appeared so, qualities Gavin appeared to be trying hard to distance himself from.

So, Gavin, I've chosen to resign. At least that much of his speech was prepared. *Why?* Brian hoped all the answers to Gavin's questions would come to him in time. *The main reason? My family.*

It was nearly 1:00 a.m. when Brian got settled in his room at the Plaza. From the hotel, he watched the ghostly specter of the nation's capitol as the city rose before him, backdropped against the gray night. It was both remarkable and corrupt. It took his breath away.

He held a pint container of milk, studied the night, and confirmed that the fog had moved on. It was hard to believe anything could be wrong, but that was not how he felt. Instinctively, he knew that beneath the innocuous lights, people were leading harried, unfulfilled, and often harmful lives. It was not hard to imagine that somewhere out there, someone had just died or was about to die.

Brian turned from the window and sat on the edge of the bed. He called home to say he had arrived safely.

Chapter Eight

Tuesday, November 16

Lynn was already up making breakfast. She peered at Randy, waiting, he was sure, for some comment about the Bible. He smiled immediately.

"Good morning, Lynn."

"Good morning . . ." Her blue eyes narrowed, as if she wasn't sure she had awakened in another dimension where even rotten brothers could become saints. Randy noticed her eyes were a lot clearer.

He pulled a glass out of the cupboard and placed it under the tap. He swallowed a couple of vitamins and washed them down, noticing that Lynn watched from the corner of her eye. After that, he came by and planted a kiss on her forehead. He heard movement down the hall. Scarpetti and Leaman were on their way to the kitchen.

"I started reading the Book," Randy whispered as he pulled out a chair at the table and sat down. Lynn was smiling. Though he could not explain it, he was happier for Lynn and himself than he had ever been since their parents had died.

Lynn placed a stack of pancakes in the middle of the table. Randy was unsure of his stomach and ate only one. Sometime during the night he had awakened with the thought that the Freedom Society already knew he was an FBI agent and that as long as they kept vital information from him, there was no reason to do anything about him yet. The more he had turned the idea over, the more it began to sound credible. The key, of course, was that whatever the Freedom Society was planning, it had to be happening so soon that getting rid of him would cause more problems than it would solve.

Scarpetti and Leaman also sat at the table, and they all ate in silence. Randy glanced at his watch and realized he needed to hurry. He grabbed his jacket and a sack lunch Lynn had made for him.

Lynn walked him out to the 4Runner. His eyes went from her face to the house. "I wish they were already gone for the day," Randy said. "I hate to leave you here alone with them. I should have thought of it sooner than now."

"Don't worry, I thought about it. The same thing occurred to me last night." Lynn shrugged. "So I called someone to come and get me."

"Who did you call?" Half his anxiety suddenly fell away, like an avalanche of snow sliding off a mountain.

"I made a friend. The woman who talked to us outside Club Rio that day." Lynn said this tentatively.

Randy smiled, relieved. He remembered the woman vaguely. "Good. It's a relief for me to know you won't be here alone with those two."

Randy glanced at his watch again and then hopped into the 4Runner. He left Lynn standing in the driveway, watching him as he pulled out. Before he had gone a block, he saw an elderly woman pass him and pull into his driveway. *Good,* he thought.

* * *

The phone pierced the morning like a Confederate battle charge. A hand, evidently lost, emerged from the covers to silence the alarm clock that wasn't there. When the phone rang for the third time, Brian had finally gotten his wits about him enough to yank the receiver from its cradle. He fully expected to hear Ann's voice.

"Hello?"

"Brian! You made it. How's the room?"

"Hello, Gavin." He wondered if his disappointment was noticed. "Room's great."

"Good, good." Gavin sounded as if he were bouncing off the walls. "I want you to come down to the Rayburn Building first thing this morning. I have tremendous news!"

"We're just finalizing a few items for the rally and your meeting with the pope, correct?" This event had been in the works for months, all the details hashed out, finalized, and paid for by millions of dollars. No matter the money or planning, Brian feared a monumental headache.

"Yes, of course, but that can wait. Be at Thurgood's office at nine sharp this morning."

Brian's silence lasted too long.

"Are you still there?"

"Uh, yes. OK, I'll be ready."

"I'm sending a car. It'll be waiting for you. Nine sharp, remember."

Brian nodded. Sprouts of hair were tugged in the crosswinds, and he wondered why he nodded to someone on the phone. He hung up.

The Rayburn Building was one of the House office buildings. It sat third among the trio of House buildings if one were traveling west on Independence Avenue. He wondered why Gavin wanted to meet him at Thurgood's office. Thurgood should have been back in Massachusetts by Saturday.

Brian flipped the television on for the morning news to fill the background. As he brushed his teeth, the meteorologist promised rain in the afternoon. He checked his eyes. Tired looking. A hint of redness. Hopefully they would undergo a transformation between the hotel and the Rayburn Building.

Minutes later, as he emerged from the shower, Brian just missed hearing a field reporter for CNN come on the screen to give an update on the curious disease spreading on the East Coast. The station went to a commercial just as he switched it off.

While buttoning his white shirt, he entertained the idea of calling Ann and the kids, but when he glanced at his watch, he realized he was short of time. He decided he would rather call after he had finished meeting with Gavin and could relax.

Sometime before he left for home, he was going to have to break the news to Gavin. *Maybe today,* he thought as he tied a perfect Windsor in his tie and slipped into his jacket. A close inspection in the full-length mirror on the back of the bathroom door showed a fit man of thirty-five in a gray suit and red tie with gray and white stripes. His face held a grave expression—the look of a person with a deep sense of foreboding about the future.

A few minutes later, he was standing in front of the Plaza whistling tunelessly. But he drew no stares. People were used to worse, he supposed. His eyes picked out the black limo as it swung into traffic at an intersection, and he watched it glide to a stop in front of him. Brian stepped inside when the driver opened the door, and then they were off into a sea of traffic like a nuclear-powered boomer heading out of dock.

"Sir, the *Washington Post* is in the rack, if you like. The coffee is hot, and I took the liberty of bringing along some Danish."

Brian ignored the coffee but chose a cherry Danish and opened the paper. Two minutes later, he was gravely reading about the strange disease ravaging the coastal cities that had already claimed the life of the vice president.

* * *

As Randy climbed the steps and entered the bus depot office, he was met by a white-haired man in a crisp, dark blue uniform with a name tag that read *Dimetri* over the word *Supervisor.* In an overtly friendly manner that bordered on uncomfortable, Dimetri shook Randy's hand.

"You must be the new man. I've been expecting you. Your name is . . . ?"

"Randy Burton."

"Randy. Yes. I should have remembered. Did, actually, just wasn't absolutely sure." Dimetri grinned. Randy grinned back, beginning to like the man.

"Ready to start? I've put you on the bus maintenance detail. Preventive maintenance. Stuff like that."

Randy nodded.

"First, I want you to meet everyone." If Dimetri had been heading out of the building for a reason, he forgot about it. He led Randy back up the steps into the building.

The office smelled like the office of an auto-repair shop—a greasy, oily smell. Behind a gray metal desk sat a middle-aged woman with light brown hair who was as friendly as her boss. Her name was Martha Reynolds. Randy shook her hand as he quickly stepped around her desk to keep up with Dimetri.

Dimetri led Randy into his office. It was sparse, utilitarian. Dimetri was a man who had little time or inclination to decorate his work environment. A window at the back looked into the shop area. Randy backed out, and they walked down to a far door.

The door stood open, and voices and laughter rolled out from the room. Randy guessed it was the break room even before he saw it. Dimetri led him inside and introduced him around. Out of the two men and one woman, there wasn't one of them he thought he wouldn't get along with. He shook hands. They were nice folk. He paid Dimetri a compliment on the way out to the shop.

"You must be a very good boss," he said.

Dimetri gave him a curious look.

"Everyone seems very happy."

"Oh," Dimetri grinned. "A happy workplace is good. Not as much sickness. Everyone likes to come to work at a happy place."

They entered the shop area. There were five bays, two occupied with buses, one with the front tires off and the other with its hood up.

"Max has been working on a tricky faulty indicator lamp for the warning flashers on Bus 22. Max puts in a new lamp; it burns out. Round and round." Dimetri grinned. "Lucinda is putting new brakes on bus 3. Hector . . . I don't know what Hector is doing. He could have barely finished repairs on one of the buses."

Randy nodded as they walked past the buses. Dimetri took him out to the yard where the buses were parked for the night and on weekends. "There are twenty-five buses. All have their own parking place. Of course, we only run twenty-three buses, leaving two in reserve. Used to be twenty-one and twenty-two regulars, but with enrollment shooting up like it has lately, we've got to run more buses. That's some of why we hired you. We can't afford to have buses breaking down, so what we're going to do is make sure they're in top shape all the time. When there's a problem, we fix the problem when it comes up and keep these buses going. Doesn't matter how small the problem is."

"I understand," Randy said. He noticed drivers parking in a small lot outside the ten-foot high chain-link fence. His eyes roamed the razor wire strung tightly in three strands along the top of the fence, angled outward at a forty-five degree angle. He pointed with a nod of his head. "Pretty tight security."

Dimetri nodded. "Yes. These days you never know what folk are going to do. Two buses once had their brake lines cut. Luckily, the drivers were new and took inspecting their buses very seriously. They noticed the fluid on the gravel. We put up the wire the next day."

"It's hard to believe that a Christian school campus would

have to worry so much about security."

Dimetri shrugged resignedly. "I don't expect the old days to return."

"No?"

Dimetri smiled, but this time with sadness. "No. Where I come from, the old days were nothing to speak of either. I think of better days ahead, not the old days."

The past Dimetri spoke of, Randy was left to imagine. He looked grim, his eyes empathetic. He changed the subject.

"How long have you worked here?"

"Twenty-five years."

Randy whistled in admiration.

"Sounds like a long time, but to me it only seems like yesterday that I started. I've been the supervisor for fifteen years."

As they talked, they walked among the buses. Randy looked behind him. A gate beside the shop was unlocked. This was how the drivers came in to claim their buses. At the far end of the lot, Dimetri unlocked the main gate. Randy helped him roll back the panels, and then they headed back to the office with Dimetri joking that the safest place to be when the buses were leaving was in the shop or office.

"I want you just to help out in the shop this week. Get a feel for where everything is, how we work and keep the paperwork straight. That's what I hate the most, paperwork. Never had to worry much about it when I was just a mechanic." Dimetri gave Randy a friendly slap on the back. "Glad to have you aboard."

* * *

They looped around the Capitol grounds and approached the Rayburn Building in the one-way traffic traveling east to west.

"May I keep the *Post*?" Brian asked, emerging from the limousine.

"Yes, sir."

Brian shook the driver's hand. "Thank you."

"It was my pleasure, Mr. Willis. I'm glad to have met you." Brian started away, but the driver continued. "You read about that disease . . . ?"

Brian held up the paper. "Yes, I did. Sounds very serious."

Before Brian could get away, the driver said, "I think it's part God's doing, if you know what I mean."

"No, I'm not sure I follow you."

"Don't you think God is trying to tell us something? Last couple of years seems like there's one disaster right after another. Two years ago, my parents lost their home in one of those tornadoes that left thousands homeless in the Midwest. Worst year for tornadoes there ever was. And that's just part of all the disasters that have been happening lately. Then those three hurricanes that hit the coast between Texas and Florida killed another thousand people. Remember?"

Brian looked at the man, his forehead wrinkling, his stomach rolling and twisting. None of how he felt came because what he had just been told was news, but because the driver was echoing ideas that were being placed before the country. Ideas from Gavin's mouth. *And,* he thought, *ideas I helped craft.*

"Not much is happening now," he suggested.

The driver nodded his head at the paper. "Right, 'Cept that disease."

Brian agreed with a reluctant shrug. "The CDC *is* pretty quiet. If it were serious, they'd be on it like saints to a crown giveaway. And it's not headline news."

"*Pppst . . . ,*" the driver sputtered. "Probably everybody is too scared to admit that they don't know how to handle it. Only thing that's going to put all this crazy stuff in check is prayer and righteous living. World's gone to pot, and I think God is getting angry."

"So you think God is playing hardball now and wants us to appease Him or He'll kill us all." Brian thought he had taken the man's logic too far, but he got a dense look and was shrugged off, like he'd hit the nail right on the head.

The limo driver shut Brian's door. "Only some of us," he muttered in low tones, like this was the first time he'd expressed his feelings out loud. He walked around and got into the car.

But it will be easier to say it next time, Brian thought. *That's the danger.* As he headed toward the Rayburn Building, he said under his breath, "Next thing you know, we'll be calling for human sacrifices to appease God."

The incident with the limo driver only caused Brian more apprehension about seeing Gavin. It had been such a relief to finish in Idaho and go home, if only for a few days. His decision to quit the Coalition had given him more peace of mind than he imagined, and now he looked forward to just being a father and husband. Still, there was Gavin before him, and he didn't think for an instant that the Religious Coalition leader would let him go so easily.

Brian had been to the Rayburn Building not more than a dozen times. This was the slowest he had ever walked its halls. His watch told him he need not hurry to arrive at the Speaker's old office by nine o'clock.

Punching the elevator button, he stood with his attaché case gripped in front of him with both hands. As soon as the doors opened, he stepped inside, turned, and depressed the second-floor button. He made the ride alone and could not recall a time when he had ridden in any of the elevators alone. This time he was grateful for the privacy. He was sure his mood toward meeting Gavin was displayed on his face as distinctively and as depressingly as a painting by Hieronymus Bosch.

At Thurgood's door, he stole a deep breath and walked through into a dark, deserted outer office. Across the room, the door to the Speaker's office stood slightly ajar. He strode across the outer office and tentatively nudged it open.

Gavin was perched on Thurgood's old desk with his back toward Brian. Like a praying mantis, his head drifted back and forth on corded neck muscles as he surveyed the Capitol and its lavish grounds through the window.

"Come in, Brian," Gavin said. "I've been expecting you."

Brian entered the room, left his briefcase in a chair beside the door, and wandered closer to the massive cherry-wood desk, his eyes sweeping over a familiar gallery of law books and political treatises that gilded the many levels of bookshelves. Although the office seemed much more sterile minus the Speaker's presence, it seemed Thurgood had left quite a lot behind too.

Gavin heaved a sigh and stood, turning to face Brian. He perched himself on the edge of the desk again. "Davis called to say you were on your way up."

Davis was the limo driver, Brian decided, realizing he had not learned the man's name.

There was a long, weighty silence when Gavin seemed to be waiting for Brian to say something more. Whatever was expected, Brian did not deliver. Finally, Gavin eagerly slapped his palms together. "You must be extremely tired after all the speeches we've given over the past year. You certainly deserve a long vacation." His sharp eyes studied Brian for a response. A moment later he motioned for Brian to take a seat in one of the two chairs in front of the desk. They were not nearly as plush and comfortable as the high-backed leather chair adorned in brass rivets behind the desk, the chair Gavin settled comfortably into. Gavin adjusted the green blotter in front of him, an unnecessary distraction since no one had probably used the office since Thurgood had left. Brian waited for Gavin to tell him what the excitement was about, but he said nothing, just smiled oddly. It was enough to push Brian into talking just to lessen his discomfort.

"What is it you were so eager to get me here to tell me?"

Gavin looked up, and his smile grew wider and more toothy, as if he were holding a million-dollar lottery ticket. "I have a surprise for you, a huge one that not only will be exciting to you but to the whole world." Gavin jumped to his feet, unable to contain his enthusiasm now that he had the opportunity to build upon his little mystery. "This is something we have to play just right, media wise. That's why I want you to be one of the very first to know." Brian leaned forward, eliciting a grin from Gavin. "So you are interested, even if it's just a tiny fraction?"

Brian nodded, realizing his curiosity was indeed aroused, much as he hated to admit it. He had to know. He was now fairly certain Gavin's excitement wasn't because of the pope's visit. That had been planned for at least a year and hadn't garnered this much enthusiasm from Gavin.

"OK, so tell me what's up," Brian said.

Gavin paced around the room, walking behind Brian and then circling around behind the Speaker's desk. Brian wondered who would next move into this office; he wondered how long before the Speaker passed away. Would there be a respectful period of time before the remainder of Thurgood's effects were boxed up and shipped home? Brian waited patiently. Gavin's pacing seemed an effort to prolong the suspense he appeared to be trying to generate. Brian let him. If half his mind were not wrestling with the timing of how to break the news of his resignation, he might have been more than mildly curious.

Gavin returned to the Speakers' chair. "You're a hard cookie, Brian," he said. "I was hoping to pump you up for this somehow, but it's about all I can do to keep your attention."

"Well, maybe you should just tell me up front what this is about, Gavin. I'm finding it difficult to be excited about something you've only eluded to. I'm not really sure you have anything that will surprise me."

Again, Gavin's face broke into a wide grin. "Oh, you'll be surprised, my friend." His eyes lifted from Brian, hesitated, and then swept the room. He leaned back in self-satisfied repose and interlocked his fingers. The base of Brian's neck tingled suddenly, encouraging him to turn around, exactly what Gavin was hoping for with his subtle cues.

* * *

Randy Burton didn't like taking chances with his cover, but

then, he also suspected his cover had already been discovered and that it was only a matter of convenience the Freedom Society did not eliminate him. This didn't help his situation as far as Lynn was concerned either. Ever since Lynn had come to him for a place to stay, he had vacillated on whether or not he should allow it. But if he refused, he couldn't explain to her why not, and he certainly couldn't send her someplace else, because there *was* no place else. He was really the only family she had left. But he feared for her safety and wished there *was* someplace else she could stay until this was all over. *What about that woman, Alice Nolan?* he thought. He would have to bring it up.

The Freedom Society had not seemed to object to his letting Lynn stay with him, and he reasoned Dietrich and others might have been more suspicious if he had not allowed it. From all angles, it was good for his cover. It was still bad for Lynn.

He thought about this on his lunch hour as he drove down Belmont, jogged over on Fourteenth to Chapin Street, and then parked at Meridian Hill Park. He took his lunch and ate while watching a few straggling leaves float to the ground, and he took a few moments to relax and watch the clouds drift by. They were altocumulus clouds, drifting quickly, and he wondered if there might be some inclement weather on its way. After twenty minutes, he rose, stuffed his trash in a nearby receptacle, and stepped into the restroom before heading back. It was there that he hid the carton containing the fingerprints he had taken out of the Ranger. With any luck, the prints, when run through the FBI's AFIS (Automated Fingerprint Identification System) would turn up information on Scarpetti and Leaman, possibly linking them to past crimes.

Back at the bus depot, Randy punched in on the time clock in the break room and headed out to the shop. He was alone in the shop when he used the phone to call Watters.

* * *

Special Agent in Charge Dave Watters was sitting at his desk in the Counter-Terrorism Unit of the FBI headquarters when he got the call on a secure line. He answered and listened carefully to the extremely short call. When he hung up, he stood and retrieved his jacket from the back of his chair and left the building. He didn't tell anyone where he was going. This was the tightest operation he had under his command, and he chose to oversee it personally. It was also proving to be the most critical at the moment, although for reasons he had not yet completely put together. All Agent Burton could tell him was that something was going to happen very soon and that he felt he wasn't trusted.

Could there be a leak? he asked himself. Burton had suggested it. Watters rolled the thought over and over in his mind on the way to Meridian Hill Park.

* * *

Brian turned to see who was behind him. He froze in that position. The man who stared back had a peculiar glint in his eye, partly because he enjoyed the look of surprise on Brian Willis's face and partly from knowing a secret millions would kill for.

"Hello, Brian," Speaker of the House Donald Thurgood said as he strode briskly across the room toward his chair. "I can tell that the next time you expected to see me was at my funeral."

The icy force that held Brian finally released him. He turned around in his chair, pushing himself up to regain his composure. He watched the Speaker. After a moment, he nodded. "Yes, I-I guess that's true." He thought of the *Time* article he had read on the plane. "But you were very sick. The cancer was extremely aggressive and had spread through your whole body. No one expected you to live more than a few weeks. The doctors were certain . . ."

"So . . . what happened?" The Speaker had his elbows on the

desk and waved out his open palms in a gesture to indicate surprise. He and Gavin were staring over the desk at Brian, giving Brian the impression they didn't intend to let him out of the office until he had fully accepted and believed in Thurgood's miraculous recovery. *Shouldn't be too hard,* he could imagine them thinking, *after all, we all believe in miracles.*

Brian nodded. "What did happen? You look healthy. You look . . . you look better than ever."

Thurgood smiled. "You're right; I do look better than I have for some years. And I've never felt better in my life. Praise God! I've been healed."

"How many people have you told?"

Gavin's eyes rolled upward, as if he were reading the names of a select few off the ceiling. Brian had an idea, after replaying the phone conversation that morning, that there were not many who knew. Maybe only one or two. Thurgood and Gavin wanted the rest of the world to find out in a well-planned media blitz, hence the reason for Brian's induction into their secret.

Gavin said, "We've been very quiet about this. I'm sure you can guess why. If the wrong person were to find out and then told someone else, soon there would be a considerable amount of conflicting reports. The news would be fragmented, and the Speaker's healing would be largely believed to be a hoax. We'd lose impact."

Brian nodded. "I understand."

"It's been a trick to keep this hidden as well as we have, but luckily it's much easier for the Speaker to pretend to be deathly sick rather than the other way around. He's managed to walk in and out of the building without too much notice, and those he has met have been sufficiently fooled. It can't last forever, however.

"Brian, listen carefully. I have developed a plan, and I want you on board with it. I want us to use the media to better advantage. With a little timing, the United Religious Coalition can triple its exposure and become a major political force overnight."

While Gavin talked, Thurgood settled into his chair and watched Brian. Brian could feel the older man's eyes—cold and professional. Their steady probe unsettled him. He sensed no camaraderie, although he had once worked for the Speaker. Thurgood was a changed man.

Brian took a breath to calm himself, and then he ignored the Speaker. He concentrated on Gavin, who had come around the desk and propped himself in front of Brian. "Any idea how we can bump up our exposure?" Gavin asked.

Brian looked at him, shrugging.

Gavin went on. "What if we announce the Speaker's miraculous recovery at the rally on Friday with the pope?"

The idea hit Brian like a meteorite. It was so simple, yet the results had the potential to captivate the nation. He was surprised he didn't think of it himself. Maybe if he wasn't planning on leaving, he'd feel more on top of the game. Brian swung his eyes from Gavin to Thurgood, who had not blinked an eyelid while watching his reactions, then back to Gavin again.

"So?" Gavin shrugged. "Can you make it work?"

"It's a sound plan. Really, it's so opportune it begs to be done. But . . ."

"We want you on board with us, Brian. I get the feeling lately that you're slipping away. The Coalition needs you. Your work is a big part of the reason we've gotten where we are today. Isn't that right, Speaker?" He gave Brian his most candid look, one that would put every car salesman Brian had ever known out of the business.

Thurgood nodded stoically.

Steel claws squeezed Brian's chest, the familiar indication that he was being manipulated. He adjusted himself in the chair, felt the sticky sensation of perspiration under his arms and the bottoms of his legs, and cleared his throat. He wanted to get up and move around. "I'm sorry, but I had planned to resign."

To his credit, Gavin didn't flinch. His fake smile held perfect symmetry. "Wishing for more time with your family?"

"Yes," Brian said.

"I want you to listen to what I have to say. I think you might be pleasantly surprised."

"I'm listening."

"Few people in our organization have been as devoted as you, Brian. Over the years you've proved yourself over and over to me. When I look at our success in raising the moral standards in this country, I realize that much of it was due to your diligence. You have nothing to be ashamed of. You've helped make Christian values into American values."

"So you see why I need to quit," Brian broke in. "I've got to take those values home to my children. They're growing up without me, and that's not right. I don't want the Willis home falling apart because I'm gone all the time trying to change the world. It would become a traumatic paradox for me. Believe me, I've thought about it."

Gavin raised his hands in a gesture of understanding. "I fully respect your decision. How would it look if the Coalition only preached about family values?"

"Then you'll accept my resignation?"

"Not so fast. You're jumping the gun on me a little here. I want you to hear what I have to say first."

Brian shrugged. He'd listen, but he was not prepared to change his mind, not after moving ahead this far. More than ever, he wanted out.

"A man with the convictions you have is a valuable asset for the Coalition. It's important for you to remain visible. People know you."

Brian lifted an eyebrow. Gavin noticed it and charged forward.

"Sure they do, Brian. You're becoming an icon. Like me. The press respects you; they trust you."

"You don't believe they trust you? We've been fighting for the same cause, Gavin. The Coalition stands for God, life for unborn children, families, community. The list goes on. These are not things people grow suspicious of." For the moment, Brian talked around his own suspicions just to see where this was headed.

"I know," Gavin shook his head, lightly conceding the point. "But the nature of the media practically demands they distrust me. And it hasn't helped that so many religious leaders in the past compromised themselves with fraud and sex scandals. It casts suspicion on the rest of us. It's my position, my increasing power. They could see it as a good enough motive to scandalize me. You can keep that from happening."

A slight smile escaped Brian. He'd seen where Gavin was heading and reached the destination well ahead of him. "And you think I, in some way, satiate the press."

"Of course, Brian. You're a natural. You're young, bright, handsome, and squeaky clean."

Brian thought what Gavin really meant was that he was still young enough to look naïve and could still be considered an idealist, meaning, in short, he wasn't smart enough to be self-serving. "Meanwhile my marriage is in freefall because I didn't have time for my family."

"We'll fix that. It's not a problem."

"Now? Or after it's too late?"

"Now, of course. But I need you to stay."

Brian sat there without speaking, long enough for the silence to become uncomfortable. Both Gavin and the Speaker were staring. Why did they want him so badly? He tossed that question around but could find no answer other than he was awfully good at his job. And they needed him.

"Let's say we talk about an increase in salary." Brian got set to shake his head, but Gavin continued. "We really want you to stay with the Coalition, Brian. Especially through the next few weeks. After things settle down, after the fervor over the Speaker has subsided, you'll take more of an advisory role. You could work from home. Sound attractive?"

"Well, yeah."

"Good." Gavin smiled, concerned, like one sincerely worried

about his friend's future. "I know you and Ann will appreciate the extra salary."

Brian wasn't thinking about money. He was thinking how much he wanted to get out of this office and find some place to think things over. He was just realizing how much had really been thrown at him in the past thirty minutes, and he wondered if it might have been planned that way. He had a funny feeling that something was not exactly right, but he couldn't pinpoint it.

Brian rose from his chair.

"Where are you going?" Gavin stood with him.

Brian's imagination had begun to visualize Ann's disenchantment with him should he commit anything more to Gavin without talking to her first. "I'm sorry, I can't make a decision without consulting my wife first."

"Brian, I need you on this now!" Gavin pounded his fist for emphasis.

Surprised, Brian turned and gave Gavin a long look. The flash of anger had been there, if only for that short burst.

Gavin spread his hands apologetically. "I'm sorry. It's just that we have a lot happening at the rally on Friday. Surely you understand the kind of pressure I'm feeling."

"Yes, I understand. But, you also have to understand that I can and will walk."

"OK, OK. Maybe I've pushed too hard for too long." Gavin put his arm on Brian's shoulder. "You've been with me a long time, Brian. I'd like you to stay." He gestured toward the Speaker. "The three of us."

Brian's eyes narrowed. "The three of us?"

Gavin nodded, smiled. "I'll explain things later. Let me know what you decide." It was a smooth way to take back control. Brian was both confused and curious, but he couldn't jump back into the discussion without fearing he might commit himself to something he'd later regret. He did need to talk to Ann first. If he stayed, it would all become academic. Ann would kill him.

Gavin steered him toward the door. In a whisper, he said, "Brian, there are plans I can't tell you yet. Trust me. I want you with me. You won't regret it, and neither will your family."

Before leaving the inner office, Brian picked up his brief-case. Alone in the hallway, he understood himself enough to know he'd been hooked quite artfully. Gavin had not tempted him with money; he'd tempted him with curiosity. And Brian well knew, because he thought it so many times when his children got into things—*curiosity killed the cat.*

He wasn't alone in the hallway long before making his way back to the elevator and down. When the doors opened and he stepped out, he nearly ran into a fit, tall man wearing a charcoal-colored suit. His face was handsome and familiar, but Brian couldn't place just how at the moment. There were bound to be many people in the Capitol who were familiar. Brian caught only a quick glimpse of him before he was out of sight in the elevator, as if he were trying not to be seen. Curious, Brian stood around and watched until the elevator stopped on a floor. It wasn't until he was out on the street that he placed the man: Kent Aldridge, the director of the FBI.

Chapter Nine

Wednesday, November 17

Mr. Lincoln became a refuge for Mara in the days following her meeting with Amy. The day after their talk, she had wandered over to the Jefferson Memorial and sat on the bank of the Potomac, watching the water swirl by and wondering what on earth to do next. She was afraid to stay, and afraid to go back home. Amy's words about the virus kept returning and playing over and over in her head. What chance did she have? What chance did any of them really have?

"We've even started going to church," Amy had said. *"We think maybe God is trying to tell the country something. I don't have any real medical hope that we'll be able to stop this thing, but I know God can stop it if He wants to."*

"Is that where it's at, God?" Mara had whispered quietly. *"Are you trying to tell us something?"* As she sat there, a bright yellow paper floated gently past her. As if it was the sign she'd been seeking, it got caught in one of the little eddies just beneath her. She could see that it was some sort of flyer. As it spun lazily around, she had reached down and grabbed it.

GOD HAS A MESSAGE FOR AMERICA. HE'S GOING TO DELIVER IT THROUGH GAVIN LARSON. THERE WILL BE A RALLY ON FRIDAY THAT WILL MAKE HISTORY. FOR THE FIRST TIME EVER, THE WORLD RELIGIOUS LEADERS WILL UNITE. MAKE PLANS NOW TO ATTEND.

Mara had mulled over the words. She couldn't risk going back home so soon, so she decided to stay and check out the rally. It couldn't hurt. In the meantime, she intended to bury her nose in her Bible. Maybe she'd even get in touch with Amy again and go to church with her on the weekend.

It became a sort of routine. In the morning she'd get up, get dressed in leggings and a T-shirt, and go for a run. She'd managed to book a hotel only minutes away from the monuments, so every morning her route took her past the country's historical landmarks. Their geographical locations were like the stations of the cross, she mused, as she wound her way through the park and by the Vietnam Memorial. Her run always included a dash up the steps of the Lincoln Memorial, where she raised her arms in salute, Rocky-style, before descending.

After a quick shower, she packed a light lunch, her Bible and a notebook, and returned to the Memorial. Finding a spot on the steps, she dug the Bible out and began reading. Now and then she made notes in the margin or in her notebook. She found that it helped to take notes. It was a habit she'd gotten into in med school, and it had always proved useful since.

At first she'd just read randomly, but that brought up questions. She'd always considered herself a good Catholic. She'd been baptized as an infant, taken her first communion, and had her confirmation, all at the same beautiful church with the same priest. She'd attended catechism longer than any of her friends.

For a little while her parents had been involved in the charismatic movement, and they'd gone to prayer meetings and retreats. Mara had set up a shrine in her room with the open Bible as a centerpiece and Mary and St. Francis looking on benevolently. Whenever she could, she'd coerced her little friends into playing "prayer meeting" where they got the "Holy Ghost" and spoke in "tongues." She preached at them until they lost interest and left.

For her confirmation, her parents had presented her with a beautiful rose-colored leather Bible that she had, over the years, read to pieces. Every morning her mother would wake her up early and she would read it for fifteen minutes. Fifteen minutes was all her parents required, but sometimes Mara got caught up in the stories and read for half an hour or more.

Initially, with Mr. Lincoln looking over her shoulder, she attempted to repeat this pattern. But it seemed as if someone had changed the words of her Bible in the years it had sat neglected on her shelf.

"Remember the Sabbath day by keeping it holy. Six days you shall labor and do all your work. But, the seventh day is a Sabbath to the Lord your God."

"And on the Sabbath day he went into the synagogue, as was his custom."

"When the Sabbath was over, Mary Magdalene, Mary the mother of James, and Salome brought spices so that they might go to anoint Jesus' body. Very early on the first day of the week, just after sunrise . . ."

A light burned dimly in the back of her mind as the beginning of an idea began to get brighter. The Sabbath: wasn't that what Dani had called Saturday? The more Mara read, the more convicted she became and the more excited she got. What else did the Bible have to say that she had missed as a child?

She spent long hours meditating on the fresh, stimulating ideas that virtually leapt off the page. When she wasn't spending time with Mr. Lincoln and God, Mara holed up in the Library of Congress doing as much research as she could on filoviruses. She spent hours surfing the Internet, reading every document, no matter how obscure, that mentioned anything about filoviruses or the current, as yet unnamed, epidemic.

Even as she sat before the swiftly changing screen, a cold soda beside her on the library table, she could feel a wave of excitement building inside her as she anticipated the upcoming rally. On Friday she would get some answers. In fact, she was quite sure she would come face to face with God.

* * *

Brian had spent most of Tuesday resting. He had also spent a good portion of it on the phone with Ann. He hinted about Gavin's proposal for him to stay with the Coalition, but she would not even consider it, even if it did mean working from home. Ann was clearly tired of Gavin Larson and the Coalition. Brian suggested they talk about it when he returned home, that he did in fact tell Gavin he had to discuss it with her first. Brian also spent a great amount of time typing e-mail to Ann, as well as to Matthew and Hannah.

This morning, he focused on Friday's rally. Newspapers in all fifty states were carrying ads promoting the rally. The three major networks and their affiliates were running a series of ads with highlights from Gavin's religious rallies across the country. The blitz was designed to focus the American people on Friday's climactic rally. It was all costing big bucks, and it was expected to attract almost a million people.

Brian had been eyeing a Post-it note on the coffee table. At ten minutes after nine, he dialed Dale Meltzer's cellular phone number. Meltzer was now coordinating everything from the site of the rally, which would literally cover the entire Mall grounds from the Capitol building to the Lincoln Memorial.

"Hello, Meltzer here."

"Dale, this is Brian. How's your headache?"

"Worse. The pope will add another half a million bodies to our original estimate, easy. I'd say even more. I'm trying not to scare myself though. For the past two weeks I've been trying to project the size of the crowd, but I'm afraid I've been underestimating quite a bit."

"How many people do you estimate?" Brian asked.

"Right now I'm figuring well over a million."

Brian whistled.

"I've scoured the country for more big-screen televisions, anything over thirty feet, and they've been shipped. We'll be working throughout the night. It's awfully tight, but we're going to make it."

"Keep me informed of any problems," Brian said.

"I'll do that," Dale said and hung up.

He didn't say anything to Dale, but at some point during the rally, every eye in front of every big screen would be fixed on a completely healed Speaker of the House. He was still wrestling with the right words to put in Gavin's speech. Several times he started rough drafts but so far hadn't come up with anything he liked.

He made a dozen more phone calls as the day wore on. He spoke to the mayor, who assured him several hundred law enforcement personnel were scheduled to be on the streets Friday to serve as traffic and crowd control. The mayor was confident his staff was well-organized and prepared, just as he should have been. This final rally had been planned a year in advance.

By afternoon, he had grown tired of his hotel room and left it to go for a drive. It wasn't until he was out of the parking garage that he finally made a decision to drive by First Christian, where he had graduated from academy. He hadn't seen the school in years.

Brian parked the rented Taurus in a tight spot recently vacated on Clifton Street. Although he had been lucky to find a parking space at all, this one gave Brian a horrible view of the main campus. Most all the satellite buildings were new since he'd been a student at First Christian, and those were what he could mostly see from where he was. Instead of a feeling of nostalgia, he felt more like a tired tourist. He switched off the ignition and sadly shook his head. He'd come here to gain his bearings, and now, in a sudden wash sparked by so many changes, he felt more lost than ever.

Suddenly, he jerked and realized he had nodded off for well over an hour. He rubbed his face as people do who are not fully awake and still a little disoriented. He stopped short of talking to himself, though, and was amused that it even mattered. They said talking to yourself only became a concern when you found yourself answering back.

When he felt sober, he reached for the ignition and started the car. He checked for traffic and began to pull out when he saw a familiar face. *Randy! Randy Burton!* Randy Burton and Brian had been in the same class at First Christian.

Brian slammed on the brakes, stopping halfway in the road. After returning to his parking spot, he jumped out and ran across the street. He heard the distinctive *beep, beep* of a car alarm being disarmed as Randy neared a black 4Runner. Randy hadn't seen him.

"Hey, Randy? Randy Burton, is that you?" For an unsettling moment Brian thought he'd made a foolish mistake.

The man turned around. "Yeah? Who are . . . Wait, I know you." Randy tapped his temple. "Brian! Brian Willis."

Brian grinned, and the two men shook hands.

"Never in a million years would I have expected to see you trotting off the school grounds," Brian said. "This is the first time in ages I've been back."

"A few weeks ago I wouldn't have expected it myself. Just took a job as a mechanic in the bus depot. Second day on the job. So how are you anyway? Caught you on television a couple of years ago and about fell over. News clip or something, but I only caught the tail end of it and never tried to figure out why you were on the news."

Brian laughed. "Boy, I couldn't begin to tell you what it was about, Randy. I've been interviewed by the media so many times I can't remember most of what I've said."

"What do you do that keeps you in the news?" Randy asked

curiously. He folded his arms and leaned against the 4Runner. To Brian the posture had a defensive quality, as if Randy felt uncomfortable. Brian buried his hands in the pockets of his slacks. "I work with the United Religious Coalition, its public relations guru, you might say." Actually, he liked the idea that Randy didn't know who he was. For someone with a high-profile job such as his, he preferred anonymity to spotlight and had no ambitions toward fame. "It's not as wondrous as it might seem."

Randy grinned. "Did I say I was envious?"

"No, you didn't."

"But it doesn't compare to being a grease monkey. I know that. I always knew your ambitions would take you a lot farther than most of us." He jerked his head toward the bus shop. "Me, I'm happy with my head stuck under the hood of anything with a motor."

"You know, Randy, I believe it. I'm tired . . ." Brian stopped short. Turning around, he viewed the school buildings. He realized he didn't feel comfortable diving into his personal feelings with someone he hadn't seen for nearly fifteen years. "I'm in D.C. on business. How would you like to meet for dinner and do some catching up?"

Burton shrugged. "Sure. Sounds good." Brian couldn't tell if he seemed reluctant or not. But if so, he covered it well.

"Good, then. Meet me at the Marco Polo at seven this evening. I'll have a table." With that, they shook hands again, and Brian trotted across the road toward the Taurus while Randy climbed into his 4Runner.

* * *

Randy Burton was stunned, so much so that he left the radio off and drove home in complete silence. How much of a problem it would create running into Brian Willis he could only imagine.

When he arrived at home and pulled into the drive, Scarpetti's Ranger pulled in behind, whipped around on the grass on his right side, and screeched to a stop in front of him. Scarpetti and Leaman jumped out and flanked the 4Runner until Randy got out.

"What was that?" Scarpetti demanded. "What happened in the parking lot at the school? What did he want?" Scarpetti fired questions like an automatic weapon. His attitude made Randy nervous.

Although Scarpetti might have been a good foot thicker than he was, Randy at least felt lucky they were the same height. He stood toe to toe with Scarpetti. "I didn't know that was going to happen. It was a freak coincidence."

Leaman had parked himself on the passenger's side of the vehicle, possibly afraid to become involved in the escalating tension between Scarpetti and Burton. Finally, Scarpetti opted for a more diplomatic approach. "So you two know each other."

"We went to school together. We were in the same class. We weren't friends, close or otherwise."

"But you know who he is now." It was neutral, neither a question nor a statement.

"Yeah, I know who he is. He works for the United Religious Coalition. Is that a problem?"

Scarpetti was no dummy; he wouldn't touch that question. He had to let the subject go or end up answering more questions than he was asking. One thing Randy had learned about Scarpetti: The man liked to have the edge, and that meant keeping as much information to himself as possible.

* * *

He had found the doctor. It had been an amazingly simple operation, and now as Dietrich sat in a chair, pretending to read a book but in reality watching her at a computer terminal at the Library of Congress, he felt almost disappointed that the hunt was over. The only thing that saved him from complete remorse—and from silencing her permanently—was the fact that although he had been following her for two days and gone through the contents of her room at the hotel while she was away, he could find no evidence of Dani. It was as if Dani had vanished. And that was not possible.

He mulled over the possibilities. Maybe the good doctor had gotten sick of her and left her somewhere along the road. No, she was too *nice* to do that. More likely that the little wretch had run off. That seemed to be a pattern with her. When the going got tough, she got going. If that was the case, she could be anywhere, but Dietrich highly suspected that if she had run off, she would be heading west. Probably to her old man.

Mara leaned back in her chair and tapped a pencil against her teeth. Dietrich's eyes narrowed as he watched her. Later he would access the computer's Internet temporary files and go through the information she was at this moment looking so puzzled about. So far about the only thing she had done was research. Lots of research about filoviruses. She had also pulled every scrap of information, no matter how remote, that dealt with the present virus.

Dietrich doubted that she was merely curious. She was onto something, he just wasn't sure what. Without a professional opinion, he was at a loss. Later, after the rally was over and he could concentrate on it again, he would go to their contact at USAMRIID and get some answers. Right now he was content to keep tabs on Dr. Benneton and bide his time until the rally was over.

That she had stayed in Washington this long suggested that she might be going to the rally. There would be time after that to find out what he wanted to know. In the meantime, she might yet lead him to Dani or at least provide a clue to where she had gone.

But Dani and Dr. Benneton were secondary worries at the moment. In two days he would pull off the assassination of a lifetime. And there were still a few details to attend to. The most worrisome was the continued deterioration of the link they had set up with Burton through Dave Watters. The two of them were much too close to catching on. If that happened, there could be some major problems before the rally, and Gavin would not like that.

Dietrich stood up and stretched. He set his book on a nearby table as he walked out of the Library of Congress. Shrugging his collar up, he strode briskly toward the Washington Monument to check on things for the rally. The air was cold, and he gritted his teeth as he headed into a brisk wind.

There was only one thing he had to take care of before he could fully concentrate on the job ahead of him. He pulled a cell phone out of his pocket and snapped it open. He punched some numbers and waited for someone to pick up.

"Dave Watters? I've got some information of vital interest to you about the Freedom Society. Randy Burton asked me to get in touch with you. I don't want to talk on this line. Can you meet me at the Arlington Memorial Bridge tonight after dark? I'll find you."

Dietrich snapped the phone shut and put the phone back in his pocket and concentrated on the next few hours. They would be crucial. After this it should be smooth sailing until the rally. And then it would be time to think about Dani again. She could wait. Until then.

* * *

In Washington that evening, the sky had become completely overcast again. But it wasn't too cold to walk, Brian thought, as he left the Plaza. Choosing the Marco Polo gave him the chance to leave the rental at the hotel and walk the eight blocks to supper, a quiet, relaxing stroll that he enjoyed immeasurably. Arriving at the Marco, he glanced at his watch. He was early, but upon inquiring about his reserved table, he was told a quiet location in the back was just now being made ready. Soon he was ushered through a maze of tables and booths consisting of heavy dark woods and rich burgundy upholstery until he was deposited at a dimly-lit booth with an overacted sweeping of the hand by the maitre d'. It was the kind of atmosphere he would have much rather enjoyed with Ann.

He had only to wait ten minutes before a figure slipped into the booth across from him. He'd had his head buried in a booklet, a brief overview of a Remnant believer author's interpretation of the last days according to Revelation.

Randy unbuttoned his jacket. "What's that?"

Brian twisted the cover toward him as if he had just discovered, with Randy, what was in his hand. *"You and Revelation."*

"The world coming to an end?"

Brian lifted an eyebrow. "What makes you say that? Have you studied Daniel and Revelation in the Bible?" Somehow he'd gotten the impression Randy was never terribly serious about religion.

"Don't get excited. I was just joking." He acted as if he were backpeddling and using a fire extinguisher to kill any sparks that could potentially ignite a Bible study.

"OK, OK, no talk of religion," Brain said. He nodded toward a menu. "Let's order first and then talk about the old days."

"Deal."

When their waiter arrived, Brian ordered the lasagna. Randy ordered fetuccini alfredo. Moments later, they had cold water on the table and a glass of wine for Randy. Brian leaned forward.

"I can't tell you how shocked I was to see a familiar face from academy. I was just there to see what the old school looked like."

"Well, you can rest easy knowing I was just as surprised. A couple of days earlier and you wouldn't have seen me there at all. But life is full of surprises. I would never have dreamed I'd be working as a mechanic at the same school I graduated from." He shrugged and leaned back.

"Do you like it?"

Randy smiled and nodded without hesitation. "Yes, I do. I never did as well with people as I did with engines. I'm trying to think. You weren't a gregarious type, but you did well with people."

"Yeah, I guess," Brian said.

Randy squinted, smiling wryly. "Yes, I can see you as a minister. So, this United Religious Coalition . . . what's it all about?"

"I can't believe you've never heard of it."

"Well, maybe I'm farther away from God than you think," Randy replied.

"I didn't think there was anyone who didn't know about the Coalition."

A peculiar look. "In your world, maybe, but there are plenty of people who don't give it a thought one way or the other."

For a moment there was silence as Brian sipped his water. Like a twenty-one gun salute, a staccato of laughter exploded from a large table twenty feet away. Both men turned to stare.

"I don't know. It hasn't seemed that way to me," Brian said.

Randy shook his head as if only a moron could miss the obvious. "With what you do, your whole world revolves around religion."

There was a brief moment when Brian felt like disagreeing, but he couldn't see much point in it. If Randy felt uncomfortable talking about religion, then he had obviously given it some thought, if only to turn away. Brian felt saddened by this and somewhat frustrated that he could not pursue the subject of God. Maybe if he'd approached Randy about God and had left organized religion out of it when he first opened his mouth, Randy might be more open now.

"OK, I see your point," he conceded with an assuring smile. "Let's talk about . . ." And suddenly he couldn't think of a thing to talk about other than the weather. What was there to talk about when you decided not to mention religion or politics anyway? "Do you know anyone who's been plagued with that disease that's hit the coastal regions?" he asked, centering on a subject.

Randy laughed, but it was polite, and Brian did not take it

the wrong way. He saw it more as a way to divert the conversation from weightier matters.

"Sorry," Randy apologized, "but that didn't strike me as dinner conversation."

"So, what do you want? It's the only story I read in the paper and the only newsbite I caught from the television. Love the weather."

"There you go," Randy said. "Turned out to be a pleasant day, didn't it?"

"The cool November air reminded me of some good times at school."

The left corner of Randy's mouth curled as he remembered fondly. "I had some good times there, but I never went back until now. Never looked up any of our old classmates either." He absently played with his water glass in the puddle of sweat it made on the table. "Did you?"

"No."

Surprised, Randy glanced up. "Why not? You . . . I would have figured *you'd* have stayed in contact with some of the class."

"I tend not to look back much."

"Catches up, though, doesn't it?"

"What do you mean?"

"You were there today."

Brian nodded. "Uh-huh. I guess it did, finally." He took a moment to search Randy's left hand. "Did you ever marry?"

Randy Burton pursed his lips, something like he'd had some chances and wasn't sure if he had regrets. He shook his head. "No, not even engaged. There's not much in my life to talk about. After academy, I joined the army and became a helicopter mechanic. Stayed in five years. I worked for a Ford dealership in Miami for another five years. Eventually, I worked my way back to Washington, D.C."

As they ate, Brian told Randy how and why he had become part of the United Religious Coalition; how he had met Ann while volunteering at a soup kitchen in D.C. That not long after Mat-

thew was born, he began working as the public relations director for the Coalition and moved to Chicago.

"Why Chicago?" Randy asked.

"The Coalition needed to be perceived as being as separate
as possible from the political strings of Washington. Gavin felt
that for the Coalition to attract grassroots America, it needed to
keep a fair distance from Washington. You see, the plan was to
create an influential interest group that would have politicians
begging for its support instead of the reverse. Thus, when the
Coalition was ready, it could step onto the political scene already
wielding enough power to cause change."

This was the part of the scenario Brian was most uncomfortable with, where religion seemed to fork and most people con-
tentedly chose the road that made their Christianity a social
status. Love for God became secondary. Love for one's fellow
human was a distant third. Brian went silent. He set his fork
down and pushed his plate away.

Randy listened intently, and he was good at it. Brian went
on. "There is a world of difference between Christianity . . ."
Suddenly he stopped. "If you're not comfortable with talking
religion . . ."

"No, I'm fine. Go ahead." Randy waved him on. "I don't know
much about the Coalition, but it sounds as if you don't approve
of how things are going."

"I don't. Christianity and 'religion' are two different things.
Religion means devotion, and it can be to an institution, such as
a country or even to an organization like the Coalition. It can
even mean devotion to a faith, or even at its most basic, the laws
of that faith. When the Nazis came to power before World War
II, they were devoted to the idea of creating and maintaining a
supreme race. It was a religion to them. Now we think that such
a thing could never happen again because we are much too en-
lightened." Brian wagged his finger. "Believe me, the more 'en-
lightened' someone thinks he is, the more single-minded he's
apt to be. You have heard of the Freedom Society, correct?"

Randy nodded, his eyes widening a bit.

"Those are the groups of people that scare me the most, yet the Freedom Society has organized many of Gavin Larson's rallies. They'll be involved in more yet, and the more exposure these people get from the Coalition, the more credibility they gain. I don't know who founded the Freedom Society, and I don't particularly care. But I'll tell you one thing, right now Gavin could influence a mass of people to do anything he wants, and that includes the Freedom Society."

Randy had become pensive, causing Brian to think he had gone too far talking about religion. He smiled, immediately dropping the topic, hoping to lighten the mood again. "I think I'm just tired. I need some time with my wife and kids. Maybe I need a change of scenery. *Maybe* I'll become a missionary."

There was a lengthy pause before Randy engaged himself in the conversation again. "Could be you would be a great minister with your own church somewhere, someday." Randy shrugged while Brian narrowed his eyes and considered it.

"Could be."

The two schoolmates warmed to a level of eclectic topics distant from their personal lives. Often they touched on the epidemic, but neither knew enough about it to be particularly worried. Brian could not get over the impression that Randy's side of the conversation was too sanitary to be genuine. But then, they were merely acquaintances in academy. From what he could remember, First Christian was not where Randy Burton had wanted to be. He was one of the more frequent troublemakers.

With little in common, the conversation soon dried up to a trickle, cluing both that it was time to call it an evening. Brian had already charged the meal and gratuity. He took the receipt from the courtesy plate and stuffed it into his wallet along with his UBC.

"It was good to see you, Randy," Brian said. When he had put the UBC away, he had removed a card with his name and office number on it, which he put into Randy's hand. "I call in twice a day for messages, so if you need anything, leave me a number, and I'll get in touch."

"Thank you. I will. And thanks for dinner."

Standing, Brian reached out and shook Randy's hand. "Take care of yourself."

As they left, Brian followed Randy out. The restaurant was filled to capacity. They walked by a booth where one of the men made eye contact with Randy, as if they might have known each other. This didn't make as much of an impression on Brian as the second man, who seemed to be making a concerted effort to avoid eye contact with either Randy or Brian. A low-voltage tingle found the base of Brian's neck. He had seen that face before!

When he walked out into the night air, he was already feeling a chill. Randy said Goodbye again and hurried off to find his vehicle. Brian paused, glanced back at the Marco Polo, then headed toward his hotel. He came upon an alley, considered its tunnel of pitch blackness a moment, then, in a matter of two strides, hid himself.

Feeling ridiculous, he hugged the edge of the brick building for nearly ten minutes while watching the Marco Polo, afraid of even his shadow. But after all, his shadow was stretched down the dank alley, and the alley *was* something to worry over. During the past few weeks, he had felt less and less in control and suspicious of everyone: Gavin, his friend Tyler Brownell, Speaker Thurgood . . .

After ten minutes Brian felt relatively invisible. Seemingly, the activity on the street was going on oblivious of him. Five minutes later, the men he was waiting for came out of the Marco Polo and stood for some time under the awning. *Waiting for someone?* Brian wondered.

They could not have intended to follow either him or Randy. If that had been their intention, they would have emerged shortly behind Brian. Probably he was just over the edge, imagining things. He jumped at some noise down the alley, like someone hit a dumpster or something else heavy and metallic. He realized suddenly that he probably made a striking silhouette against the streetlights. Now he wanted to leave for the comfort and safety of his hotel room, but he couldn't move, at least not until the two men had gone. Unfortunately, they seemed to be waiting for someone. They would most certainly see him if he left, unless he left through the alley.

Since exiting through the alley was certainly not an option, Brian decided to study them. The taller one, he determined, was the one in charge. He appeared to be the most agitated, while the shorter man was content to let his companion do the worrying. They were both clean-cut and healthy-looking. Even wearing jackets, they looked tough and muscular. One of them he was sure he recognized. But from where?

Minutes later, a 4Runner rolled up outside the restaurant and picked up the two men.

What?

This revelation caused Brian's knees to buckle. He slid down the wall until he was resting on his haunches. *How did Randy fit in with those two? Why were they watching him? What was going on?*

After the 4Runner sped away, Brian returned to the Marco Polo and found the maitre d'.

"Sir, I need some help."

He got a dull look, but the man nodded. "Yes? What is it?"

"I was eating here with a friend about half an hour ago. Our waiter's name was Tony. Is he still here, and may I speak to him?"

"Tony works till eleven."

Brian waited for him to say more.

The maitre d', who had been carefully watching the doorway for customers, said, "I've got work to do. Excuse me." He went forward and greeted a couple, an Armani and a fur, who wore their wealth like peacocks. Brian faded into the background until the maitre d' returned, the fellow making no attempt to hide his disappointment that Brian was still waiting.

"Follow me. We'll see if Tony wants to talk."

They found Tony, an empty tray in his hand, flirting with a waitress with calflike brown eyes and straight, very dark brown hair cut to frame her face, the perfect cut for her.

"Tony, someone to see you." Surprisingly, the maitre d' left Brian in the kitchen and returned to the front.

Tony's girlfriend left, and the six-foot college student looked Brian up and down. "Hey, you were here an hour ago."

"Half an hour. But the time doesn't matter. What matters is that you remember."

"Sure, I remember."

Now the hard part. "And do you think you might remember who else was in the restaurant at the same time? Specifically, two men, young, looked like bodybuilders."

"You know, I can't remember waiting on a party of two men, except for you two. But," he concluded seriously, "Maria might remember. I think she had the table you described."

"Where's Maria?"

"Well, that was her, the one I was talking to," Tony said, as if she would still be standing there if Brian hadn't chased her off.

"Thanks," Brian said. He stepped out of the kitchen and surveyed what could be seen of the dining area. Quickly, he searched through the restaurant, catching an occasional curious look at his apparent aimless wandering.

When he found Maria, she was serving a table. He waited, and when she returned on her way to the kitchen, he flagged her down.

"Hi," she bubbled. A chronically happy person. Brian frowned.

"Hi. I was wondering if you could help me. Tony said you might."

"Sure."

"Two men were at one of your tables about forty . . . forty-five minutes ago. Do you remember them? Have you seen them around? Did they do anything odd?"

Eager to help, Maria also adopted a serious expression, much like Tony's, only decidedly more genuine. "You'll have to ask me those questions again, mister,'cause I didn't catch them all."

"Do you remember two men dining alone at one of your tables?"

"Uh, yeah, I guess I do. I thought they were sort of creepy."

You're not alone, Brian thought.

"Then you don't know who they are."

A shake of the head. "No, never seen them before."

"OK. Anything odd that you remember them doing?" Maria caught a portentous look from the maitre d'. She grabbed Brian by the arm and led him through the kitchen doors toward the back until they were out of the way.

"They didn't leave right away, I mean, not after they paid for their meal."

"Cash?" Although he didn't know why he wanted to know. Seemed useful.

"No, UBC."

"And then they hung around before getting up and leaving." So had he and Randy, and he'd never thought of it being conspicuous.

Maria shook her head, like he'd just missed the grand-prize phrase in Wheel of Fortune. "No, they didn't leave, but they didn't stay at their table either. It seemed real important they get to another table before leaving."

"What?"

"They went looking at another table. Checking it out or something. I thought it was strange. But that's all they did, just looked around."

"One of Tony's tables?"

"Yeah. How'd you know? Are you a cop? Did they do something?"

Right now Brian wished he *was* a cop. He wished he *knew* a cop, someone who would listen to him and take him seriously. "I'm not a cop, and I'm not aware of what they did," he said. Maybe he'd seen too many cop shows on TV, but he pulled a ten out of his pocket and put it in Maria's hand. They were ten or fifteen feet from a back door. "Can I go out that way?"

Maria glanced around and gave him a shrug.

"Thanks." Brian smiled and slipped quickly out the back.

By the time he reached his hotel, Brian was tired of his heart being in his throat. He'd held his breath through the lobby until he was inside the elevator, and then he half-expected to find someone watching him in the hallway on his floor. But everything appeared quiet when he left the elevator and as he let himself into his room.

Brian picked up the phone. He had three messages, all from home. He dialed home, and after four rings Ann was on the line. He kept his cool.

"Ann, how is everything at home? How are the kids?"

"We're all fine, Brian. Are you all right? You haven't called. I was getting worried."

"I'm sorry. I tried around noon to get you, but you weren't home. Then I went for a drive and ended up at my old school."

"Well, I'm glad you're back safe and sound, although I wish you were back here safe and sound."

"That's not all. Totally by coincidence I met one of my old classmates. We had dinner."

"Oh? Who?" Ann asked.

"His name is Randy Burton. He went to First Christian his senior year, and I haven't seen him since." Until this moment, he had been debating telling her more, that he was suspicious and worried. But there was no sense in worrying her unnecessarily. He had also decided he couldn't very well tell her about Speaker Thurgood yet. There was no way they could afford the long-distance telephone charges it would take to explain that phenomenon.

"How are you with me staying in Washington until after the rally?"

"Oh, Brian, I'm not going to do very well with it. You know that." Clearly, he was not going to score any points with her until he was completely finished with the Coalition.

"Sweetheart, I couldn't have left the Coalition in a lurch. You know I'd have to give two weeks notice, anyway."

There were a few seconds of complete silence, like the vacuum of space. "I guess I was hoping too much for the impossible. I'm all right, really."

"I wish I was home with you and the kids now." Brian had a hard time keeping the catch out of his voice.

"Are you OK? You sound a little upset."

Actually he was a wired, adrenaline-pumping head-case. "I'm fine, just tired is all."

"I know, Hon. I'll let you get to bed. But first I wanted to tell you about an idea. This spring, let's take the kids on a cross-country vacation."

"God knows we need it. It's a great idea, Ann. As soon as I get home, we'll plan it. In the meantime, ask Matthew and Hannah some of the places they'd like to see."

"You mean it? Oh, I think it will be so much fun." Brian could imagine his wife's beaming face. *At least the conversation is ending on a positive note,* he mused with a smile. After a warm exchange of I Love Yous, Brian replaced the receiver on its cradle.

Lying back on his bed with the lights turned out, he replayed the evening. Randy had not come to the restaurant alone. They, or rather, Brian, had been under some kind of surveillance. Randy Burton had been aware of it. He tried to recall what they had talked about. Nothing important. He had been wary of sharing too much personal information.

Brian was now almost positive there had been a listening device, otherwise there would have been no reason for the two men to go back and "check" the table. *But why?* Brian thought of his job, the Coalition. He was a known person in the Christian world, but he was not a politician, not a bureaucrat, not a technological wizard with secrets to sell. He was the commonest of common people. He didn't know what was happening. He just kept reminding himself he wasn't imagining things.

* * *

Scarpetti sat in the rear seat as Randy drove back to the house and listened to the tape they had recorded of Willis and Burton's dinner conversation. Randy watched him through the rearview mirror, but Scarpetti was his usual unexpressive self. He glanced at Leaman, who was riding shotgun and apparently trained not to speak unless ordered to by Scarpetti. He was like an attack dog that would snap into action the instant his master gave the command.

The microphone hidden at the booth before Brian arrived had transmitted to a reel-to-reel at Scarpetti's table. Randy would have refused to wear the wire had he been asked. He didn't know how long he would have argued the point before giving in, though, but the issue had never come up. Scarpetti did not trust Randy and was having a hard time digesting his explanation that seeing Brian at First Christian was a one-in-a-million fluke. Therefore, he did not trust Randy with a wire anyway. Of course, Randy knew the conversation would be recorded, he just couldn't look for the microphone and not be conspicuous.

He settled into his seat and drove. He watched the city lights. He studied people on the streets. He turned the radio on as a distraction and listened to depressing news about murder and drugs. When he was distracted and depressed enough, he switched it off.

When they arrived at the house, Scarpetti put the tape in a small leather bag strapped around his waist, and they went inside. Randy went directly to Lynn's room, knocked lightly, then opened the door a crack. "All right if I come in?" He heard a faint Yes.

Randy entered and closed the door. Without turning on the lights, he went over and sat on the edge of the bed. He didn't speak.

"What's the matter? Where did you go tonight?"

"I went to meet an old classmate for dinner."

A bank of silence descended. Now, as his eyes were adjusting to the darkness, he thought he saw Lynn smiling at him.

"I like you much better now, big brother. You've changed."

"Have I? I wonder how."

"You never would have come to me just to talk. That's nice. Before you'd tell me to get lost. It seemed like you didn't really care. You just kept me around 'cause I was your sister, like it was something you had to do."

"You've changed a fair amount too, Lynn. I've watched you struggle to stop using drugs. The withdrawals haven't and won't be easy. People don't just up and quit. It can be a horrible struggle." He paused, as if a nucleus of thought was working its way to the surface. "Whenever I saw you stoned, a fist of anger would grind its way up into my gut, and I would lose all reason. It was crazy thinking, but sometimes I thought things would be easier if you died. Last time, when I found you on the floor, I realized how much I had let you down by ignoring you and your problems."

He could hear Lynn let out a long, pent-up breath. He didn't let her speak.

"Lynn, can you forgive me for those thoughts and for the way I've treated you? I guess I feel like I've betrayed you by how I felt and by not doing what I could to help."

Randy felt Lynn's hand touch his arm. "You don't have to ask. I have already forgiven you. And I've already forgiven myself too. That was the hardest part. I'm starting over. I think you are too. I think God is working on us."

A self-depreciating chuckle escaped Randy's lips. "I don't know why He wants to work on me."

"Well, He loves all of us, you know," Lynn said.

"All of us? What about Scarpetti?"

"Yes, I guess so. You don't like him much, do you?"

"I don't like him at all. I don't trust him."

"Maybe he'll change too."

"Yeah. Right," Randy glanced at Lynn. She was smiling again, and he grinned back. He got up to leave.

"If you don't like them, why don't you quit whatever you're doing?"

Lynn had to be more than curious about his job, but she had never outright asked about it. Probably she was afraid to know. "I can't, Lynn. It's really too important. Trust me." And then he slipped out and went to his own room. He could hear Scarpetti and Leaman in the kitchen just before he entered his bedroom.

* * *

Dani lay on her back while the baby hiccuped. Her stomach jerked rhythmically, and she sighed. It seemed as if this baby always had the hiccups. One hand wandered free from the covers and caressed her abdomen idly.

In the other bed she could hear her father's deep, even breathing. He had been asleep for about fifteen minutes. She'd been keeping track. Just as soon as she thought it was safe, she planned to sneak out of the room and get out of here. He wasn't going to take her to Washington, D.C., if she could help it. Her hands patted her belly reassuringly. Her father didn't know how dangerous D.C. would be. For him. For her. Or for her unborn baby.

A chilly feeling of foreboding swept over her as she thought about the baby she would have and the short months remaining before it would be born. What then? She scrubbed the broken barbed wire tattoo as if by rubbing hard enough she could wipe it off. How she wished she had never wanted it, that she had never agreed.

Angrily she rolled onto her side, jacking one leg up to support the awkwardness of her belly in this position. In the slant of light coming in the window of the hotel room, she studied her father's face and was shocked to see how old he looked. In the grimy yellow light, his skin seemed deeply furrowed and she could see more strands of silver in his hair than she remembered. His unshaven face was grisly, and even in repose he looked tired, a grimace of perpetual pain etched around his eyes and mouth. He moaned in his sleep, and she started.

No, no! her mind screamed. *Don't wake up now!*

But he didn't wake, just squirmed and fell back into a restless sleep. Awake she almost always hated him, but sleeping, Dani was surprised to find a tender pity fill her heart for him. They had never been close. He had always been too demanding, too suspicious, too hard on her.

She'd thought it was bad enough until he joined the Remnant believers. Then he became almost fanatical, tightening his grip even more, figuratively beating her up with his Bible. She couldn't take his God. He was too strict and vengeful. But a strong part of her wanted God desperately. That was when she found Shon and the Freedom Society and Gavin Larson.

In the Freedom Society she found God to be idealistic and loving. He didn't want to exact vengeance on her. He loved her, and he wanted her to have a good life. But before that could happen, people had to be good. And it was part of their responsibility to make people see that if they would only be good, God had a wonderful life waiting for them.

It wasn't until the end that she began to see the ugly side of the Freedom Society. Then they made her father look like a psalm-singer by comparison. He may have been strict, but at least he didn't blow the brains out of those who didn't listen to him.

Jack's breath sucked in with a small snore, and Dani studied him. He really did want what was best for her. She knew that. If he didn't, he would never have sold his precious antiques and come to look for her. He loved her. He just didn't know how to show it.

She felt a pang of remorse as she silently slipped off the bed. Her sandals were on the floor, and she searched for them with her feet. Quietly she crept toward the door, picking up her duffel bag off the floor where she'd left it, packed and ready to go. Gripping the handle snugly, she crept to the door.

Her fingers reached out and closed around the doorknob. Letting a breath out slowly, she turned the handle. On the other side of that door was freedom.

"Dani." It wasn't a question.

Dani cursed under her breath. For half a second she wondered if she should make a break for it.

"Close the door."

There was no way she could out-run her father. She closed the door and shot him a murderous glare as she stomped back to bed, flinging herself on it, mattress springs squeaking with protest.

Jack looked at her, his face stern in the moonlight. "Don't try that again. Promise me."

Dani glared at him stubbornly.

"Promise me," Jack repeated.

"I promise," Dani agreed reluctantly, knowing full well that if the opportunity arose, she would break it without even thinking twice.

Content, Jack rolled over and went back to sleep while Dani stewed before finally dropping into a light slumber.

Chapter Ten

Thursday, November 18

The next morning, Lynn tapped lightly on Randy's bedroom door. "Are you awake?"

"Uh, yeah, I think so." Randy rubbed his face as Lynn marched through his room and opened the one bedroom window.

"Fresh morning air," she told him, like it was scientific compound he had forgotten from school.

"Is that important?"

She snatched a pillow and tossed it in his face, more like threw it, something reminiscent of the pillow fights in their childhood. And curiously, there was a redolence to the air that triggered more vivid memories of that time.

"Do you smell it?" Lynn asked as she plopped on the side of his bed, one leg curled up underneath her. "It reminds me of Thanksgiving time."

"And air so thick you could drink it. But then it would kill you."

Lynn's soft laugh was full of cheer.

Randy was curious, and he looked at her, registering each stroke and twirl her mood seemed to give her. "You seem way too happy."

"I know."

"Why?"

"Oh, come on, Randy. Do you suspect a new exotic drug?"

"No, well, at least nothing I know about. I don't think there's a drug that can make anyone as happy as you seem to be this morning."

Lynn lowered her eyes. It was like watching the final curtain come down in a play, the mood shifting dramatically from fantasy to reality.

"I'm sorry. I didn't mean to ruin your wonderful morning."

"You didn't. Don't worry. I was just thinking about how quickly things have changed for me this past week." She got up, folded her arms, and paced at the end of the bed. "I guess I don't always believe it's real. Maybe it won't last, I tell myself. I saw you ask the same question, you know. It was in your eyes, and, well, sometimes your eyes give you away."

"I'm a cynic. A Doubting Thomas."

"Oh, so you remember Doubting Thomas from Sunday School?" Lynn caught him out of the corner of her eye with a mischievous look.

Randy shrugged. "A little. The point is that even if . . . even if I sometimes might react that way, it's not your problem. It's mine. I'm the one who is the cynic. I'm the one who at some point has to take people at face value. You are doing great, Sis, and I'm very, very proud of you."

"I had an anxiety attack last night, but it wasn't as bad as last time. Alice told me if I can last three days without shooting up, my symptoms wouldn't be so bad. With God's help, I know I can quit."

* * *

"Where are Scarpetti and Leaman?" Lynn asked while they

were eating breakfast.

"Don't worry about them. I'm sure they'll eat later. Besides, I like the company I've got right now better."

"Well, so do I, but I'd also feel better if I knew what they were doing."

Randy nodded, agreeing, then became serious. "So would I."

Lynn leaned forward and whispered. "I still don't know why you are working with them."

"I know, Lynn, and someday I'll tell you. But right now, maybe the less you know, the safer you are."

"OK, so you're doing something dangerous."

Randy gave her a smile and a neutral shrug. He wouldn't talk about it.

"OK, so you're not going to tell me."

Randy shook his head. She fought down the urge to keep prying. She was just worried, was all. And so was he, she could tell. He finished his breakfast then planted a kiss on her forehead when he stood up. She smiled and walked him out to the 4Runner.

"I know you're worried about me," he said as he unlocked the door and slid in. "But don't be."

"I am worried, and I can't not be. But I can pray. I know that whatever you're doing is something good."

"Is that what's bothering you? You think I might be doing something illegal?"

Lynn hesitated. Then she shrugged and said, "I don't think you are." But she was sure he got the point; there was an awful lot of bad history that kept her from accepting his word on blind faith.

"Did you call Alice to come over?"

"No. Not today. I forgot about it earlier."

Randy glanced at the house and rubbed his hands over his face. "Lynn, I hate to leave you alone, especially should Scarpetti and Leaman show up."

"I know you do. But, they haven't done anything."

"A Twix candy bar doesn't always snap in the same place either."

"I'm staying out of their way. They haven't done anything, OK?"

Randy didn't answer, just continued to stare at the house.

"I'll be fine, I promise."

"OK, but call Alice as soon as you get inside."

"I will, Randy." Though she knew the time, she glanced at her watch anyway. It was a big hint for Randy to leave.

"I'd better get out of here," he said, swinging the door shut. As he backed out, he mouthed the word *Remember*.

"I will. I will."

Lynn waved after her brother then returned to the house and started cleaning up the dirty dishes. It didn't take her long at all to make the kitchen spotless. When she was finished, she poured herself another cup of herbal tea and sat down and for a few moments took pleasure in what she had accomplished. She had discovered that giving herself many small goals daily, such as cleaning or cooking or studying her Bible, gave her the strength she needed to fight the symptoms of withdrawal. Sometimes she worried about what might happen should she not meet some of her goals. Would her guilt cause her to begin using again? *Maybe,* she reasoned, *and maybe not.* She couldn't recall ever hearing that it would be easy. If she didn't have God and Alice to turn to, she knew she could never quit on her own.

Alice had also encouraged her to begin writing poetry after learning that for Lynn it once had been a passion. She thought of the poem she was working on now, something she wanted Alice to read called, *Where My Father Goes*. It was almost finished.

Oh no! She had forgotten all about Alice! Jumping up, she picked the receiver off its hook on the wall and dialed. The phone rang twice, and then the answering machine picked up. She hung up, stood there, and held the receiver in her hand. *Now what?* Well, there was nothing she could do about Alice being gone.

But before putting the phone away, she hit redial again.

Answering machine.

Great.

There was certainly no sense in trying again. Lynn looked at the receiver as if it had a mind of its own. Calling a third time was not something she would normally do. But this time she simply could not return the receiver to its cradle and felt terribly impressed to try again. For the third time she pressed the redial button and waited.

"Hello," an out-of-breath voice said. Alice was huffing like a marathoner.

"Alice, it's me, Lynn."

"Lynn? I'm so glad I made it to the phone. I've been grocery shopping."

"So early?"

"I like to before it gets really busy."

Lynn told her Randy was at work and that he wanted to know if she could call to spend the day. "We could study more," Lynn said.

"I'd like that, Lynn. I've been thinking that you could live here for a while until those men are out of your house."

"Randy's been a lot different lately," Lynn said. "I think it's safe enough here, and I'd like to spend time with my brother. I think he might be interested in what I've been learning too."

For a moment there was silence, and Lynn knew it was because her friend didn't trust Randy much, if at all. "I'm glad," she finally said.

Lynn smiled. She loved Alice Nolan. She loved that Alice cared so much about her. "Thank you for saying that."

"You'll be all right, but just to make sure, I'm coming over right now. If those two men you've told me about try anything, they'll regret the day they meet up with old Mrs. Nolan."

Lynn smiled. As soon as she hung up, she went to the front door and flipped the deadbolt. *Good.* Now she was safely locked up until Alice arrived.

* * *

The paper was spread out in the break room when Randy got to work. Martha came in and took a section back to her desk. Randy flipped through what was left on the break-room table but found it hard to concentrate on news so far detached from his current situation.

"Here is the rest," Martha said as he passed her desk on the way to the shop.

"Thanks." As he thumbed through the metro section, however, one story nearly floored him. Shaken by the article, he smoothed the paper down on Martha's desk, staring into the face of Dave Watters. The caption read, *David Watters, Special Agent in Charge of the FBI's Counter Terrorism Taskforce—Missing!*

Randy imagined that a taskforce had already been created to investigate Watters's disappearance. Would they know about the agents who were in the field? There had been five undercover agents on each of two teams in the taskforce when Randy went undercover in the Freedom Society. As far as Randy knew, he was one of only two agents who went undercover in the Freedom Society. He read the article again, and the thought occurred to him that Dave Watters was the only agent on the taskforce with whom he had a personal relationship and whom he knew how to contact secretly. But with Watters missing, he couldn't even do that. He wondered if anyone else under Watters's command knew how to contact him. Did they know the code words? Did they even know where to reach him or how involved he was in what he felt was quickly becoming a major conspiracy to be carried out by the Freedom Society?

Suddenly he felt completely isolated and out of time. He needed fast answers, and there was only one way. He began thinking through what he must do as he turned around and left the office. He climbed into the 4Runner and exited the bus depot grounds. A block away, a red vehicle pulled out of its parking space. Randy was halfway back to the house when it struck him that his cover was indeed completely blown.

He drove fast with the radar detector active. With rare luck, he managed to hit most traffic lights green and pulled onto the driveway of the rented property less than twenty minutes after leaving the school. Lynn's friend's car was parked out front. He raced through the front door into the living room.

To his left, Lynn was wrapped in a blanket on the couch. She held a cup of hot tea that smelled like peppermint. She looked calm and smiled at him curiously. Alice was sitting next to her, her eyes narrow, measuring him.

Randy tried to appear calm as he approached them. Bending down, he kissed Lynn on the forehead while holding an eye on Alice. From the look she was giving him, he thought she might pop him on the side of the head. It didn't take a panel of psychologists to conclude that he hadn't treated Lynn well in the past. He decided to make the first move toward an amicable relationship and reached out an open hand.

"Your name is Alice," he said. "I'm Randy, Lynn's brother. We met in front of Club Rio several days ago. Lynn has said an awful lot of good things about you."

Alice was staring pretty hard at him, and she didn't offer to shake his hand. He found the situation very uncomfortable, even if it was deserved. But at the moment, there was no time to talk. They all heard a vehicle pull into the driveway. Randy glanced down at Lynn. The sound had obviously made her uneasy.

"You OK?"

She smiled bravely. "Just jumpy. But yeah, I'm OK."

Randy squeezed her shoulder and then looked out a window. It was Scarpetti's and Leaman's Ranger pickup, but only Leaman was inside. Leaman yanked the Ranger around Randy's 4Runner and buried it in the garage. The garage door rolled down.

"Who is it?" Lynn asked.

"Leaman," Randy said. Thinking this might be the opportunity he needed, he headed toward the kitchen. Alice jumped up and followed him.

"What should we do? Should I take Lynn away from here?"

Randy considered her idea for a moment then said, "No, you two stay here until I return. He's not coming inside." Alice gave him a look, like *Right, I'm going to trust you*, but he didn't have time to explain himself before he went out the back door.

Randy kept an eye on the garage side door while he walked around to his 4Runner. He opened the passenger door and reached underneath the seat for his Glock 9mm. It was in a holster with a clip on it that could be slid inside his pants at the small of his back. Then he pulled out a pair of handcuffs he had stuffed up underneath the seat.

He pulled the Glock out of its holster and crept along the wall. When he came to the window, he ducked down and took two quick steps that put him on the opposite side of the door. There were only three ways in or out: The main garage door in front, the window, and the side door. He was able to cover two points and could hear the main door if it was opened. Leaman was still inside. He couldn't know Randy intended to arrest him, but Randy was sure Leaman knew he was an FBI agent.

Randy tried the doorknob and found it unlocked. He threw it open and stepped back out of the line of fire. Trying to see inside the garage was like peering into a well. There was not much to see past the first few feet. He frowned. It was dangerous, and he could feel it. A knot of fear blossomed like a black rose in his chest.

"Leaman?" He waited a few seconds. "Are you coming out?"

Leaman replied from the shroud of blackness: "I want you to come inside, Burton. I want to talk."

This was something Randy was not about to do. Leaman had seen him leave the school and had followed him to the house. He had to know that Randy knew too much. Suddenly Randy's mind clicked. He returned to the 4Runner and opened the driver's door to get at the visor. Then he went back and knelt down at the right front corner of the garage where he could watch both the front and side of the garage and squeezed the button on his garage door opener.

While the door crawled agonizingly slowly along its metal tracks, it generated a tremendous amount of noise Randy had not anticipated. He might as well have been in the middle of a carnival. Unable to hear, he felt exposed and foolish. But he couldn't do anything about it now, so he crouched down a little tighter for cover.

As soon as there was enough light spilling into the garage, he took a quick look and then pulled himself back behind the wall. He didn't see anything, and he hadn't drawn any fire. He tried it again, just as the door jerked to a stop fully open. Leaman was making a try for the side door.

"Leaman, freeze! FBI!"

Leaman took another generous step toward the side door then hesitated.

"Put the gun down! Now!" Randy barked again.

"OK, OK!" Leaman cautiously set his gun on the workbench.

"Back away. Lace your fingers on the top of your head."

"I'm doing it! I'm doing it!"

Randy kept his shooter's posture as he walked between the pickup and bench toward Leaman. "Just stay cool," he said calmly. He always feared a prisoner would become desperate and make a foolish attempt to either get away or try to take him down. Because he'd lived within the ranks of the Freedom Society for so long, he knew many of its members were not afraid to die.

Before he cuffed Leaman, he ordered him to remove his wristbands.

Leaman glared at Randy as he loosened the bands and let them fall on the floor, revealing the broken barbed wire tattoo of the Freedom Society.

Randy put him in cuffs. He took Leaman's gun and told him to walk back through the garage ahead of him and into the house through the back door.

Alice opened the door for them before Randy had to worry about it, and when she eyed him critically, he said, "Don't say it. I know I told you I wouldn't let him in the house, but I meant that I wouldn't let him come in on his own." He gave her a wry smile, but she blew out a breath of exasperation.

"Come on, Lynn, we're leaving. That brother of yours is determined to keep your life in perpetual danger."

"What happened?"

"Nothing. Get things together you want to take."

Randy heard Lynn protest, but Alice was moving along quite swiftly, gathering up their jackets and her purse. He shoved Leaman into the living room amid the flurry of activity. Looking uncertain, Lynn was being swept along in Alice's wake. Randy sat Leaman down and holstered his weapon. He met Lynn's eyes, which expanded like ripples in a pond when she saw Leaman.

"Don't worry, he's cuffed."

"Maybe she's not worried about *him*," Alice snapped.

"Please, Alice, stop it." This from Lynn, who had started shaking and grabbed her stomach. "And you too, Randy."

"Lynn, are you feeling all right?" Randy asked, moving to her side.

She gingerly lowered herself into the chair and doubled over. Her cheeks had flushed, and her forehead was glistening with sweat.

"She's having some symptoms of withdrawal, probably made worse by the excitement," Randy said. He put the back of his hand to her forehead. "Alice, will you take her to her room and make her comfortable?" Alice nodded. Turning back to Lynn, he said, "You'll be fine. You've been doing great hanging in there. I know it's tough, but you're doing great."

"Thank you. I wish I could say it got easier." Her eyes filled with tears, and she tried to hold back a sob. She meant it. It was so hard. . . .

All the years Randy had ignored Lynn and her growing drug problem because he had been so wrapped up in his career had cost them dearly. He ignored it because he didn't want it known at the Bureau that his sister was an addict. What he really should have done was deal with it head-on before her dependency got too bad.

He stole a glance at Leaman, who seemed to have welded himself to the couch. Then he noticed Alice hovering like a winged carnivore, which explained Leaman's cooperative behavior. They locked eyes for a second, and Randy nodded and gave her a cock-eyed grin.

"Alice is no pushover," he told Lynn. "I'm glad you know her." He stood and helped her to her feet. Alice took her down the hall. When they were in Lynn's room, Randy turned his attention to Leaman. "Leaman, it looks like we've got some things to talk about."

Leaman shrugged.

"There's no way on this earth, man, that I'm telling you anything."

"Then you'll be sitting there an awfully long time." He already looked uncomfortable sitting on his hands.

"OK with me," Leaman said and looked away.

There was something in the way Leaman acted that brought a sudden rush of anger. Maybe it was the stupid fleeting half-grin Randy saw.

After a few moments, Leaman looked back and narrowed his eyes. "Come on. You got the drop on me. You proved you're a tough man. If you still think you're man enough, let me go, and you can try to beat the answers out of me."

Afraid he would lose it and do just that, Randy got up slowly, giving a patient grin, letting Leaman know he was in control. Then he went back to Lynn's bedroom.

"Hi, kid, how're you doing?"

Lynn smiled. "Oh, I'm tough. Didn't you know?"

"I knew it."

Lynn reached out, and Randy took her hands. "You seem different again. You seem tougher," she said.

"I'm supposed to be convincing Leaman of that."

She gave him a particular look, the kind of look that begged for honesty when that's all there was left. He realized then she deserved at least that much. She seemed to recognize a pivotal moment had come. Her eyes went to Alice, whose face was un-readable, and then back to Randy, who took a seat beside her on the bed.

Alice cleared her throat and got up. "I'll keep an eye on that man out there."

"Thanks," Randy said.

"What do I do if he moves?"

"Yell."

"I'll do that." She looked down at Lynn and added, "At least my day today isn't boring. I always fear that."

"She's different," Randy said after Alice had gone.

Lynn nodded. "She's very caring and really concerned about me. She's taught me all sorts of stuff about the Bible. Mostly, she's taught me about Jesus. Now He seems so real. Without Him, I couldn't ever quit using drugs, I don't think. Randy? I like the way you've changed, but I-I guess I don't really know who you are either."

Randy let out a long sigh like *here I go*. "OK, remember that summer before I graduated from First Christian, the year Mom died? You were in eighth grade. We spent almost the whole sum-mer together doing things. I didn't want anything to happen to you. Remember how sick Mom was the year before, so she sent us to live with Dad?"

"Uh-huh." Lynn looked at her hands. She started rubbing her fingers, a nervous habit.

"We all knew that she wasn't going to get better, but no one said so. You know, if someone had said it, it would have been like sealing fate somehow."

"I know."

"She asked me to watch out for you that summer. I think she knew she only had a month or two left to live, and she didn't want that summer after school was out to be completely ruined. So what did she do? She asked me to keep an eye on you, and most of all, make that summer fun for you."

"She asked you to take care of me? Like a job?"

"It wasn't like a *job*; it was fun. Well, after a while it was fun. There was a lot going on. Mom had died, and you didn't like the idea of hanging out with me, but then, you were having to adjust to new friends too."

"What's all that got to do with now?"

"Maybe nothing." Suddenly Alice knocked, and the door opened. "This guy's getting fidgety," she said. "Shouldn't we call the cops or something?"

"Alice, I am somewhat of a cop myself." Randy lifted his eyebrows and shrugged. It all came across very sarcastic, not at all how he had intended.

"It was just a question."

"I know. I'm sorry. But if we call the cops right now, I think it will only cause more problems than it's worth. The local law will have no reason to hold him and will be forced to let him go, and I may not get any answers I need."

Alice leaned out to look down the hall at Leaman, and then she poked her head back inside. "Don't you have some superiors to answer to?"

"Are you afraid I'm a rogue FBI agent?"

"Mostly, I think you're just a rogue. I have no idea if you're really an FBI agent or not."

"Cute."

"What is going on? How can you make him talk to you when you're in here?"

"Uh . . ." Randy held up an index finger. "Can I have just a few more minutes to talk to my sister? Just a few? And Alice, I'm hoping he gets tired of sitting on his hands. He may be more willing to say something after a while."

Alice let out another exasperated breath. "Oh, all right, but I'm not your prisoner's baby sitter. Do you understand that?"

"I understand completely," Randy said. Alice left the door ajar when she returned to the living room, and Randy relaxed and tried to remember where he left off. "I better make this quick. When we went to live with Dad just before Mom passed away, he sent us to First Christian. So I spent my senior year, my last year in high school, in a Christian academy where I didn't know anyone and didn't care if I did or not. I knew Mom wasn't going to live much longer. I had decided that after she died, I was leaving forever. Maybe join the army or something."

"Why?"

"I blamed Dad for him and Mom getting divorced. I hated him for not being there when Mom was sick. I think I even blamed him for Mom getting cancer in the first place."

"What about me? You were just going to leave me alone too?"

Randy looked away. "I have fond memories of that summer we spent. But when you went back to school, I left home and went to college. I got wrapped up in my own life. I guess I went ahead and did what I wanted to do. No one else mattered."

"You never came back, at least not completely. I think that during the years I was still going to school, I only saw you when you came to visit at Christmas."

Randy put his hands in his pockets, paced some, then sat down again beside Lynn. "I should have come back more often. I shouldn't have forgotten about you the way I did."

"You shouldn't have forgotten about Dad either."

"You're right. I shouldn't have. I shouldn't have blamed him for breaking up our family. I shouldn't have blamed him for Mom's death. It wasn't right, but I was looking for excuses. I found them, and I lived off them for a long time."

"It wasn't anybody's fault they split up. They had lots of problems neither of them knew how to fix. As for Mom, she smoked. She smoked a lot, and really, that's what killed her. It wasn't her fault either. She couldn't help it when she needed to smoke. I know how she felt, I guess, and I don't blame her too much." Lynn took a breath. She was looking back, trying to make sense of the past. "She tried to quit lots of times. Remember?"

"Yeah, I remember she'd throw out all their cigarettes and claim she wasn't going to light another one. Never lasted long."

"Don't hold it against her. She tried as best she could. Some people just can't make it back out. The addiction is stronger for some than it is for others. Lots of times it just depends on how much help they get, like being in the right place at the right time. You know?"

Randy nodded. "Like Alice has been helping you."

"Uh-huh. She keeps encouraging me and praying for me. Most of all, she's my friend. She doesn't condemn me, and I don't feel alone. You wouldn't believe how much God helps get me through the bad times. I couldn't make it on my own, 'cause sometimes I need something so bad it hurts. You saw me a little bit ago. I know the symptoms could have been a lot worse. I just do a lot of praying . . ."

Randy reached out and hugged Lynn gently. His eyes went to the window, to the gray sky beyond, cold in its own way but nothing that could change the brotherly love he felt for Lynn.

"Lynn, I'm a special agent with the FBI's Counter-Terrorism Taskforce. For a few of the years that I haven't been around, I've been inside the Freedom Society. An undercover agent. That's what I have been doing here, but things have been falling apart. I don't know how long the Society has known about me, but I think it's been a while." All of a sudden, Randy felt lightheaded, as if he had just envisioned his imminent death. A piece had just fallen into place. He jumped to his feet. "Lynn, I've got to make a phone call."

One of the key elements to this whole puzzle was the bus schedule. Another, the fact he was working in the bus depot. That's what had clicked. There had to have been some sort of logic to that, and he thought the most logical rationale was that he was being set up. He had been kept just far enough out of the loop that he would have no idea what was going to happen, but he was closely enough involved to become a prime suspect. He felt like a pawn in a game of chess.

But there was something else too, and he had stumbled onto it quite by accident. He grabbed the phone off the wall, pulled out his wallet, and dialed a number. When a voice on the other end of the line answered, he left his name and number and a message that it was urgent. When he had finished, he returned to his prisoner.

Leaman was looking awfully uncomfortable, his eyes pleading for mercy, because he was sitting heavily on his hands. Unfortunately for the rather solid and heavy Freedom Society man, Randy wasn't feeling particularly magnanimous.

"Tell me what the Freedom Society is planning to do, Leaman, and I'll get you off your hands. Otherwise you stay right there until the police or the FBI shows up. By the way, I haven't even called them yet."

"I'm not telling you a thing, Burton. You don't have any leverage with me. There is nothing you have the power to do that can make me talk. Tomorrow I'll be a free man, anyway."

"Not if you are an accessory to terrorism. That will still get you life in prison *without* a chance at parole."

Leaman laughed aloud, like a man who had inside information.

Randy rose out of his chair like an Apache helicopter and hovered over Leaman's face. "Don't tempt me to do more than just hold you here until your neck and shoulders go to sleep!" He stared into Leaman's eyes and saw nothing but a black wall of defiance, something like the marble wall of the Vietnam Memorial. However, instead of the names of the casualties of that war, there were the martyrs of a different kind of revolution.

In his frustration, Randy almost slapped Leaman. Instead, he left him alone and went to the kitchen, where he put his palms on the countertop and leaned on them, thinking. He was becoming convinced Leaman would not talk soon enough. There was little he could do to threaten the man, and Leaman might rather die than betray his loyalty to the Freedom Society. It was the issue with all radical groups.

He glanced at a clock on the kitchen wall. The time was almost noon. He looked back at Leaman, who continued to sit on his hands with the same defiant expression painted on his face, like a poster child for adolescents anonymous. The house was silent, almost like a morgue.

He went to the garage and backed Leaman's pickup out so he could hide the 4Runner in the garage, just in case Scarpetti returned and became suspicious.

* * *

Brian Willis normally checked with the home office at ten o'clock and two o'clock during the day. It was quite unusual for him to call in late, but if he hadn't been tossing and turning all night instead of resting, he wouldn't have ultimately dosed off from exhaustion when the eastern horizon began to gleam. He answered the wake-up call but didn't remember that it had happened, drifting immediately back to sleep. It was nearly eleven when he rose off the bed like a diver coming up for air.

Although he didn't have any appointments, he was upset to have overslept. Then, with his schedule turned completely upside down, it took him half an hour to remember to call in. It was noon when he finally picked up the phone and dialed his office, getting the message to return a call from Randy Burton. He'd forgotten about the business card he left with Randy. *What did Burton want?*

Brian replaced the receiver and paced the hotel room. He felt anxious. The fact that he hadn't eaten anything all morning became increasingly evident as the acid in his stomach began to burn. He looked at himself in the bathroom mirror. "You're a braver man than this, Brian. Get yourself together." He listened to the words, but the face staring back at him remained tense.

It wasn't just Randy Burton's call. It wasn't just not understanding why Burton had been spying on him. It was Gavin Larson and his United Religious Coalition too. Gavin was focused on uniting all religions under one leadership that would become a large enough political group to create public policy. The more Brian analyzed the Coalition's rapid growth, and subsequently, Gavin's rising popularity, he was uncomfortable with the speed at which it had all happened. How was Gavin generating so much public support so quickly?

He tried to settle down and work on the speech Gavin was to give on Friday but found it nearly impossible to concentrate. It became an act of sweating droplets of blood to produce a passionate speech when he felt his efforts would only help to mislead people. And he couldn't help but continually think about Randy Burton's call. Finally, he gave up entirely, plugged his laptop into the phone line, and dialed up to retrieve his e-mail from the Coalition's own Internet server.

His computer downloaded one message. This was from Tyler Brownell. *Brian, you'd better wise up. I don't know what you're trying to do, but Gavin knows about it now. You did not return all the information I sent to you. There are three files missing, which I assume you are well aware of.*

This did not set well, especially considering the mood Brian was already in. His blood boiled, and a thick sweat broke out on his forehead. He found the reply button and jabbed the enter key and began typing: *Tyler, you're a coward.* He sent the message before he had a chance to think about how childish it was. And while he was doing childish things, he typed another message—one Ann would have loved to help with even though it was only two words—and sent it.

Brian got up and began pacing again. It was becoming an all-consuming routine. It didn't seem to help him sort out his problems either. The only thought that kept shooting through his mind—like a comet now—was that he was very much alone and had no idea whom he could trust with his fears, except for God. Brian immediately dropped to his knees and began to pray.

When he was finished, he knelt there in the middle of the hotel for several moments with the strong impression that he should contact Randy Burton regardless of his fears. He felt much calmer about the decision now, and as he knelt there, he knew he felt the presence of God. Sometimes, he realized, in the midst of life's most confusing and trying moments, one simply forgot about his Lord and Maker.

* * *

Brian decided the safest course was not to use his own phone, just in case. He walked four blocks before ducking into a coffee shop looking for a telephone. As he punched in the number and waited for an answer, he watched the street. He had walked into a run-down section. It was polluted with torn newspapers that appeared to be racing erratically down the street in front of an increasing breeze. Debris filled the gutters, and listless people with blank looks watched it all in a state of near catatonia.

"Burton, this is Brian Willis."

"Yes, Brian! I'm glad you called. I was beginning to think you hadn't gotten my message."

Brian took a deep breath as he tried to think. Before calling, he had scripted exactly the words he had intended to use, but they had all vanished. "I didn't intend to call. I got your message hours ago."

"Is something wrong?"

"Listen, I know that you taped our conversation at the restaurant. I also watched you pick up two men after I left who were in the restaurant at the same time we were. They're the ones who set up the microphone at our table."

"Man, I'm sorry, Brian. I didn't realize you saw any of that."

"I don't think 'sorry' covers it."

"No, I suppose it doesn't. But right now I don't have much else to offer. I need you to believe I had nothing to do with recording the conversation."

"You knew about it," Brian snapped.

"Yes, but—"

"Enough!" Realizing he was yelling, Brian looked around the shop. Yes, he had managed to draw the attention of practically everyone. He lowered his voice and turned back to the pay phone.

"Why did you return my call?" Burton asked.

"I don't know. Because I wanted you and whomever you work for to know I'm not an idiot."

"That's a good thing to know. Makes me feel better about asking for your help."

"What?"

"You heard me. So keep listening. I know you're not going to hang up and walk away, so don't argue either. Just hear me out for a minute."

Brian glanced at his watch. "A minute's about all you've got; then I hang up."

"The reason our conversation was being taped was less to hear what you had to say than to hear what I said."

Brian let a few moments pass while he tried to understand this. "I'm not sure I follow."

"My job at the school's bus depot was a cover that was set up by the Freedom Society to help carry out an act of terrorism. The two men you saw are members of the Freedom Society. They arrived several days ago to help me finish a job. Are you with me so far? I'd rather not explain all of this over the phone. In fact, there's every possibility my phone is tapped right now."

"I'm hearing you, but I'm not sure why I should believe this. However, your story *is* too entertaining not to see how it turns out."

"I'm dead serious. If you want to know how it turns out, you're going to have to work with me."

"I'm not budging until you tell me something more convincing," Brian snapped back.

"Did you happen to notice the wristbands on one of the two men in the restaurant?"

"Yes," Brian said.

"Underneath the bands are Freedom Society tattoos, a broken strand of barbed wire."

Brian broke into a cold sweat. The seconds ticked by as a piece of the puzzle clicked into place. *Desmond Krane's tooled leather wristband wasn't a tacky fashion statement. It was covering a tattoo.*

"Are you still there, Willis?"

"Yes, but how are you involved? If you don't really work for the school and you're supposedly undercover in the Freedom Society, then—"

"The FBI, Counter-Terrorism Taskforce, and I swear we don't have a lot of time to yack over the phone, Willis."

Taking a couple of deep, calming breaths, designed primarily to help him keep his head, Brian said into the phone, "You've got my undivided attention now."

"OK, how does this grab you? The reason Scarpetti and Leaman, the two men you saw at the restaurant, bugged our conversation was because Gavin Larson, your boss, also pulls the strings of the Freedom Society. The Coalition is a political monster, but add to that the muscle of the Freedom Society, and you've got a lot of power. Too much. It's the kind of faction our forefathers were afraid of when they wrote the Constitution."

"I understand the history lesson fine," Brian said. "I'm just not sure I understand who and why."

"About the 'why,' I'm not sure, either, which is the reason I'm asking for your help. The special agent in charge has disappeared. That worries me. I was and hope still am, in deep cover. I don't know who my boss kept informed, and call me overly cautious, but I don't want to accidentally start a leak that's going to ultimately drown me."

Brian remembered a story in the *Post* from that morning. "Are you telling me Dave Watters was the agent overseeing your undercover operation?" The pause on the line told him it was fact, which at the moment didn't really help to convince him Randy Burton was telling the truth. Burton could still be pulling an elaborate scheme.

The more he thought about it, though, the more he believed Randy Burton. And if he disregarded Randy's plea for help, he might never find the answers to his own growing suspicions. "Give me an address," he finally said, taking a scrap of paper and pen out of his suit jacket.

* * *

Brian very much wanted to take his rental car, but he would have had to go back to the hotel for it. He decided a cab would actually serve him better. When the cab slowed down and pulled into the driveway of the residential address Randy had given him, he gave the driver one of his cards with the fare.

"What's this?" The driver held up the card. He was a short, stout Russian immigrant, somewhere around fifty years old, Brian believed. Brian felt he was a man of integrity and would not toss the card or forget about it.

"I need a favor." Brian handed him a twenty. "Take a good look at me; remember my name. It's on the card. Keep your eyes and ears open so that if I turn up missing, you know to contact the police."

The driver's eyes narrowed. He pursed his lips and shook his head, a gesture that meant he thought Brian was a lunatic, but then, in his occupation, he met a lot of lunatics. He nodded. "I'll go to the police," he said.

"Thank you." Brian tapped the card. "On the back is the man I'm going to meet right now. I know this is his real name, so be sure the police have it."

The driver shrugged. "OK."

Brian got out. Before he rang the doorbell, the cab was gone. The neighborhood was terrifically quiet, and his worry made it seem ominous. Then the door was opened cautiously by an older woman who looked tired, upset, and most of all, scared. Brian knew for certain he was at the right house.

Randy Burton strode over and shook hands with Brian as

soon as he was inside. Brian returned a fake smile then surveyed the living room. One of the two men from the restaurant was sitting on his hands on the couch with a deeply painful expression. Brian's eyes swung to a young, petite woman who bore a remarkable resemblance to Randy.

"Brian, this is my sister, Lynn. Alice Nolan is a friend of Lynn's, and as you can see over on the couch, our man Leaman, who isn't talking much right now. Come with me, Brian." Randy waved him down the hall.

"What about this guy? Should you leave him alone?"

Randy half-smiled. "Alice will watch him. I think he's almost more afraid of crossing her than of crossing me."

In a back bedroom, Randy shut the door. "This man Leaman is carrying a Freedom Society tattoo on his wrist. You can look at it when we go back out if you want to. But for right now, I want you to know what I know. I have spent the past two years in a Freedom Society boot camp in Michigan working my way into a position of trust."

Brian interrupted. "Why did the FBI put you undercover? Did it already have a reason to believe the Freedom Society was a violent organization?"

"We believed there was potential for violence, but we had no evidence the Society would ever become a problem. In fact, the Society has been very careful about keeping a clean image."

"Why infiltrate it then?"

Burton gave Brian a look that clearly showed frustration. "Look, I need you to grow some trust here, Willis. I don't have much time."

Brian was stung by the rebuke but still uncommitted.

Randy Burton continued. "After the Federal Building bombing in Oklahoma, the Counter-Terrorism Taskforce began investigating every militia group, every radical organization, and every threat against the government, no matter how insignificant they appeared to be. Most of the time the investigation does not require agents to go undercover, because the FBI is quite successful at developing informants already within the organization. However, one characteristic of the Freedom Society and maybe a few other highly focused and well-organized groups is the extreme loyalty of its members. The FBI is much less successful at developing reliable sources of information within these kinds of groups. Oftentimes the informants purposely give false information, making it necessary to put agents undercover. It tends to be a big cat-and-mouse game on one level, but more plots than you would imagine have been exposed by the Counter-Terrorism taskforce.

"Six months ago, completely by surprise, I was taken into an office to meet a man I had never seen before. He said his name was Dietrich and asked me how I felt about the government and if I believed America could be kept from deteriorating as a world power. The Freedom Society believes the government is far too liberal, and as a result, is weakening America by protecting the rights of minority groups with broad, divergent ideas. The theory is that America has lost the unity that once made it a solid nation, its moral backbone being strangled by a government that has gone too far to the left. The problem is that once you begin to buy into these people's way of thinking, you no longer make your own decisions about right or wrong. Someone else does.

"After eighteen months in the Society, I knew the party line by heart and told Dietrich exactly what I thought he wanted to hear. A few days later, I was selected to work on a special project. One has to part with reality to sound fanatical, but I must have faked it well enough to be convincing. And there were probably other factors. The point is, I had gotten on the inside."

"What do you think the other factors were for putting you on this special project?" Brian was honestly curious.

"I believed one reason was because their plans had already been set, which meant they knew they wanted to use First Christian. Somehow, they plan to use the school's bus system. I'm sure that through their background check when I joined the Society, they discovered I had graduated from First Christian.

The FBI, of course, changed any of my background that linked me to the FBI Academy and altered my college records to show that I had taken a vocation. I was fairly innocuous during my college years anyway." Burton watched Brian and smiled a little.

Now, Brian thought, came the big question. "Why do you need my help?"

"We know the American people do not think of the Freedom Society as a violent organization but more of a government watchdog. It also takes on a lot of community service projects and has its members become active in their communities. Lots of volunteerism. And everyone likes a volunteer," Burton said.

"When you approached me at the school, I assumed I was being watched by Dietrich's men, Scarpetti and Leaman. I knew instantly who you were. You're pretty high profile, and I didn't need 'high profile.' And considering that the Freedom Society has been avidly supporting the Coalition, it made my situation a bit dicey. I had no other option but to allow them to eavesdrop on our conversation to keep them from getting suspicious. It didn't occur to me that my cover was probably already gone."

"I think I understand that part." Brian folded his arms and began to pace. "Naturally, they would be suspicious of me if I were not on the inside." Brian flinched as if hit by an electrical current. "How do *you* know I'm not on the inside? If you weren't certain, you'd be taking an awful risk telling me what you know now."

A mixture of surprise and relief flooded Burton's expression. "Thank you for finally realizing that. Now maybe we can establish some kind of working relationship."

"You're going to ask me to risk my life."

Burton frowned. "I sincerely hope there is no risk to you. I've involved enough innocent people with Lynn and Alice. First of all, I think we should work on figuring out what kind of terrorism is being planned. Now that you understand whose side I'm on, you may have information that could help us figure this puzzle out before it's too late. Come into the kitchen. I want to show you something." He glanced at his watch, and Brian took a quick look at his also. It was nearly eight o'clock.

As Brian watched Burton unroll a map on the kitchen table, Lynn made sandwiches and raspberry Kool-Aid. He accepted a glass, held down one end of the map with his fingertips while Burton placed weights at the corners, and studied the intricate web of colored lines. "What is it? Times, routes . . . Is the Society planning to blow up a few members of congress or Supreme Court judges?"

"No, unfortunately it's nothing quite so simple." Burton cracked a grin.

"Sheesh, there's a lot of lines drawn!"

"They're all school bus routes for First Christian," Burton said.

"What? Bus routes? But why? Kidnapping?"

"I don't know. My first guess was ransom, but that doesn't wash. Besides, the Freedom Society seems almost better funded than the United States military, and the kind of exposure it would have following the kidnapping of a busload of kids would ruin its reputation. Politically, it's suicide."

Brian sat down. Cupping his face in his hands, he continued to study the map. "What do the colors represent?"

"The ages of the children."

"Doesn't help."

"I do believe that whatever happens will involve children mostly in the fifth- through sixth-grade age group because they will be the easiest to handle."

"Sounds logical, especially if it were a kidnapping."

"Which we've ruled out." Burton sighed, rubbing his face. "I've been over this a dozen times. It was important for me to get a job at the bus depot, but I was never told why."

Brian jerked his head up. "To hijack a bus *before* it's full of kids!"

"Right. That's what I thought. You're coming up to speed quickly."

"These are things you're way ahead of me on. You get paid to investigate crimes. I'm just trying to cope. When this is all over, when tomorrow is finished and the pope goes home and Gavin becomes leader of the religious world, I'm going into seclusion with my family."

Burton had gotten up to get a sandwich. He had an eye on Leaman when suddenly he spun around. "What did you say?"

"I'm just trying to cope."

"No! You said 'tomorrow when Gavin becomes leader of the religious world.' I want you to tell me what Gavin Larson has been up to." Burton pulled over his chair and leaned over the table, staring intently at Brian. "You mentioned Gavin and the Freedom Society at the restaurant last night. Have you noticed anything peculiar within the Coalition?"

Brian thought a moment then nodded. "Gavin Larson has been particularly secretive lately. I've come to think there is a lot more going on than I know about, and I'm talking about things that are not legal." Brian paused, leaned back from the table, and returned Randy's stare. "I have reason to believe hundreds of thousands of dollars from charitable contributions may have been diverted somewhere other than the charities for which they were intended. In some way, I think it connects with the death of Stan Shultz.

"It was something I was following up on at my office before flying out here to Washington. I had planned to talk to Desmond Krane, the man who runs the M Street Shelter. I couldn't say for sure without thoroughly examining the shelter's financial books, but I doubt it received even half the funds the records I took from the Coalition office reported." Brian paused. "And there's something even more interesting: The manager of the shelter, Desmond Krane, is a member of the Freedom Society. He's got a wristband like Leaman's."

"If you're right, that connects Gavin and the United Religious Coalition to the Freedom Society in an administrative way. Do you think Shultz might have known about the diversion of funds, maybe even sanctioned it?"

Brian shook his head. "No, I don't believe he would have allowed it. Shultz was an honest man. He was a firm Christian. If I were to believe anything, it would be that Shultz may have accidentally discovered what was happening. Maybe why he was getting suspicious. Could be why he was killed."

Randy leaned back and let out a long breath. Brian could see that he was somewhat overwhelmed.

* * *

Lynn heard it first, then Randy, who had seen his sister catch the faint noise—the low purr of vehicles out front. Randy carefully swept back a corner of the curtain with the back of his hand.

"We've got trouble."

Brian had been leaning against the corner wall that led down the hallway. He stood abruptly. "What kind of trouble?"

"It's the FBI. Looks like a Suburban, so there may be at least three."

"Anyone you know or who might know you?" Brian asked.

Randy shook his head. "It's too dark."

"I was afraid of that."

Alice looked from Lynn to Brian to Randy, like someone who'd missed the punchline of a joke. "Please tell me why the FBI being here is such a bad thing."

Randy spun around and gently grabbed Alice's arm. "First, let's get out of here. I'll tell you later. You, too, Lynn and Brian. We don't have any time to spare."

Alice pulled away and grabbed her purse. "What about this man?" She asked about Leaman.

"We'll let the Bureau worry about him."

Alice frowned deeply. "I don't understand why you're in such a hurry to get away from the FBI, since you're supposedly an agent of theirs."

Brian stepped in quickly. "Really, Alice, let's not worry about it now. If it's worth anything, I trust Randy. We're not criminals." He glanced briefly at Randy as they headed out the back door. "At least, I don't think we are. But there's just no time to sort out who the bad guys are from the good guys at the moment."

"Oh, all right. I guess I can trust *you*, Mr. Willis."

Out the back door, Lynn took up the lead to the garage. Randy held the door while Brian followed Alice out. Brian's mind conjured up images both ominous and terrifying. The Freedom Society was like the teeth of a lion about ready to launch an act of terrorism against innocent people. When he thought about the lives that might soon be snuffed out, like so many raids, shootings, and bombings had done before, he felt sick.

As Randy ran around to the driver's side, Brian let the women in on the passenger's side. Alice climbed in first with remarkable agility. Then Lynn slid in beside her. As he jumped into the front seat, Brian heard Alice ask, "How are you feeling, dear? All the excitement isn't making you sick, is it?"

"No, Alice. I'm fine. Really."

Randy started the 4Runner and stabbed the garage-door opener at the same instant. He threw the vehicle into reverse and punched the accelerator, leaving the lights off so only the back-up lights glowed in the dark. A man dressed in a dark suit and a woman agent with blond hair who were walking up the driveway dove out of the way. Once he had cleared the two agents, Randy gunned the 4Runner into the street, skidded the front end around, and found first gear. In a matter of seconds, they were careening around the corner at the end of the block and heading south. Randy put them on Highway 1 going southwest toward Logan Circle.

The four of them rode in silence for the better part of ten minutes. Alice sat stoically in back, her purse sitting in her lap and her hands folded on top of it. Lynn was watching for flashing lights, with an occasional curious look toward her brother.

Brian broke the silence, broaching a subject he felt sure had crossed Randy's mind.

"This vehicle sticks out like a sore thumb. I think we should stop by the Plaza and pick up my rental."

"That's a good idea." Randy studied his mirrors. Just past Logan Circle, he turned left on Fourteenth.

"Mr. Randy Burton," Alice said. "You *are* going to tell me what's going on, *right?*"

Randy nodded. He cleared his throat. He began with his assignment in the Freedom Society, his fear that an act of terrorism was being carried out at that very moment, and lastly, that his boss within the FBI's Counter-Terrorism Taskforce had disappeared. He added scattered bits of information about Gavin Larson that Brian had been able to provide, along with the fact that Donald Thurgood had apparently been blessed with nothing short of a miraculous healing.

As Brian listened again to Randy's fantastic story, an obscure nudging began to linger on the edge of his consciousness, yet it was not strong enough for him completely to grasp. Unconsciously, he began to chew on the inside of his cheek, thinking, trying to pull it in. Randy droned on. Alice asked one or two questions. When Brian focused his eyes through the front window, he saw the Plaza Hotel loom before them just moments before Randy turned into the mouth of the parking garage.

"What's the quickest route to power in any government?" He looked casually out the window.

A few moments of dead silence. "A coup d'état?" Randy said.

"Or succession."

Randy stared at him.

Randy, who seemed to be getting more nervous with each passing minute, drove around a bit in the garage, never coming too close to the Taurus Brian pointed out as his. Nor was there a parking space available. The city, even one the size of Washington, D.C., and its surrounding suburbs, was noticeably more crowded. From the looks of the parking garage packed with vehicles, the Plaza probably had no empty rooms.

After several nervous moments while each of them probed the garage for signs of trouble but found nothing suspicious, Randy relaxed. He pulled up in front of Brian's rental. Brian hopped out and strode quickly to his car. Before sliding in, he said, "How long until they know to look for this vehicle?"

"Not long, I'm afraid. But let's hope by then we know enough to stop whatever is going to happen."

Brian pulled out and followed Randy out of the garage. His paranoia growing, he carefully watched his rearview mirrors to make sure they weren't being followed. Before the Taurus turned onto the ramp out of the parking garage, someone already snapped up Brian's parking space.

Ten minutes from the hotel, Randy pulled into a parking lot that drivers used for ride sharing. The lot was mostly vacant this late at night, but soon it became obvious what Randy was doing. He pulled in between a Ford Bronco and a full-size pickup with a fiberglass shell. From either side, for as long as the pickup and Bronco stayed put, Randy's rig was well hidden.

"Let's hope that works for a few hours," Randy said as he, Lynn, and Alice got into Brian's car.

"It was a good idea," Brian said.

"When can I go home? Maybe Lynn should stay with me." Alice's voice sounded strained with weariness.

"That's not possible," Randy replied quickly. He pushed himself off the back of the seat with his elbow to see Alice. "Your car is in front of the house. I have no doubt agents were posted there minutes after we left."

"I knew you were going to say something like that." Alice sighed.

Brian asked, "Is there some place to stop to get something to eat and think this out?"

Randy eyed him askance as he changed lanes. "Willis, get a grip. This isn't the movies. This is real. If the FBI catches up to us, we'll have a lot of explaining to do and any hope we have of preventing what's going to happen may be gone."

Brian wiped his face with his left hand. "It just doesn't seem real to me."

"My church isn't too far away. It would be a good place to stay and get some rest," Alice suggested. "We might even be able to find something to eat there." She looked at each one of them. "I have a key."

* * *

Alice let them into the multipurpose room and then switched on the lights. There were some cots somewhere in the building, she told Randy and Brian, but she didn't know exactly where. They left in search of the cots.

Fifteen minutes later, Brian was setting up four rickety beds. Randy brought in blankets and put a couple on each cot. It was almost 10:00 p.m.

"Brian."

Wearily, Brian looked over.

"Go call your family, man," Randy said.

Alice had made hot cider, and she brought a cup to Randy. She looked after Brian. "He's a good man," Alice said. "I wonder how he got mixed up with Gavin Larson."

"I think he wonders the same thing. But you're right. He is a good man. He's a Christian, and he's doing the best he can. Like we all do, I guess." Randy paused, looked up at Alice, and said thoughtfully, "Do you think God respects our desire to do better more than He cares how well we succeed at it?"

"Oh yes. I think so. God doesn't have a merit system. That's sort of a human invention in conjunction with the devil, I think."

"What do you mean?"

Alice sat down on the cot beside Randy, and Lynn sat down on the floor, folding her legs up. "Randy, humans are always thinking backwards." With a mystified expression, she shook her head. "A person who is completely honest with himself knows he ultimately has only two choices in life. He can choose to do what is good for himself, or he can choose to do what is bad for himself. Oh, he can fool himself, many people do for a time, but down deep they always know what is good or bad. We're not just talking about being a Christian. It applies to all humans who have the ability to reason in whatever they do."

Randy agreed.

"So, God has only wanted one thing since before he even created us."

"What's that?" Lynn asked.

Alice smiled. "To love us and to have that love returned. He didn't even ask us to love Him first. Think about Adam. Adam woke up to a beautiful garden. It was already finished. All the animals were there. The sky was already blue. God didn't create Adam first and say, 'Well, if you jump when I say jump, I'll snap my fingers for some green grass, and you won't have to walk on sharp rocks anymore.' " Lynn laughed. Randy chuckled. "That's a merit system. It's not God's system."

"What you're saying is that God already accepts us, and by honestly choosing Him, He takes us even with our faults. What about the sins we commit?"

Alice leaned over to set her cup on the floor. She smiled wryly. "This seems to be a big secret to most folks. You would think there is nothing He can't do, right? Well, He can't *make* anyone love Him. He can't save anyone who doesn't want to be saved. There is no merit system, because the choice is fully and completely ours."

Randy thought deeply about the things Alice said as they sat in silence. Another piece of the puzzle began to fit. Lynn was thinking hard, too, he saw, and he smiled to himself. Then he considered Alice, not only her willingness to sit near him after their rocky start but her growing acceptance of him, and he marveled over the immeasurable rewards that came from knowing good people.

After a few moments, Lynn looked up at him. Her blue eyes,

clearer now than they had been for days, moved to Alice.

"Alice, Randy, I-I want to be baptized. Can I? I want to be baptized into the Remnant Church."

* * *

Jack drummed his fingers on the steering wheel and brooded. Beside him, Dani slept peacefully curled up on the seat, her hand tucked up under her chin like when she was a child. In the intermittent wash of the streetlights, her face looked calm. He could almost make himself believe that she was happy. Almost.

What had she gotten herself into? Assassins, murders, sinister plots, how could his little girl be mixed up in such horrible things? Was it his fault? Had he driven her to this?

Jack gripped the steering wheel and fought a wave of anguish. Tears welled up in his eyes, and he could taste their saltiness as his mouth opened in a soundless scream. *Oh, God!* he cried. *Please help me! I can't do this alone. You know how much I want to show her Your love and my love, but it never comes out right. I can't keep messing up. There isn't time. Thank You for watching over her this far. Tell me how to watch over her now. Tell me what she needs most. Thank You. Amen.*

Jack sank into the seat behind him with a feeling of relief. Somehow he would show Dani how much he loved her and how much God loved her. With God's help he would find a way. He glanced over at her, wondering how she could sleep in such an awkward position, wondering if he would have a grandson or a granddaughter. They had hardly spoken about the unborn baby.

In fact, the only thing they had talked about was the plot to assassinate the president. Using techniques he had honed during his years as a policeman, Jack had questioned Dani's story from every angle, made her go over and over the night she'd seen the information that led her to believe there was going to be an assassination. He made her relate every word Shon had said until he knew them by heart.

She'd done so almost mechanically, never tripping up, never altering her story in the slightest. In the end she had convinced him of the validity of the plot. He just couldn't figure out what the Freedom Society, the Coalition, or even Gavin Larson had to gain by it. After all, it wasn't like Gavin Larson would, by default, become the president.

The Coalition had its fingers in a number of political pies, but all of them were to benefit the family or some other benign cause. None of them were in any danger of providing a foothold in the workings of government or apt to gain power with the death of the president. And the current president's politics, as far as he knew, mainly agreed with the Coalition's. President Fairfield was a very pro-family president.

Jack squeezed the steering wheel in frustration. There was something here he was overlooking. There had to be. He glared out at the road as if it held the answer. The twin beams of the headlights pierced the darkness, and the broken centerline flashed by as the miles between them and Washington, D.C., were eaten up. Soon he would be there and then maybe he could find some answers. He just hoped that they wouldn't be too late.

After they dealt with the problem in D.C., he would take Dani home. At least he would take her back to Idaho. A feeling of depression settled over him as he realized that a house was all he had to take her back to.

He glanced at Dani again and found her eyes on him. He swallowed hard.

"You're awake," he said.

"Yeah," she mumbled sleepily. "How much farther?"

"Only a few hours now."

"Are you going to make it in time?"

He noticed how she formed the question in the singular. "Yes, I think we'll make it in time. The trick will be finding someone who will listen and be able to help. How are you feeling?"

"OK, but my hips hurt."

"Do you want to try sleeping in the back seat?"

"No." She fought with the seat belt and shifted her weight to the other side. "I'm OK. Wake me when we get there."

"OK, honey," Jack said. In the distance he could see the first faint shimmer of morning silhouette the horizon. The headlights pinned a green highway sign. Washington, D.C.—120 miles.

Chapter Eleven

Friday, November 19

Brian didn't sleep well, but he didn't think Randy had slept at all. A few minutes after five in the morning, Randy shook him awake. "Let's go."

Brian's eyes flashed open. "What's wrong?"

"The rally today. Whatever the Freedom Society is going to do, it's got to happen today. Everything points to it. The bus routes have been bothering me all night, so I'd like to go by the depot and look around and maybe put my mind at ease."

Brian swung his feet to the floor and put his shoes on. "What about Alice and Lynn?"

"Let them sleep. I left a note asking them to stay here until we get back."

Brian stood and followed Randy out the door into the crisp night air. The carbon-dioxide had lifted some, he noticed as they hurriedly climbed into the car.

As soon as Brian pulled up in front of the bus depot office, Randy jumped out and ran to the door. He drew his Glock 9mm and held it pointed at a 45-degree angle to the ground with his arms locked. Randy's sudden reaction surprised Brian. He ran up to the left side of the door while Randy reached out and tried the handle. "It's locked." Not missing a beat, he backed off the steps and disappeared around the corner. As Brian rounded the corner right on Randy's heels, he noticed what must have triggered Randy into action. All of the mercury vapor lamps had been knocked out, and the yard was pitch black.

"Someone's been here tonight," Randy said. "And I'll bet I know who."

"Scarpetti?"

Randy nodded. "I'm pretty sure. And unless I miss my guess, there is surely a bus missing."

"I still can't figure that out. Why steal a bus? What are they up to?"

Randy shook his head. "I don't know. That's what you and I must figure out."

"And if we don't?"

Randy stopped and turned to face Brian. "After last evening, it's become pretty clear you and I are on our own. We can't rely on the FBI, because it would take much more time than we've got to figure out what's happening. I think we have to assume that there is a circle of power growing that has begun with Gavin Larson and includes Speaker Thurgood. If what you told me about Gavin wooing the Freedom Society is even remotely possible, he might well have succeeded in creating an organization with enough public support through the Coalition and enough force through the Freedom Society to radically change the power structure of the nation. What happens when he makes his move? How will he make his move? I don't think there is any way we are going to know that before we run out of time. Also, how and when did the Freedom Society learn I was an agent? Some militias encourage law enforcement personnel to secretly join their ranks."

Brian, standing with his hands on his sides and partially

bent over like a football player huddling up to get a play, studied Randy's eyes. He knew Randy was a cautious man who wanted to be sure he knew the score before he committed himself to action. But this was something big, something ominous, and time was running out. It seemed Randy was coming to the conclusion that he didn't have time to exercise caution.

"You know, we've got to start making some assumptions awfully quick, or we're going to be too late to do any good."

"I'm aware of that," Brian said.

As they continued walking the perimeter of the fence, Brian stuffed his hands in his pockets and looked wherever Randy shined his flashlight, knowing all the while that if there was anything out of place, he wouldn't realize it. He was just about to turn around and head back to the 4Runner when Randy grabbed his shoulder and aimed his light at a black hole one space from the last bus lined up against the fence. The missing bus.

"That would be one of the two buses the school has for backup."

"But that doesn't make sense. Why all the routes and times just to steal a bus that doesn't even have a route?"

"I don't know." Pulling back the sleeve of his jacket, he looked at his watch. "We don't have much time. Drivers are going to start showing up in another half-hour. Martha should be here at any time."

By the time they returned to the front doors, the secretary was sliding in her key card to let herself in. She wheeled around, startled. "Oh, Randy, you scared me!"

"I'm sorry. My friend and I thought there was something suspicious happening in the yard."

"Well, if there's anything suspicious, Dimetri already knows, because he phoned me very early this morning about it. He got a call that the lights were out. He came to check it out." Martha rolled her eyes, like she thought Dimetri's dedication was outdated.

Brian let Randy walk ahead of him, following Martha inside. She flipped on lights as she talked.

"When did he call?"

"Maybe two or three o'clock." Randy headed into Dimetri's office and scanned the shop through the window. "Why? He would have gone back home if there wasn't anything wrong. Wouldn't he?" Martha asked.

"I would assume so." Randy looked puzzled, which worried Brian, since he had come to rely on Randy to fill in big chunks of the plot for him. "Call Dimetri and see when he left. I want to talk to him."

"Well, OK," Martha said, apparently not sure if she liked taking orders from the new guy who had only worked two days. She picked up the phone.

Brian followed Randy to the shop. "What's the matter?"

"I don't know."

Out in the shop, the two men looked around. It was empty, save for tool cabinets, barrels of oil, and auto parts lining shelves. The place was spotless.

"There *is* a bus missing. It's certainly not here. If someone stole a bus, and Dimetri *was* here, then the place wouldn't have been locked up and dark. Dimetri would have called the police, fretting over the disappearance like the mother of a kidnapped child."

Brian frowned. "I see."

Frantic, Martha met them in the doorway leading back to the offices. "Dimetri's not home. His wife doesn't know where he is, and now I've gone and worried her. Is everything all right? Why did you want me to call?"

"Tell Dimetri's wife you'll call back. We'll check out the yard."

On the way out, Randy grabbed a second flashlight from one of the tool cabinets and tossed it to Brian. They split up, each taking a side of the yard. Brian had gone all the way to the gate without noticing anything unusual when Randy called out from the opposite side.

"I've found him." Brian trotted over. "Cover him with your jacket," Randy ordered, sweeping off his leather jacket and tucking it around the old man. Dimetri had been beaten and left lying on the ground. "Stay with him while I call the paramedics."

Ten minutes later, the paramedics arrived ahead of a police car and pulled into the bus yard through the gate. The cruisers pulled up, and two officers got out. As soon as the paramedics arrived, Brian felt inadequate, so he pulled back a few steps and watched. His eyes roamed the bus yard, and he thought he saw Randy walk out of the office and continue walking east toward Eleventh Street. *What was he doing?*

"Are you the one who called this in?"

Brian jumped. He turned to see the fresh, young face of a rookie policeman. "Uh, no. A man named Randy Burton called."

"Do you know where he is?"

"Check in the office."

The rookie glanced toward the depot buildings then pulled out a notebook to write down facts that he would later put into a report while his partner started toward the office.

* * *

Nancy Wanetree, whose own child attended First Christian, pulled into the bus drivers' parking lot and shut off her car. As had everyone else, she noticed the flashing lights of the paramedics and police cruisers. Her fifth-grade daughter, Angela, was also watching with a great deal of fascination.

"What happened?" Angela asked.

Only half-listening, Nancy shook her head but didn't answer. "Come, let's get going. You know I like to make a thorough check of my bus on the first day of the week."

Angela groaned. "I know. That's why I have to get up half an hour earlier."

Nancy smiled and locked the car up when Angela finally extracted herself from the passenger seat. "I know you're never happy about this, but please move a little faster. I'm afraid I'm not going to have enough time."

"OK, I'm hurrying."

As Nancy headed up the steps into the office, a tall man about thirty or so with blue eyes and short hair passed her on his way out. He smiled, and they exchanged Hellos.

"What happened here?" Nancy asked Martha before going out to her bus.

Martha checked her name off the daily driver list. "Oh, somebody beat up Dimetri and stole a bus." She talked like it would take a lot more than that to ever shock her. "There's nothing to worry about. Dimetri will be fine."

Nancy took her daughter's hand, and they went out to her bus. Since it was a cold fall morning, it would take a while to warm up the bus. Nancy climbed in and started it while Angela located her favorite seat—naturally toward the rear—and slid in. While the bus warmed, Nancy began her routine of checking gauges and making sure the safety guards were all functioning properly. Soon she would step outside and begin an external check, which began with the lights.

* * *

When Nancy Wanetree pulled in and parked her vehicle, Scarpetti stepped out of an Escort wagon and began walking toward the school grounds, the bus depot in particular. Although he was taking a great risk just being there, he felt a unique exhilaration for what he was about to do. This day would bring with it an event that would affect not only the nation but the whole world, and he was to have a significant part of it. In the process, he would earn the coveted symbol of sacrifice and devotion to the Freedom Society. He pulled his knit cap down below his ears and raised the collar of his coat until his face was almost completely hidden.

With ease, he walked past the police cruiser and through the gate the buses passed through each school day. He passed the young policeman who was questioning Brian Willis. He didn't look at Willis. He was risking enough.

The "accident," Nancy coming around the rear of the bus at the same time as Scarpetti, happened perfectly.

"Excuse me, ma'am," Scarpetti said. "I didn't see you. I should wake up."

Nancy gave a startled laugh. "Oh, that's all right. I'm fine."

Scarpetti turned concerned. "Does everything check out fine?" He knocked on the back panel of the bus, right on the number 22.

"Seems to be fine so far. I look things over pretty carefully, just to make sure." She had noticed the maintenance uniform underneath his coat. "Are you the new mechanic?"

Scarpetti nodded pleasantly. Always conscious of timing and how easily people were to manipulate in their moments of need, he offered to help. "Let me help you finish up. I'll watch the lights while you're up front flipping switches. That'll save you some time and get you back on schedule."

Gratefully, Nancy accepted the offer and climbed back into her seat, pushing the brakes, switching on the flashers and blinkers. Everything worked. Then Scarpetti poked his head in the door and offered to check underneath for any signs of leaking fluid.

"I worry about the brakes," Nancy said.

"I would too," Scarpetti said. "They're the most important. I'll take a good look." He crawled underneath and double-checked the plastique explosives wired to the frame of the bus. It all looked ready to go, just as he and Dietrich had left them during the night. Leaman was supposed to have helped, but after Burton had arrested him, Dietrich took over Leaman's part of the operation as well as his own. Scarpetti didn't bother looking for leakage before he crawled out. "Everything looks fine, ma'am."

"Thank you. I really appreciate your help."

Scarpetti humbly waved off Nancy's expression of pleasure. A moment later, as if he had just forgotten something very important, he knocked on the folding door. Nancy opened it, and he stepped inside. The bus was running, and she was ready to leave.

"Did we forget something?"

"Well, yes you did. You forgot to take me along on your route," Scarpetti said.

"B—b—but I don't understand. I don't know anything about this."

"Well, we can say you're the first to know," he said with a much harsher tone. He glanced at Angela sitting at the back of the bus, unable to hear the conversation transpiring between himself and her mother because of her stereo headphones. "If you don't do everything I tell you, when I tell you, then your daughter will die. Then, of course, you will die." Scarpetti emphasized the point by jabbing a gun barrel in her kidneys.

Scarpetti sat down behind Nancy, enabling him to whisper directly into her ear. He noticed with satisfaction the color drain from her face like mercury in a freezing thermometer. Several hours of observation had helped Scarpetti and Leaman determine that Nancy Wanetree would be no trouble. Nancy's daughter was added leverage. Scarpetti smiled. It was remarkable that even with Leaman getting caught, everything else was working out quite well. The driver of Bus 22 was going to do exactly what she was told.

"Now, I think it's time we left. There are going to be some children eager to get on your bus this chilly fall morning. Don't you think?"

Nancy didn't acknowledge. She put the bus in gear and drove toward the gate, silently pleading for someone to realize that the man sitting behind her was not supposed to be there. The young policeman glanced up, smiled foolishly, and then eagerly waved her through.

Her only hope, it seemed, lay with the man who was answering questions being put to him by a police detective. But he watched the bus drive through the gate, make a right turn, and drive down the road. Nancy Wanetree was on her own with a cold-blooded killer. What he planned to do, God only knew. And then she remembered something about her bus that this man could not know. She did have one more hope after all . . .

* * *

"I was afraid I'd be recognized if I stayed at the depot too long." Randy Burton said this as Brian pulled over and picked him up on Eleventh Street.

"It's a good thing I saw you leave. What do we do now?"

"I don't know. I just don't like the way things are turning out. I went to a lot of preliminary work for the Society for it to steal a bus that doesn't have a route. It doesn't make sense."

"Then we missed something," Brian said. "I don't know what it is, but we missed it. I keep thinking that I know where all of this may be heading, but I can't put my finger on it."

Randy looked at his watch. "Speaking of missing things, Gavin Larson's rally begins in an hour."

Brian shrugged. "As of yesterday, you may consider me unemployed. I e-mailed Gavin a two-word speech. 'I quit'!"

Randy grinned. Then his expression turned solemn, and he began to get increasingly fidgety.

"What's the matter with you? Should I pull over?"

Randy's face paled remarkably, like someone having a heart attack. "I don't know. I don't know what's wrong. Anxiety maybe. It just all of a sudden hit me with such force that we are out of time."

"Well, think! Where do we go from here?" Brian's voice raised an octave and, as tense as he felt, sounded harsh. Randy glared and took a deep breath.

"OK, OK! What I want you to do is make a right here. Let's go with the hunch that the bus with the largest percentage of fifth- and sixth-graders is the most likely target. The buses that pick up the most children in that age group are Bus 9 and Bus 22. It's a mad grasp at probably nothing, but let's check them out."

In less than fifty feet, Brian pulled sharply over to the curb to let Randy drive, which Randy willingly did. It was easier than giving directions, and Randy knew the routes by heart. The trick was trying to remember where each bus would most likely be at a certain time.

Bus 9's route was southeast of First Christian and didn't go beyond North Capitol Street to the east. Since they were already pointed south on Eleventh, he kept going, cutting left on M Street. He pulled over near New Jersey Avenue.

"I don't see a bus anywhere," Brian said. "Is it ahead of us or behind us?"

"I think it's behind us." Randy drove to the corner of First and Pierce, where a small cluster of children waited. "These are First Christian students. The bus should be here any minute."

* * *

Dietrich was nowhere near Scarpetti and Bus 22. He was in an industrial area parked in a vacant warehouse, smoothing the second large "chartered" decal out to its corners and strapping several pounds of explosives underneath a second bus. When he had finished, he stepped back and patted the side of the bus, admiring his work. A few moments later, he drove away from the warehouse toward the White House.

At eight o'clock that morning, he dialed a number from his cellular phone.

"Scarpetti here."

"Any problems?"

"None. The driver is being very cooperative. We should be at our destination within fifteen minutes."

Dietrich smiled, gratified at the news. He pulled the phone

away from his ear for a few moments and concentrated on driving. The traffic was growing significantly worse, all siphoning toward the religious rally. He brought the phone back up. "Scarpetti, this is our last contact." Several seconds of silence followed, which he understood. Scarpetti's job was the most dangerous. He might not live. But he was devoted to their cause, and if he lived he would receive the coveted tattoo of a Freedom Society patriot. "Good luck," he said, and terminated the call.

Dietrich drove quickly to Pennsylvania Avenue. At one time it had been blocked off, but since President Fairfield had been elected, she re-opened it. She felt it didn't present a "family" image to be unable to drive by the front of the White House. Dietrich was glad she was so tenderhearted. It made things easier.

Aside from the shuttle buses, Dietrich's school bus was one of the only vehicles on the road. As expected, school buses had been called into action to shuttle people to the rally. He studied the army of police personnel on every corner, their attention directed toward the mobs of people who had left cars parked blocks and even miles away, and decided this could not have been planned any better. He was lost in a sea of anonymity.

* * *

Randy was accurate in his estimation about Bus 9's arrival, but he had missed his guess in other ways. As the bus pulled to a stop, he got out and trotted up, flashing his identification for the driver. There was nothing amiss, although he'd given the kids something to talk about that morning.

"Wrong bus, huh?" Brian asked as soon as Randy was in the car.

Randy shook his head ruefully. "I missed it by a long shot." He didn't say any more on the drive to find Bus 22. He wasn't through berating himself for his mistake. It also made him wonder if he wasn't wrong about that bus too. What if he was? What if it was all just a poor guess?

"But why kidnap these kids? Ransom?" Brian asked.

"The kids are hostages for bargaining." Randy had been thinking this through. It helped to express his theory out loud.

"How can you be sure?"

Randy glanced at Brian. "I can't. But the Freedom Society has put a lot of time into setting up this operation to just take a busload of kids hostage for ransom. No matter what horrendous amount of money they ask for, it won't be worth that kind of publicity. This bus is either a decoy or coercion, but it's part of something much bigger than ransom!"

Randy took what he hoped was the quickest route to Eighteenth Street, praying he wouldn't be too late to find the bus. Unfortunately, its route was completely on the other side of First Christian, between Meridian Hill Park and the Zoological Park.

Traffic was not moving fast enough! The lanes going south were heavy. *At least going north will be easier,* he thought, remembering the rally was the big attraction this morning. "Somebody is going to have to do something about Larson," he said. "He should answer to an investigation into Stan Shultz's murder."

"I understand," Brian said.

As they crossed Seventeenth Street, which ran north to south, Brian pointed at a bus waiting to make a right turn onto K Street. "That's odd. Wait—."

"Bus 22," Randy shut him off. "The warning flashers are going when they shouldn't be, and it's headed away from First Christian. It must be a signal from the driver."

"But if Scarpetti has hijacked the bus, surely he'd know the lights are flashing."

"Not if the indicators on the dash don't work. Dimetri mentioned the interior indicators were giving one of the mechanics problems. We've got the right bus." Randy stated as he pulled over on K Street to wait. When Bus 22 drove by, he pulled out, accelerating until he was a couple of cars behind it. They made a quick left turn. They were back on Seventeenth Street, which restarted after a short jog to the west.

The intersection of Seventeenth Street and Pennsylvania Avenue became a problem. Sixteenth Street was shut down beyond Pennsylvania, and traffic cops were directing all traffic left onto Pennsylvania. Randy expected the bus to turn with traffic. However, it made no indication of turning as it pulled into the intersection and kept a straight heading, winging one of the two traffic cops on the way through.

Randy stopped the car. "Brian! Get out! Explain the situation to one of the cops. I'm following the bus."

Randy sped away almost before Brian exited the vehicle, but it didn't take long for him to catch up to the bus again. Although the road was congested with a sea of people, it parted easily in the face of several tons of bus. Randy pulled up into the bus's wake. When it turned right onto Constitution, he began to think that he needed to have an edge.

He heard sirens in the distance and decided they were evidence Brian had successfully convinced the traffic cops of the crisis. Pedestrians who were crowding over Constitution Avenue scattered off the road as police cruisers came from the west. Two cruisers had pulled onto Constitution behind Randy too. If he was going to do anything, it had to be now.

Randy pulled up on the left side of the bus to go around.

But suddenly, the bus veered and forced him all the way to the left. Randy yanked hard on the steering wheel, trying to stay out of the way. He shot across the street and collided with the curb. The car bounced back into the street and hooked itself underneath the left front of the bus, causing the bus to pull hard to the left, jump the curb, and drag the Taurus with it across Constitution Gardens.

The impact yanked the steering wheel from Randy's hands; then the airbag exploded, shoving him against the headrest and blocking his vision. He fumbled for the ignition to shut off the car, but other than that, he was helpless as the bus threaded its way through two rows of trees, the left rear of the Taurus hitting a tree trunk on the second row. In less than ten seconds, the front ends of the bus and the Taurus were submerged in the lake surrounding the Declaration of Independence Memorial.

* * *

It was called "the magic box," a device roughly the size of a cigarette package and a nightmare for Secret Service and FBI wiretapping efforts. When the device was wired to a cellular phone, a person could change his number every three or four minutes. Because of this tiny high-technology gizmo, Dietrich felt comfortable about the use of cellular phones, at least during this operation. And without a solid number, it would be impossible for the Secret Service or D.C. police to triangulate his position. He wandered around the grounds near the Vietnam Memorial and then walked the length of the Lincoln Memorial Reflecting Pool back toward the Washington Monument. With this amount of people, it was not a casual walk as he wove in and out through the sea of bodies.

Although it was difficult, he enjoyed the anonymity. Every few minutes, he glanced at the bus. For the time being, it remained untouched.

The phone rang.

"Is everything in place?" the voice asked.

"Yes."

"Begin."

It was time to make the first call.

* * *

Mara could feel the excitement coming from the people already beginning to assemble at the rally. It rippled across the sea of humanity like shock waves. She was running late, she knew that. It was silly, really. She'd stayed up late the night before doing some research and overslept. Now she was going to get a lousy position from which to watch the rally.

Oh, well, she thought. Maybe they would have some big screen TVs set up. She was so occupied with this thought as she walked past the foot of the Reflection Pool that she barely realized the drama unfolding directly in front of her.

With a sickening squeal of tires, a car careened across the street, nearly colliding with a small battalion of police vehicles headed toward her, sirens blaring, lights flashing from the opposite direction on Constitution Avenue. Mara stopped, staring dumbfounded with shock as a car and bus collided, rolled across the park, and splashed into the lake near the Declaration of Independence Memorial. Pale, frightened faces peered out of the windows.

The police cars all squealed to a stop and formed a horseshoe, blocking the bus and car from the pedestrians on the road side of the accident. Some officers on foot were already cordoning the area off. Mara was jogging up to the row of police cars before she fully comprehended what she was doing.

"I'm a doctor," she said breathlessly as she approached a burly officer holding a walkie-talkie.

"Stay back behind the line, lady."

Nonplussed, Mara gaped at him. "But—" she began. The sound of a round being chambered in an automatic rifle jarred her. Slowly she looked around, and for the first time noticed that nearly all the police officers at the scene had guns drawn and were taking up positions around the perimeter of the bus. "What are you doing?" Mara asked in panic. "There are children in there. They could be hurt."

The big man took his eyes off the bus for a fraction of a second. "Look, lady, this isn't a good place for you to be. We've got a terrorist situation here. Now stay back." He turned and shouted, "Has anyone got me an ID on that car yet?"

An officer who looked hardly old enough to be out of police academy trotted up. "The car's a rental, Sergeant. It's licensed to a Brian Willis. We ran a check on him and he works for the United Religious Coalition."

"What is he doing?" Sergeant Franck muttered under his breath.

* * *

Dietrich reached for the cellular phone the second it trilled. As he put it to his ear, he expected to hear Gavin Larson's voice.

"Scarpetti here. Burton rammed us, and the bus is stuck in the water near the Declaration of Independence Memorial. The police are setting up a perimeter right now."

"How? What? What happened?" Dietrich couldn't help the confusion in his voice.

"Looks like Burton figured it out. He used Willis' car to angle the bus, trying to stop it. Don't know how he found us, but it doesn't matter now. Nobody's moving in on us. The cops seem to be more cautious than Burton."

"Keep calm," Dietrich said first, then considered the incident. "Is Burton moving?"

"If he is, it's not much. Could be hurt pretty bad. The bus went over the front of the car before we hit the water."

Dietrich considered this. "Don't let anyone get close to you or the car. If he's hurt, let him die."

He turned around for a glance back at the bus he had just parked. The keys were still in the ignition, although he'd left the ignition disabled so the bus wouldn't be easy to move. That wouldn't stop someone from trying to tow it though. That may become a problem. They had planned to have a driver stay with the bus, but that was a part of the plan that had been abolished when Randy Burton caught Leaman. Dietrich grinned to himself. If he could adapt to such problems, Scarpetti could adapt as well.

Dietrich wasn't worried too much about things happening so fast with the kids. So the police found out a few minutes earlier about them. It would take time to get a negotiation team on the scene, and by that time the president would already be doing what he ordered her to do. *Or not,* he thought, *though unlikely.* But if not, she and the rest of the world would know he had been serious all along. The real goal in the idea of using a busload of kids was that no one, absolutely no one, was going to want to be responsible for getting any of them hurt. Frankly, he was surprised no one had thought of this sooner. Admittedly, he would never have put such a strategy together, it just never would have occurred to him. *Gavin Larson has some brains*, he thought, as he put the phone away.

He checked his watch. Another thirty minutes until Gavin was scheduled to begin his speech.

* * *

"Everything in front of the tape is the kill zone," Sergeant Frank was shouting. "Shoot to wound unless there is a direct threat to a hostage. I want a hostage rescue team here now! Has this guy tried to reach anyone yet? Get me a mobile phone." While he was talking, the door of the Ford Taurus slowly opened and a man's form sagged onto the ground where it lay motionless.

"He's hurt," Mara cried. Before anyone could stop her, she dashed under the yellow tape and sprinted toward the car, vaguely aware of the police officer's voice shouting at her to stop. She ignored it. But bullets pinging up turf on both sides of her brought her up short. She stood for a moment trying to decide what to do.

Inside the bus she heard the terrified screams of children. The man on the ground twisted suddenly, and she could see his face. "Go back," he hissed. "He'll kill you. Go back!"

That decided it for her. She turned on her heel and ran back.

"Do you have a death wish, woman?" Sergeant Franck roared as he grabbed her arm and yanked her back under the police tape. "The last thing I need is two bodies out there!"

"He's not dead," Mara panted. "He doesn't even look wounded. He told me to get back."

"He told you?" the officer demanded.

Mara nodded.

"Hey, Sergeant, that guy on the ground is trying to tell us something," an officer interrupted. He handed his field glasses to the sergeant, who squinted through them at the figure lying beside the car.

"What is that he's doing? Sign language? Get me an interpreter."

"I'm no interpreter, but I know some sign language," Mara offered. "I had a deaf friend in college. I took one semester, but then she moved away, so I stopped. I'm awful rusty, but I'll give it a try."

The police sergeant grudgingly handed her the field glasses. She held them up, the entire scene swimming before her eyes in blurry movement until she focused in on the man beside the car. He held one hand up and was fingerspelling.

"F," Mara repeated dutifully. "B, I. FBI. That's it, over and over."

"FBI?" Sergeant Franck repeated. "Hey, is Willis an FBI agent?"

"No," came the reply, "but we've had a report that someone named Brian Willis was picked up at Seventeenth and Pennsylvania Avenue. He claimed the man in the car was an FBI agent."

* * *

"It's true," Brian Willis said as he walked over to the police officer. He had just arrived in a police cruiser from Seventeenth and Pennsylvania Avenue where Randy had left him. "Sir, my name is Brian Willis. The man under the bus is FBI special agent Randy Burton." Willis took out his Illinois driver's license as he talked. "The Freedom Society has stolen two buses. This one and an empty. I'm not sure how, but this may involve President Fairfield."

* * *

Dani held onto her father's fingers in a death grip as he towed her though the monstrous crowds. "You don't even know where we're going," she complained. "Or what we're going to do when we get there." Eyes wide, she looked at every face around her, certain she would see Dietrich eventually and then the adventure would be over for her permanently. Part of her admired her father for what he was doing and part of her was angry with him for it. She wasn't sure which part was stronger.

"Look," her father was saying. "There's a whole bunch of police cruisers. Let's start there."

"Sure," Dani muttered. "Why not. The police protect and serve, right? Maybe they will protect us while they're at it."

As they approached the semicircle of police vehicles, Dani became aware that the police were not there merely for crowd control. These officers had guns drawn, and they were hiding behind their vehicles and any other cover the terrain offered. A sick feeling began in the pit of her stomach and expanded. "I don't like this," she began, but her father cut her off.

"Not now, Dani. We're almost through, and then we can leave." He pulled her along as he approached a policeman issuing orders into a two-way radio. Dani panted to a stop beside him and, surprisingly, found herself standing face to face with Mara, who seemed just as surprised to see her.

They stood gaping at each other for a few minutes before Dani felt a wave of shame wash over her. She dug into her pocket and pulled out the money Mara had given her. "I wasn't going to steal this," she said. "I just forgot I had it until it was too late."

Mara took the money slowly. "Why?" she asked simply. "Why did you run away from me?"

Dani bit her lip. "I didn't want to come here."

"Then . . . why are you here?"

Dani jerked her head at her father, who was talking animatedly with the police sergeant. "My father made me come. I tried to get away from him too, but he's too smart for me. He knows me too well." She shrugged her shoulders. "He's determined to save the president. I just want to get away from here."

Dani's eyes roamed over Mara's shoulder. "Why is that man under the bus waving at you?" Dani asked.

* * *

Mara wheeled around. "He wants to go under the bus," she said loudly.

"What? No!" Sergeant Franck blustered. "Tell him to stay put for the time being," he said to Mara. He turned to Jack and Brian.

"Mr. Talbot? Mr. Willis? Step over here, please." Sergeant Franck walked a short distance from the tape. "Right now I don't care how either of you is involved in this. I just want to get those kids off that bus alive and safe. Can either of you tell me anything I don't already know?"

"Sir?" Franck's Containment Officer broke in. "We have contact with one of the hijackers."

"There are two?" Franck grabbed the phone and held it to his ear for a moment. The call terminated abruptly before he spoke a word. "He says there is a bomb on the bus and the bus will be blown up if he isn't allowed to speak privately to the president."

"It's a ruse. It's not the children they're after; it's the president," Jack said firmly. "My daughter was with the Freedom Society, and they are the ones responsible for this. She said their aim is to assassinate the president."

"Get me Kent Aldridge," Franck snapped.

* * *

President Fairfield had already been up for hours, although

today was scheduled to be a light day because of the religious rally. Her staff had suggested no public appearances. The publicity of the Rally would overshadow everything else that went on in the country. The president was better off making no news at all than making news that no one noticed.

She returned to the first family's living quarters by ten o'clock to find her husband had already left to teach his classes at Georgetown University. She had forgotten to kiss him Goodbye, not as if he wasn't used to it, she mused. But she still regretted it. Her two children, Jenny and Mark, were at school, and for the first time in a long time, she felt relaxed, wondering what she would do with the precious free minutes she had right now.

She didn't know. But in less than ten minutes, she went from reading Jane Austen to being immersed in a blissful dream of a day at the lake alone with her family. The piercing ring of the phone jolted her sharply from the lake to reality. "Hello?"

The other end of the line was held by the director of the Secret Service, Arnold Day, a man whose dedication to the protection of the president was both unquestionable and legendary. "Ms. Fairfield, there is a crisis in Constitution Grounds that seems to have taken a turn that involves you."

"What crisis?"

"A busload of kids has been taken hostage."

Immediately, the president feared the worst, that her children were somehow involved. But that was unreasonable. Her children went to and from school in Secret Service suburbans with a detail of agents for protection. "How does it affect me?" she asked tentatively.

"It appears one of the men responsible has informed the authorities he will only speak directly to the president."

"Should I be involved?"

"No, Madam President, you should not involve yourself. You cannot allow yourself to negotiate with terrorists."

"Then, Mr. Day, why have you informed me of this crisis if I am not to become involved in it?" Her question was followed by a lengthy silence.

"Because I thought you would want to know the situation. And because . . . well, because should the situation degenerate, I felt you would not allow policy to interfere with children's lives."

"Thank you, Mr. Day. You know me well. Please keep me informed."

* * *

Dietrich made the second call precisely when he said he would, and the Secret Service man answered like he was a puppet on a string, although Dietrich believed the agent was quite capable. It was just that he didn't have much information, and for any law enforcement agency, that was practically the whole battle. That's when you knew you were in control.

The Secret Service knew they had nothing under control, so Dietrich figured he had nothing to fear. This call was much like the first, with Dietrich having nothing of substance to say except that he was out there and serious, and that he expected to speak to President Fairfield when he called again. He wanted the Secret Service man to understand this perfectly. There was to be no fooling around. He would not negotiate with hostage negotiators, but he would blow up the First Christian bus full of children if everything wasn't done as he wanted. It didn't matter to him if the president decided to ruin her career by allowing innocent children to die. He made that point known.

* * *

"Madam President, this is Day again." The Secret Service man's voice sounded strained and worried. "The situation could become a catastrophe."

"Thank you for alerting me. Meet me in the Oval Office with Walt Harburg in five minutes." Walt was her Chief of Staff and trusted advisor. She set the receiver down and left the private residence. She arrived at the Oval Office at the same time as Arnold Day. Two minutes later, Walt Harburg charged in, out of breath and carrying a two-page briefing of the events at Constitution Gardens.

"Sorry I'm late," Harburg said, wiping sweat from his curly, graying red hair.

Jessie Fairfield gave a tense but warm smile. "I won't even ask where you were, but the fact that you got here in such short notice is admirable."

"Thank you." He returned a smile and nodded at Agent Day. "Let me begin by suggesting that we do not get involved in this situation. The D.C. police will get their most skilled negotiators talking to these people. There is too much potential for problems."

Fairfield made a steeple with her hands and covered her nose and mouth. She closed her eyes and called on a hidden reserve of strength. "I'm afraid that I know much less about the situation than either of you. Will you two please fill me in?"

"Certainly," Day said. He and Walt sat down on one of the two couches as the president sat across from them. "Currently there is a man holding approximately twenty-five children from First Christian hostage in their bus along with the driver. The kidnapper's first demand was to speak to you, Madam President, but he was told you were not available. Several minutes later, he contacted us again, just as he said he would. We tried a trace, but he was only on for a few seconds, just long enough to say that if he didn't talk to the president, he would blow the bus. That's where we are now. We know the man inside the bus is armed, but he isn't the man who called." Day pulled back his sleeve and studied his watch. "There are five minutes left of the fifteen he gave us during his second call."

Fairfield took a deep breath. "What is your gut instinct on this, Arnold? Is he as serious as he sounds?"

Agent Day raised an eyebrow, locking intense green eyes with those of the president. "Madam President, I believe he *is* as serious as he sounds. Furthermore, although I am not a political advisor—no offense, Walt—this is going to be a tough one for you."

"What do you mean?"

"I mean that if there is even the slightest possibility this man will do what he says, you will not be able to live with yourself knowing you didn't do something."

"Now wait a minute, Arnold!" Walt snapped. "You let me worry about the politics."

Fairfield raised her hands. "OK, that's enough. Arnold. Please tell me you are not talking about my future as far as this office is concerned."

Day's look was stern, and not a muscle had twitched in the craggy fifty-year-old face that stared across at her since Harburg's outburst. "I'm not talking about your presidency. I'm concerned about how something like this might personally affect you or anyone who holds this office. It may sound odd coming from a man who is sworn to protect the president of the United States regardless of the cost, however you want to look at it, but on this one you have to make a personal choice about whether or not to get involved. I swore to protect the president, an institution of the United States, but I will also do my best to protect the person who holds up that institution."

"I don't believe what I'm hearing!" Walt snapped. "Since when does the president of the United States kowtow to terrorists? It's preposterous! Let him make all the demands he wants. There is no way he's serious enough to blow up a whole busload of kids. Then where is his bargaining power?" Walt was glaring, and in the sudden stillness of the Oval Office, it was something quite tangible.

President Fairfield switched her gaze from one man to the other. After a long minute of silence, she said, "I'll talk to him. I will do everything I can to ensure the safety of those children."

"Madam Pres—."

Fairfield raised a hand, cutting Walt off. "I know, Walt. But this isn't so much a policy decision or a political decision as it is a personal decision. At some point, however, they are all related. If I do *not* act and those children die because I didn't do what I could have, my personal life will have ended. I would be no good as a mother, a wife, or as the president of the United States. I hope you understand that, as apparently Mr. Day does."

With his chin thrust out and lips pressed into thin lines, Walt Harburg nodded.

Fairfield turned to Agent Day. "Please set up a link here to the Oval Office." She stood, and the two men stood with her. "Walt, I want you in on this. Bring in Director Aldridge."

* * *

Police Sergeant Franck hung up the mobile phone and regarded Jack and Brian with worried eyes. "Aldridge says the president is indeed involved in whatever is going down here. These kids, apparently, are being held hostage as bargaining chips. The killer claims he will blow up this bus if his demands are not met. Do either of you know for certain whether there is a bomb on this bus?"

"I don't, but why don't you ask Randy. He's in the best position to be able to tell," Brian suggested.

Sergeant Franck turned to Mara. "Tell the agent there probably is a bomb on the bus."

* * *

Mara remembered the sign for "is" but couldn't recall ever using the word bomb in a sentence, so she fingerspelled it and ended with "on" and "bus." It was pidgin sign language at best, but it got the point across. Burton's response was immediate. He began to sign furiously.

"What's he saying?" Sergeant Franck asked impatiently.

Mara, who caught only about half the signs at the rate the

man was signing them, offered her best guess. "I think he's saying he's going to go under the bus to look for a bomb and not to shoot him."

"Maintain your positions, but don't shoot; the target is going to move," Sergeant Franck ordered. "Tell him to go ahead and hurry up about it."

Mara signed "go" and "quick."

As they watched, the man slithered beneath the bus. For an agonizing moment he was exposed to the dark shadow of the man in the bus who had shot at Mara. Finally he was past the bad spot, and he slid beneath the dark water of the pond to check beneath the engine of the bus, which was submerged.

Mara didn't realize she was holding her breath until a searing pain in her chest made her suck in a lungful of air. The man was still beneath the water. Surely he couldn't stay under much longer. Mara's muscles tightened, and unconsciously she leaned forward as if by the power of her will she could make him come out of that water.

"Lord, help him!" It was more a command than a prayer, but she figured that God understood.

When the man's head broke the surface of the water gasping for air, Mara nearly fainted with relief. He pulled his torso out of the water and began signing again. Mara felt her blood run cold.

"He says there are explosives attached to the engine of the bus," she relayed. "Lots of them."

The police sergeant cursed heartily.

* * *

"Madam President," Director Aldridge said, entering the Oval Office. Though not the youngest man to hold the office of Director of the FBI, Aldridge by far looked the youngest. He was an extremely fit man with a head of thick black hair and a dark complexion. His jawline looked chiseled from stone and fit classically with his brooding eyes. If he had not already been appointed by the previous administration, she would not have put him in his position, however. She felt he was far too arrogant to be completely objective when he should be. But he did not make mistakes, she admitted. He was a political *wunderkind*. Those were qualities she needed in this situation.

Aldridge was already up to speed, having taken briefings since the crisis in Constitution Gardens first developed. He greeted President Fairfield respectfully then proceeded to take over the situation, which seemed to put Arnold Day at some discomfort, the president thought. She knew the two maintained only a professional courtesy toward each other. Their styles were as different as night and day. Aldridge, the younger, was brash and decisive, promoting an almost Hollywood-like image as the nation's top cop; while Arnold Day, efficient and soft spoken, had invisibly protected the past three presidents.

"Madam President," Aldridge said, nodding briefly to the president. "I believe we have located the source of the threat. I have a team in position to take down the man who is issuing the threats. All I need is a little time to stall him and a diversion. What I suggest is that you play along to give us the time we need to be sure we can take him down before he can detonate the bomb on the bus full of school children."

Everyone in the room relaxed visibly at this news except Harburg.

"But the president's life will still be in danger," he pointed out.

"No, not really," Aldridge said curtly. "There will never be any real danger. This man wants to meet with the president. His demand is that she enter the school bus parked in front of the White House on Pennsylvania Avenue. We presume he intends to walk to the bus and drive them somewhere, but that will never happen. We'll take the president to the bus. She will board it. While his attention is occupied in making sure we carry out his wishes, my hostage threat team will take him down. Does this plan meet with everyone's approval?" His question was met with solemn nods around the room. Even Harburg acquiesced reluctantly.

The phone rang, patched through to the Oval Office from the White House switchboard as ordered. Two of Day's Secret Service agents had quickly installed a second phone. Aldridge calmly picked up both receivers and handed one to the president.

Aldridge nodded at President Fairfield. She took a deep breath and announced herself firmly. The instructions were brief. President Fairfield agreed to all of the caller's demands. When she hung up, she quickly sat down behind her desk. Her eyes went from Aldridge, who stood to the right of the desk, to Harburg, who sat hunched forward on one of the two couches in front of the president's seal. Arnold Day looked miserable.

* * *

Brian reached out and shook hands with Jack Talbot, Mara Benneton, and Sergeant Franck. "Thank you for what you have done here. I'm sure Randy would like to meet you as well. Hopefully, when this is over, we can all sit down and get to know one another."

Jack smiled, his expression very genuine. "I'm looking forward to it."

"Captain Franck? I'll be in touch later. There is something I need to attend to."

"You're leaving?" Mara asked.

"I've got something to take care of with Gavin Larson." He nodded to the south of the Washington Monument where the United Religious Coalition stage had been erected. Through the trees, Brian could see the motor homes that had been parked to the rear of the stage for Gavin Larson and the pope. "I'm afraid Gavin Larson is not the great religious leader he has convinced most of the American people he is. Someone has to stop him before he deceives the rest of the world, and it might as well be me. I feel partly responsible."

Brian hesitated only a moment longer. Randy would have to take care of himself. Right now it was important he stop Gavin. He turned toward the Washington Monument where he knew Gavin would be waiting behind the scenes for his big presentation. It was up to him to confront this dragon.

* * *

President Fairfield looked at each man present. "Director Aldridge has assured me there will be no real risk in this operation. He has a team standing by in position to bring this man in. Our cooperation means saving the lives of innocent children. I will not allow even one child to die. I'm not made of stone, and I am not the *institution* of the presidency! I am a flesh-and-blood human being."

Her Chief of Staff cleared his throat, preparing to speak. "The American people need to see that the president they elected is strong and unable to be coerced. That goes for law-abiding citizens as well as others who in the future might want to force the president to meet their demands," Harburg said in a firm, low voice, a tone he used quite often when he was right. "You can't let your emotions guide you on this, Madam President. Think of the precedent it will create."

President Fairfield was aware of where her Chief of Staff was headed long before he made his last statement. She glared at Harburg. A second later, his eyes widened when he realized what he had just said. "If that was a sucker punch, Walt, I just lost a great deal of respect for you.

"Walt, America is composed of human beings just like me. They love and hurt and cry and laugh no differently than you or I do. You know as well as I do that should even one of those children die, I could not survive the public backlash. Strength does not come from turning one's back on children. The 'institution' of the presidency, to which you are so devoted, could also be ruined." Fairfield raised a hand to hold off any comment before she finished, as if anyone dared to argue now. "No human being who is worthy of this office puts himself or herself before the life of a child. That is impossible to argue."

Arnold Day nodded and opened the door for his principles. He spoke into his radio to inform the Detail they were on the move. Outside the door, six Secret Service agents were waiting to escort the president down to the waiting Secret Service vehicles. There were three to be used: one Suburban in front and one behind the president's car for the short distance to Pennsylvania Avenue.

Eleven agents had taken up positions on Pennsylvania Avenue but had been instructed to keep a prudent distance from the bus. They had been warned that any attempt to tamper with it would result in the explosion of the bus full of kids in Constitution Gardens. No one wanted that. At the moment, it was better to feel things out.

And certainly Agent Day was trying to feel things out. He was a clearing house for information. Two agents had dogs trained to sniff out explosives. Although they were a fair distance from the bus, there still might be a chance they could detect a bomb. So far, nothing. Other agents were giving distressing reports of far too many people being on the street to get a fix on a suspect.

Director Aldridge held the door for President Fairfield. He was grim, yet he appeared confident. That's what Jessie Fairfield needed—someone to let her know there would be a later to think about. She thought about her children, her husband, and making time for them that evening.

"Don't worry, Madam President. I have everything under control. This will all be over shortly."

"What do you think they want?"

"We may never know." A cool November breeze stirred up some leaves, scurrying them past Director Aldridge. His look was determined. "Madam President, please let me worry about it. We'll be watching, and when we have our chance, we'll move and take them down."

President Fairfield smiled, a measure of her confidence returning. Then she slid into the rear seat, and the car moved out of the White House gate toward the bus.

* * *

Brian opened the door to Gavin's motor home and stepped in, surprising Gavin, who obviously did not expect him. "Gavin." Brian nodded curtly.

"Hello, Brian." Gavin's features seemed to have grown harsher and more shadowed in the past two days. He smiled perfunctorily as he picked up a remote control off the table, aimed, and muted the TV. "The news is startling. I hope it doesn't interfere too much with the rally."

"I'm sure none of it has terribly discouraged you, Gavin. Or surprised you."

"What are you trying to say?"

"That you engineered all of this. Through the Freedom Society, you formed your own armed police force, much like Hitler did in 1927 with the Schutzstaffel, or the SS, his Elite Guard. You did it by promising the Society power in a country that you claim you will raise up to dominate the earth. Through God, of course. Let's not forget that you're God's right-hand man. Tell me, Gavin, was it a terribly agonizing decision to have Stan Shultz killed when he found out you were using millions of dollars of his money to fund the Freedom Society instead of feeding the hungry and sheltering the homeless, the people he meant it for?"

Gavin grinned lightly, smoothly, full of guile. "Some sacrifices have to be made to achieve the ultimate goal, Brian. Surely you understand that."

"No, I don't."

Gavin sighed, like a teacher frustrated with a rebellious child.

"This country had gone much too far to the left, Brian. Someone had to bring it back into line. After all the catastrophes that have befallen America these past few years, it was ripe for a conversion, and I took advantage of the sentiment of the people. When things are good, when the economy is good, when the people are fat and happy, no one worries about the country swinging too far to the left. But when tough times come, they wake up! They very nearly trample each other to climb onto the moral bandwagon and get right with God. I am here to lead them farther than the usual disembarking point. A conservative nation is a strong nation, and by God, Brian, I'm going to make this a *strong* nation. It will become the center of a new world!"

"First by a coup d'état."

Gavin shrugged. "So be it."

"If you were to succeed in assassinating the president after the vice president has recently died, Speaker Thurgood would become president. Together, you could control the country. Surely that hasn't been your plan all along."

Gavin's smile got larger, more fraudulent. "The assassination part, yes. That has been planned for nearly a year, although we had planned to assassinate both the president and the vice president. Should Speaker Thurgood have remained healthy, the rest of my plans would have gone much quicker. He would become the president in the succession of power, and I would be his right-hand man, probably with more power at my disposal than actually being president of the United States. But once he became ill, I couldn't count on that, and so I planned to win through election."

"You? You were planning to become president?" Brian shook his head, beginning to grasp the scope of Gavin's vision.

"But, of course. Easily. With the support of the Coalition, it wouldn't have been difficult."

"Yet now that Thurgood is well, you will still have the power you covet, just as you had planned in the beginning."

"Oh yes. Without the spotlight of the presidency. I never aspired to the politics of the presidency, Brian. Only the power." He glanced at the television and then at his watch. CNN had begun broadcasting sketchy reports from the hostage scene at the Declaration of Independence Memorial and the situation unfolding on Pennsylvania Avenue.

The door opened behind Brian, and someone stepped inside the motor home. He was reluctant to take his eyes off Gavin, however. He fully intended to stop Larson, make a citizen's arrest, whatever. But Gavin Larson would not get away with the things he had done.

Gavin eyes lighted up, and he smiled—genuinely smiled—with satisfaction. "It's about time you got here, Rory," he said. "Please detain Mr. Willis. He doesn't appear to be a team player anymore."

Before Brian had a chance to turn around, he was pushed strongly from behind into a booth at the table.

"Sorry, Brian," Gavin said, patting him on the shoulder as he went by. "I'm afraid I must leave you now. The American people need to see me stepping up and taking charge. I'm afraid Kent will have to decide what to do with you once he's not so occupied."

As Gavin left, the man whom he had called by the name of Rory sat down opposite Brian. There was a suspicious bulge in his pocket and a confident smirk on his face. Brian sank into the seat, resigned to wait and see what would unfold next. When it came time, maybe he could reason with this "Kent" person. Maybe he could convince him that Gavin had to be stopped.

His eyes wandered to the television screen. A man's face appeared, talking about the hostage situation. His face was familiar. Brian soon recognized him as the man he had seen at the Rayburn Building.

Director of the FBI, Kent Aldridge.

* * *

Brian glanced at his watch. As Gavin met Pope John Xavier on the platform erected by Dale Meltzer and his crew, the silence of the crowd felt ominous to Brian.

Gavin's voice boomed through the walls of the motor home. The sound on the television was delayed a fraction of a second, so that Brian heard what was, in effect, an electronic echo. "My friends, my brothers and sisters in Christ," Gavin said. "Today is a day of tragedy and of miracles. First let us pray for the safety and quick release of the children who were taken hostage this morning. The crisis rages just a short distance away. Beyond the White House, another terrible drama is unfolding, for our president is trading herself for the lives of these children."

Gavin motioned off the stage, and Speaker of the House Donald Thurgood gravely made his way to Gavin's side. "Dear Christians, I want you to see what God will do! The more people who are united under Him, the more He will bless us! My good friend Donald Thurgood is my strongest example of the power of the Lord, and I want to call on you now to be united in righteousness!"

As Gavin continued, Thurgood walked across the platform. The gasp of surprise was audible. Seemingly overwhelmed, Gavin embraced Thurgood, who looked as fit as the day he'd taken office. "God has wrought this miracle," Gavin was saying.

All eyes were on Gavin in an air of expectation as he raised his clenched fist in the air. "The great God Jehovah will not have mercy on those who choose to break His law or the law of the land! I implore those who are responsible for this act of terrorism to free the children! Now, my fellow Christians, his excellency, Pope John Xavier, and I will join in prayer before God to intervene in this crucial situation."

Don't you see? Brian thought. *Gavin planned this.*

* * *

Randy lay back, dripping wet and freezing to death. The explosives strapped beneath the bus were no surprise. There were enough to blow the bus and probably cut into the police line. One thing he did know. He was no explosives expert, and there was no way the police were going to be able to sneak one over.

He was going to have to confront Scarpetti. He thought about what was happening in the bus. The police were keeping their distance, so they were apparently taking Scarpetti seriously. And that left only him.

He went back into the water, and with his hands he gripped the bottom edge of the bus until he had pulled himself to the folding door. The driver was staring straight ahead. He thought for a moment that she was in shock, but then she simply looked down and saw him. To her credit, she didn't act surprised. Randy motioned for her to open the door.

* * *

As soon as Jack saw the red flashers, he looked for the folding door, which was opening slowly. Immediately, he realized what was happening and that the FBI agent needed some kind of diversion to keep the gunman occupied. He turned to Dani. "Honey, I'll be back soon." He pressed his newly acquired UBC into her palm. "If something happens, you take this and go on home and find Dan Reiss. You remember him? He's my pastor. He'll keep you safe. Understand? Promise me."

"I promise," Dani said softly.

"I'll be back," Jack said.

"I know, Daddy," Dani replied, but there was no conviction in her voice.

Jack squeezed her hand before he turned and ran as quickly as he could toward the bus. Someone, or possibly several people, shouted warnings behind him, not realizing the flashers on the bus came on automatically when the doors opened, not realizing that there were only a few precious moments in which to act. He passed the first row of trees.

As he emerged through the second row of trees, the man in the bus saw Jack, and Jack was moving more slowly, feeling the strain on his leg. Now that he had the gunman's attention, he slowed to a trot, then a walk. It was odd that the only thing he could hear was his own breathing, knowing cerebrally that there were other noises, a cacophony of sounds. Before he had left the safety of the police line, Gavin Larson was calling on God. Had he gotten God's attention?

Suddenly Jack didn't think so, because he felt God right then, very deeply. It was like nothing he had ever felt before; it was something Gavin Larson could never feel. All Jack's prayers, all his talks with God, all his Bible study had never before led him to feel such a nearness to God.

He had run toward the bus for no other reason than to keep the gunman from noticing the FBI agent who was crawling into the bus through the front door. In that, he had succeeded, he noticed. He also noticed that he was utterly alone now.

As the silence settled heavily around him, he remembered that he had never told Dani that he loved her. He hoped that she knew it anyway. It was the last thought he had.

And then there were two shots fired from the bus. Jack felt nothing as his legs gave out beneath him. From his knees, he fell forward and rolled over onto his back.

* * *

Suddenly, the driver swung the folding door all the way open. *Something must have happened,* Randy thought. He reached up and grabbed a metal handrail on the left and heaved himself into the bus. Scarpetti was just pulling himself away from the third open window from the back, unaware of Randy behind him. He pulled a cell phone out of his jacket pocket with his left hand, his right clutching an automatic pistol.

Soaked though he was, Randy sprinted with the speed of an NFL wide receiver up the aisle, catching Scarpetti as he was turning around. Some of the children closest to the two men screamed and climbed over or under the seats to get out of the way. Scarpetti lost his grip on the phone, and since the bus was sitting at an incline, it slid away on the floor toward the front of the bus. Randy smashed Scarpetti's right hand down against the metal frame of a seat, knocking the gun from his grasp. He quickly reached inside Scarpetti's jacket pockets for a detonator, but he found nothing in such a quick search. Maybe Scarpetti wasn't carrying a detonator.

Scarpetti began looking around wildly for something. At first, Randy assumed it must be the gun, but as his gaze followed Scarpetti's frantic eyes, he understood. Scarpetti was looking for the phone! They saw it at the same instant, and the power light was on!

Frightened kids were unknowingly kicking it around as they frantically moved away from the combatants until it was finally kicked under one of the forward seats.

Randy's mind leapt ahead and made the connection—why Scarpetti was after the phone. *Someone else had a detonator!* Scarpetti elbowed him in the stomach and scrambled for the phone. Randy reached from behind Scarpetti's head, grabbing him with a hand over his mouth to keep him silent. Scarpetti fell forward in the aisle with Randy on top of him. "Get everyone out!" Randy screamed at Nancy Wanetree.

The driver rushed past them to the rear of the bus and threw open the emergency exit door while the children closest to the front escaped into the lake. *A few seconds more,* Randy thought and prayed.

Scarpetti lifted his feet and pushed off a seat across the aisle, and Randy was propelled backward with Scarpetti's weight on top of him. His left foot caught on one of the seat frames bolted into the floor, and his leg twisted as he fell into the seat. The pain was excruciating and instant. He reacted quickly by releasing his grip on Scarpetti and twisting his body around sharply to ease the pressure. Scarpetti jumped free and grabbed the phone. He hit a speed-dial number.

"Blow the bus now!" he yelled into the phone.

* * *

The rear of the bus was sitting with a good thirty-degree up angle, which exaggerated the distance to the ground. Some of the smaller children were frightened of the jump, so a few of the older kids who saw what was happening began helping the younger ones out—rather pushing or throwing them into the arms of Nancy Wanetree, who waited below urging them on. But they were doing what had to be done. Within seconds a variety of law enforcement personnel had arrived to assist them.

* * *

Dietrich put the phone away. He held a detonator in each pocket of his jacket. Today, the United States would suffer an inglorious defeat, and like the famed phoenix, the United Religious Coalition would rise from the ashes in its place as the most powerful entity on earth.

He watched as the president climbed cautiously from the car and made her way onto the bus. The car she had arrived in reluctantly turned and drove back. Dietrich smiled with satisfaction. He depressed the buttons simultaneously.

* * *

Randy and Scarpetti slid toward the front of the bus as they fought. From his position, Randy could see that Scarpetti's gun had slid past them and was hung up just behind the driver's seat. Scarpetti saw it too, and Randy felt him tense an instant before he exerted his considerable strength to knock him off.

But the gun didn't matter, Randy thought. He had to get off the bus!

Calculating his chances, Randy jumped back from Scarpetti and cleared the rear of the bus in three incredible strides. As he jumped from the bus, he rolled and came to his feet running. "The bus is going to blow! Everyone down!"

Every person in his field of vision dropped at the sound of his voice. The last sensation he had was of his legs churning wildly beneath him and a terrible roar in his ears.

* * *

Gavin Larson had just finished a well-rehearsed prayer in conjunction with the pope, who spoke fervently in Latin. Then the pope turned and grasped Gavin's hand, and they shared a solemn look. Brian bowed his head, running his fingers through his hair. At that moment, the motor home shook, and there was the sound of a very loud explosion . . . and a fainter echo . . .

* * *

Brian could not have explained how he felt to anyone. The past few hours had completely drained him both physically and mentally. He felt betrayed and isolated. Unable to think clearly, he felt as if he were imprisoned in a nightmare.

For ten minutes after the two explosions, the media was in complete chaos. Camera shots were all over the place as camera technicians raced to the scenes of the tragedies. Hysterical field reporters clamored to report the source of the explosions. When they began to receive unconfirmed reports that the president had been killed, the media lost even more of its composure. Finally, CNN put together a fairly coherent "Special Report."

Brian listened to field reporter Greg Harrison try to explain what had happened to the president. Suddenly, he startled his guard by jumping up and heaving in the motor-home sink. The guard grimaced and covered his nose and mouth with a handkerchief.

Twenty minutes after the bombs went off, a second man came to the trailer, and Brain was taken out in handcuffs and put into a car and driven away. He didn't see Gavin anywhere. He caught a glimpse of the smoldering bus the children had been in, but he already knew from the television that the children had been rescued. He and Randy Burton had not totally failed. Randy had saved the children, although Brian didn't know whether or not Randy had lived.

As they cleared the congestion around the Mall, Brian's head was covered with a black pillowcase, and he was forced to lie down in the back seat. He had noticed that the men carried guns and seemed to be serious, so he didn't protest. He had never felt so helpless—or confused—in his life. If he had had some idea what was happening to him, he might have felt more hope. But he didn't really have a clue, and in the back of his mind he was beginning to regret refusing Gavin's offer to be a part of his plans. He could have stayed in the Coalition, he thought, at least for a while until he knew what Gavin was doing. Then he might have gone to the police and stopped Gavin. But how could he have known? How could he have been fooled so well?

They left his head covered as they pulled him roughly from the car. Because of the lack of background traffic noises, Brian felt he had been brought to an isolated place. Both men gripped his arms hard, and he was led away from the driver's side of the car. A door was opened and then closed quickly behind them. It groaned on its hinges and sounded heavy when shut. His footsteps echoed down a long corridor.

Where were they taking him?

What was going to happen to him?

You know how it ends.
Would you be prepared to face the ultimate crisis and remain faithful?

Read the exciting conclusion to this faith-building drama
in

Midnight

Coming soon . . .